Keeper of Faith:
The Autobiography of
Tatenda Taibu

Keeper of Faith:
The Autobiography of
Tatenda Taibu

IN COLLABORATION WITH
Jack Gordon Brown

First published by deCoubertin Books Ltd in 2019.

First Edition

deCoubertin Books, 46B Jamaica Street, Baltic Triangle, Liverpool, L1 OAF
www.decoubertin.co.uk

ISBN: 978-1-909245-86-0

Cover design by Matthew Shipley.

Printed and bound by Jellyfish.

To my wife, Loveness, and my two boys,

Tatenda Junior and Gershom Paul,

who have all been by my side in happiness,

success, disappointment, danger and

uncertainty in life. To have loved ones

who love me regardless of emotions and

circumstances has made me one of the happiest

and blessed human beings alive.

Contents

Foreword
Andy Flower

IN THE 1990S CRICKET IN ZIMBABWE WAS CHANGING, AND NO ONE knew that better than my father, Bill. The generation of young black cricketers emerging from the Zimbabwe Cricket Union's development programme in the high-density areas of the major cities were the future, and along with other coaches such as Peter Sharples, Bill gave everything of himself to help these boys achieve their dreams in the game. Highfield, a township in the capital of Harare, soon proved to be a particular hotbed of talent, and in time would produce a number of the nation's leading cricketers. None of them would prove more influential than Tatenda Taibu.

I first came to know Tatenda later in that decade when I made the move to Takashinga – the first predominantly black team in Zimbabwean club cricket – who at the time were called Old Winstonians. I had been playing across town for Old Georgians, but as white cricketers I thought we needed to show, through our actions rather than words, that we were serious about developing black involvement in our sport. The young cricketers I encountered there were highly talented, technically excellent and all dreamt of a future for themselves in the game. I hoped I could enhance some of that with some of my own expertise and guidance.

Soon enough Tatenda was following in my footsteps, turning his attentions to wicketkeeping in order to supplement his batting. He was a complete natural: quick over the ground, quick hands, good balance, excellent hand-eye coordination. He had all the components to be world class with the gloves. By March 2000, he had joined the national squad as my wicketkeeping understudy in the West Indies. He was sixteen years old.

Tatenda's arrival into the national squad came at a difficult time. For years we had been paid a pittance as international cricketers, and it was only through threatening strike action during the tour of England in 2000 that we managed to start earning some reasonable money. This dispute coincided with an even more controversial issue centred around racial quotas in the national side. The recommended quota system from the ZCU was introduced for good reason: promoting black participation and providing opportunities that had previously been denied young black talent.

We were already a small cricketing nation constantly fighting to justify our international status, and as established players we believed this quota system would serve to weaken us further. We had only just started to receive a fair amount of money from our board, and places in the team were highly sought after. In truth, a number of the players really resented some of the young black cricketers being promoted.

Looking back, I wish I had been wiser in the way I responded. I think that Graeme Smith and the people around him handled a similar situation in South Africa with more wisdom and with a better understanding of the bigger picture. It must have been difficult for youngsters such as Tatenda and his friends Hamilton Masakadza, Stuart Matsinkenyeri and Vusi Sibanda, but I think they handled themselves extremely well. Tatenda was always a role model, on and off the field. This was evident even at his junior school where he seemed to naturally evolve into leadership positions. He was a gutsy individual; always confident, always smart. When he first arrived in the dressing room, and because I recognised his potential, I often tried to challenge him to think both about his game and the team dynamics. His opinion was valued from a young age.

Hopefully this stood him in good stead when he became captain in the most difficult of circumstances at the age of twenty. He was still trying to organise his game as an international cricketer, and the problems that had engulfed Zimbabwe had not disappeared. It's possible to captain successfully from a young age, take Graeme Smith at 21 as an example – but he would have had good people around to guide him. With Peter Chingoka and Ozias Bvute at the helm in Zimbabwean cricket, the same could not be said for Tatenda. That showed when he made his own stand against the board a little over a year later.

There is no doubt they would have employed their classic divide and rule tactics with him, offering a sweetened personal deal at the expense of others, and expecting silence or support as a result. Tatenda was better than that and stuck to his values and principles. As with Henry Olonga and myself at the 2003 World Cup, his own personal fight was never going to bring about regime change, and it would have been naïve to think otherwise, but he made a point of standing up for his values. Speaking out in Zimbabwe was not necessarily the route to future safety or financial prosperity, yet Tatenda wavered not in the face of severe pressure from above.

The mismanagement at the top of both cricket and government is heartbreaking to witness. It seems so entirely unnecessary. Zimbabwe is a resource-rich country with a strong foundation in good education. The parallel between the country's story and that of its cricket is obvious, and tragic. Countless outstanding people have invested heartache, blood, sweat and tears into the game in our country, only to see its assets stripped and wasted. Is it retrievable? I suppose in time, anything's achievable.

I have nothing but admiration for Tatenda. His dedication and commitment to 'doing it right' is a lesson to us all. It may not be in Zimbabwe any time soon, but his influence in the game will be felt again.

Andy Flower
March 2019

Introduction

IT WAS THE TYPE OF THING I HAD SEEN IN THE MOVIES, BUT NOT IN real life.

It was October 2005 and I had been summoned to a last-minute meeting with Bright Matonga, the Deputy Minister of Information in Robert Mugabe's ZANU-PF party. It was just before his trip to China, and I was pleased. After suddenly announcing my retirement from international cricket, I had already met with senior Zimbabwean politicians to explain my decision. Zimbabwean cricket needed fixing, and some of Zimbabwe's most influential figures seemed as if they were willing to listen to me. I had no reason to believe that this meeting would be any different.

I soon found out just how naïve I had been.

I had arrived so full of hope, and now I found myself staring down at a brown envelope. I didn't even know if I wanted to look at what was inside.

Mr Matonga had pulled it out of his drawer and thrown it across his desk to me. I had refused his offer of a free farm, and this was his next move. I half-expected it would have been an envelope full of money, a bribe to try and keep me quiet. I could have thanked him and declined the offer. But it was worse than that, much worse.

Instead what I found was an envelope full of photographs: images of dead people, murdered citizens of Zimbabwe.

I was in a panic, unable to work out the intention of his message: was he trying to remind me about how many of our people had perished at the hands of the white minority during the War of Liberation? Or could this be my own fate if I did not comply? I didn't want to stay and find out, and I could not bring myself to make my way through his whole gory album. Instead I got up and left. The reform of Zimbabwe's existing cricket structures was clearly not on the agenda. Intimidation was the order of the day.

I was acutely aware of the problems in Zimbabwean society, and indeed in Zimbabwean cricket. It was only two years since Andy Flower and Henry Olonga had been forced to flee the country after their 'death of democracy' protest at the 2003 World Cup. Neither had returned since. I had also been made captain off the back of Heath Streak and 14 other players walking out on the national team in 2004. I had seen how Robert Mugabe and his government had gone about land reform in the previous five years, brutally seizing farms in a sustained campaign of violence. I knew how Zimbabwe under this government was now viewed around the world: an undemocratic state where people were kept in check by the threat of violence and violence itself.

And yet I still believed I could change Zimbabwean cricket. After all, it was only a game: surely the government wanted the best for our sport, to help us to compete to the best of our ability? It would only enhance their reputation around the world. It seemed not. I had to make plans to get out.

When Henry and Andy had made their stand in 2003, they had each other. Whatever mud the Zimbabwean cricket officials flung at them, however much they were threatened, they could at least count on each other's support. They also had the world's media watching the government's every move. England did not travel to Zimbabwe at all for their fixture against us, citing safety concerns, and our government were well aware that everyone was watching them. Ironically, England's refusal to play us meant we reached the next stage of the competition, allowing Andy and Henry to reach South Africa and never return. Later on, with the international press long gone, would those in power be lenient with me?

It was not a risk I could afford to take. Loveness, my wife, had just given birth to our first child, Tatenda Junior. It was a beautiful moment for us, but the joy had been tempered by the fact that we were effectively on the run from our own government. What a way to bring a child into the world.

Bright Matonga wasn't the only one making threats. In fact, Temba Mliswa, a known ZANU-PF activist who had just been made executive of the newly-created cricket province Mashonaland West, had been far less subtle in his attempts to scare us into submission, threatening over the phone to beat me up and describing me as a 'black boy being used'. Loveness, meanwhile, had been taking anonymous phone calls at our home and had been followed in the street. The guards from the Central Organisation that Dr Gideon Gono had made sure were stationed outside our house had abandoned their post. Whether these threats would ever be acted upon was immaterial as they had achieved their goal. We were petrified.

I was a pioneer in Zimbabwean cricket, the first player to make it through the development programme set up by the administration in the townships. The whole programme had been created to get people like me into the game, people who did not have the benefit of privilege. I was their poster boy in many respects: in the team at the age of 18, vice-captain at 19, captain at 20. Now I was on the run, scared of what the future might hold for me and my family

1
Before the Beginning

DURING THE 1960s, EVERYDAY LIFE BECAME VERY HARD FOR THE people of Malawi, so much so that many decided to flee the country for greener pastures. It was around this time – an era in which Malawi became independent from the United Kingdom – that Manyando, my grandmother, started off on a journey with her two sons, Joseph and John. Manyando's aim was to reach the country known as the breadbasket of Africa. That country was known then as Rhodesia.

The two countries have shared a history – Malawi, formerly known as Nyasaland, had been part of the Federation of Rhodesia and Nyasaland under British rule, a federation created in 1953 and dissolved in 1963. A year later, when the country gained independence from the United Kingdom, it officially became Malawi. To this day, Malawi has a large Zimbabwean diaspora. Manyando's hope was to find fortune in Zimbabwe, but reaching it would be no easy task, especially on foot. Malawi and Zimbabwe are split by hundreds of miles and another country, Mozambique, and it was in Mozambique that Manyando decided to make a stop with her two boys. Very soon, reaching Zimbabwe became almost impossible, and so Manyando decided to seek citizenship for the three of them.

It wasn't long after settling in Mozambique that Manyando passed away, leaving her sons in a foreign land. In her absence, Joseph and John determined to accomplish their mother's dream of finding fortune in Zimbabwe, so they eventually carried on with their original journey. Upon arrival in Zimbabwe, Joseph, my father, got straight to work, not wishing to miss an opportunity to earn a decent living. He set up shop, offering his services as a barber under the temporary accommodation of a large Mopane tree – one of the most distinctive trees in Southern Africa – in the township of Highfield, based in Zimbabwe's capital, Harare. He surprised himself with his instant success; word spread quickly and soon men were queuing to sample Joseph's clipper skills.

Because of the increase in men visiting his makeshift barbers under that tree, it wasn't long before Joseph was opening his own shop in Highfield's Machipisa Shopping Centre. Every Saturday afternoon this shop would be packed with men getting their haircuts and discussing the latest juicy political and life issues. Joseph's business was expanding faster than he ever anticipated it would.

One early morning at the shop, as he was going about his daily chores, Joseph met the beautiful Margaret, my mother. Margaret was light-skinned, and for that she was considered beautiful in the township, a common view to this day. Joseph did not think twice about approaching Margaret, and she was taken in by his own handsome looks. They got to know each other straight away, and before long they were married. By this point Joseph was an established barber and had bought two houses in Highfield, and though Margaret was a qualified nurse working at one of biggest hospitals in the country, he managed to convince her to be the 'homemaker'.

Joseph was doing considerably well for an immigrant who had started out with nothing. Though Margaret was usually blind to the gossip of the neighbourhood, it wasn't long before word reached her about her husband's past in Highfield. Had she really quit her job to commit to a man who could not be honest about his own past? Questions kept flooding her head until she decided to confront him. Joseph came clean, admitting he had been married not once, but twice. With the first wife he had fathered two girls, while his second wife had given birth to two boys during their relationship.

Margaret forgave Joseph, and even looked after these children with the income made at the barbershop. In 1972, they welcomed their own child to the world, Joseph Junior. Joseph was soon joined by three sisters – Jean, Jaqueline and Julie. Things were tough for Margaret not only financially, but emotionally as well. Joseph drank heavily and was not the sentimental type, practically leaving her to raise the children alone. To add to this, Joseph Jr soon inherited his dad's habit of consuming large amounts of alcohol. My elder sisters Julie, Jean and Jackie fared better from a young age, and all later enrolled in college after mandatory education, but the financial pressures of raising a young family burdenened Mum.

I was born on 14 May 1983. My parents had been blessed with a second son, a son who they hoped would turn out to be more responsible than their first.

In their joy they named me Tatenda, which means 'thank you'. My father in particular had very high expectations of me.

Dad never talked about his early life. I have thought about it plenty, and there are certain things that just don't add up. If the records are correct, he started his barbershop between the ages of sixteen and eighteen, which seems a little young to me. When you consider that he was married twice before he met my mum, that only confuses things further. It leads me to believe that at some stage he may have changed his birth certificate; I am told that used to happen regularly when people from either Malawi or Tanzania moved to Zimbabwe.

Whatever may have happened previously, as children we all got the impression that it was too painful for him to discuss. He had walked from Malawi to Zimbabwe, which is no easy journey – 735 kilometres sit between Malawi's capital Lilongwe (established as such in 1975) and Harare – and it seemed to us that he wanted the past buried, not wishing to burden the next generation of Taibus.

As a child, I was simply not allowed to make mistakes. Dad was very tough on me. If I ever stepped out of line, I was beaten. My siblings would always tell me he treated me this way because he loved more than everyone else, and in turn he expected more of me. Whenever he wanted a glass of water, it was me who had to get it for him. Even if I was playing outside, he would get one of my siblings to come and get me just so I could carry out the task. I specifically remember him telling me at the age of ten that I was going to make a lot of money. It was, he said, a secret between me and him. I wasn't even to tell Mum. I realised from a young age that the tough stance he took with me was not because he didn't like me, in fact it was the very opposite. He wanted me to succeed in life, and he didn't want me to take the same route as my brother.

In the townships it was quite normal for the man of the house to work hard during the day and then stay out drinking afterwards. That's what Dad used to do, and it meant we didn't see a lot of him, which I was fine with. I also didn't have much of a relationship with my older brother. Joseph was a talented athlete, and he used to go down to the Gwanzura Stadium to impersonate his hero Mike Tyson in the boxing ring, but by the age of fourteen he was already a heavy drinker. I wasn't comfortable that he was already like my Dad in that regard given how young he was.

Of my other siblings I was closest to Jackie. Jean was very quiet, someone who wouldn't engage in confrontation or take sides. I was always fighting with Julie.

A year after I was born, Mum gave birth to Kudzai. Given there was only a small age gap between the two of us, people often thought we were twins.

Kudzai was bigger than me in stature, and was also a very gifted athlete, but like my older brother he struggled to control his behaviour. Kudzai was such a naturally talented cricketer, and if he were to pick up a bat or ball now, you would not think he had been away from the sport for a very long time. He used to be so confident in his own ability that he would often tell me how he was going to achieve more in the game than I would without working as hard, while he'd also tell the opposition of the day that he was going to score a hundred before the match had started. When I told him he was only creating pressure for himself, he wouldn't listen. He would later go on to earn a cricket scholarship at our local high school, Churchill, only to be expelled. Such were his talents that the neighbouring institution, then Prince Edward High School, offered him a rugby scholarship. These days, Kudzai runs an illegal lodge – effectively a brothel – back in Zimbabwe. It's not nice to say, but it's the truth.

My youngest sibling is Tapiwa, who was born in 1990, seven years after me. Later in life it would be me who looked after my little brother.

Mum was the glue who held us together at home while Dad went to work. It wasn't always easy but compared to other families in the township we didn't have it too badly. The business was doing well, allowing Dad to extend the house and buy three cars. He even had money left to buy a house for his brother. We each had a couple of pairs of shoes and a change of clothes; many in Highfield did not have such privileges.

By this stage the days of white minority rule under Ian Smith were over in our country. Rhodesia had become Zimbabwe and Robert Mugabe, the leader of the Zimbabwe African National Union – Patriotic Front (ZANU-PF), was now the Prime Minister of the country. Still, it was very rare to see a white person in the township during my childhood. It is more of a regular occurrence now, but back then you would usually have to travel to the centre of Harare to see a white person. When people such as Bill Flower – father to Zimbabwean internationals Andy and Grant – came to Highfield for cricketing purposes, it was seen as something special. It was such a rare event that sometimes the little children would sing songs when they saw a white person.

Due to recent history, Zimbabwe is often characterised as a volatile, unstable country, but throughout my childhood it seemed very peaceful. To put things into perspective, I remember being taught about potholes one day when I was in high school, when I was in the sixth or seventh grade. There were so few potholes in Zimbabwe at the time that our teacher had to use pictures from Zambia to demonstrate what they were talking about. It's obviously a trivial matter, but it paints a picture. It was called the breadbasket of Africa for a reason; it was and is rich in resources. Things such as mining, tobacco, and mineral exports were big business. There was never a thought of wanting to move to neighbouring countries such as South Africa and Namibia. Years later, during the crisis of the noughties, refugees from Zimbabwe flowed into South Africa with increasingly regularity as inflation and food shortages worsened.

I was young, but Mugabe was definitely considered a popular leader during the 1990s. A lot of what I learnt was from what you'd call street talk – that's how word used to travel in the townships. I still talk to my wife Loveness about it now: how did we know so much about everything as kids? The answer is street talk. There will have been plenty of chatter in the streets when Mugabe was given a knighthood by Queen Elizabeth II in 1994. That sort of thing affected our view of our President as well. As far as we knew, you could not be knighted without doing anything spectacular.

I grew up in a poor area, but as a family we would not struggle for food or drink. Generally, having access to three meals a day is not something you would associate with living in a high-density township like Highfield. Growing up, I don't remember seeing many people struggle for the basics. There was a real community feel to Highfield; people would chip in to help others who were struggling, and most would share together. If we ran out of sugar at our house, we would go next door and ask to borrow some.

There were certainly townships in Harare where you would find more people without accommodation than in Highfield – Mbare and Epworth are two examples – but where I grew up you would hardly find any homeless people. At the time most of the really poor people in the country would live out in the rural areas. They would come to the big city to find work and if they found that work it was likely that they found accommodation as well – even if it was just a one-room place. If they didn't find a job and therefore a place to stay, they would tend to head back to where they had come from rather than stay in the city. Back in the rural areas they may have had their own little plot of land, just enough to do some subsistence farming, but that was it.

Dad's business was extremely successful in Highfield, and because of that we were better off than the average family in our suburb. He was also a very generous man. In time he extended our four-room house into an eight-bedroom house, so he could accommodate all the extended family who always visited, and he even bought a house for his brother. He was able to purchase three cars; two he could use for his business and one he could use as a family car. These weren't luxury vehicles, but they were a sign that he was doing well.

Along with food and shelter, health is the most important thing, and that was always provided for as well. I remember getting sick and my parents not having to pay when we went to the clinic. Such a privilege is a distant memory in Zimbabwe now.

They are the things you look back on now, as a mature person, and think, 'Do you know what, things were much better then'. I still go back to where I grew up, back to my old primary school. I have relatives and friends who still live in those areas, and it's a complete contrast from how it used to be. When walking back from school I used to see houses all across the neighbourhood being extended. That is not the case now.

Another indicator of how much more comfortable people were was how full the sports grounds used to be. For someone to pay money to go and watch a football game or a cricket match live, they have to have a little bit going spare. Dad once took me to watch a soccer game, to see a team called Caps United. They played at the Gwanzura Stadium in Harare – the ground I used to run around in the mornings as part of my training – and on the day I went for the first time, it was completely packed out. I have rarely seen it full on my visits back to Zimbabwe over the years, and it is currently undergoing work after it fell into a state of disrepair. That was the sort of thing that used to keep people content. If a father is able to provide for his family, he's more peaceful, isn't he? There certainly isn't any need for him to go and steal from the shop.

I was a child intent on learning both sides of every story, and so although I took in everything I was taught at school, I always remember listening to Mum the most intently. Though politics was never a big topic of debate in our household, Mum always used to remind us that we were born free. She had seen what life was like during white minority rule, whereas we hadn't. It was an important reminder to us all: she lived through a time where black people were not allowed onto certain streets, and she didn't want us to forget. Years later, just before she passed away, Mum's mood about the state of Zimbabwe was so despondent that she openly wondered whether life during the Ian Smith era was better. Though the black population were denied many basic human rights and privileges, at least most people had access to food and other basic commodities. The war saw many horrors, but in some ways, people suffered more as Mugabe's rule continued with impunity in the later years. That my mum was questioning that very point after everything she had witnessed pre-Mugabe showed the place we had reached as a country at the turn of the 21st century.

2
New Horizons

I WAS SIX YEARS OLD IN 1989 AND IT WAS TIME TO START SCHOOL. No more afternoon naps. The world suddenly seemed a better place. For me, big school was Chipembere Primary, which was located within the local police camp. This meant that most of the children who enrolled there were from families where one of the parents was a police officer.

The main difference between schools in the UK – which my children have been taught at – and schools in Zimbabwe is the number of children in each class. There used to be around 50 other kids in my classrooms. That's a lot, and it was difficult for our teachers to deal with that.

The method of teaching was also very different. We were basically taught to cram as much knowledge into our heads as we could. We weren't taught how to learn or figure things out, just to cram. Take being in grade two or three, for example: we'd walk in the room to be told that we were doing multiples of five. We wouldn't be able to sit down until we had each answered a question relating to the subject of the day correctly.

It was quite a rigid way of doing things. When it came to exam time, we would do this thing called 'spot the paper'. That meant collecting all the exam papers that had been used on your grade in the years before and going through them methodically. We knew that pretty much all of the questions we were going to get would be in those papers. That's why we called it 'spot the paper'. There was no real practicality to it, we just had to fill our brains with information.

Broadly speaking, the students at Chipembere came from very humble backgrounds. In my grade, I was one of the few who were privileged to have the full required school uniform, thanks to my Dad's thriving business. The fact that I was sent off every day smartly turned out, with my shirt tucked in and my socks pulled up, meant some teasing, but I knew I had to do well at school and behave in a disciplined manner. Failure to do so would result in consequences at home. Mrs Washaya was my first-year teacher. She was a motherly influence and no stranger to the family – she had taught my sisters before me. She was very patient with me, so I took a liking to her and tried hard to impress. My education was off to a fine start, but like most other children of my age, I longed for break time, where with a new group of friends I would play all sorts of games, my little legs covering a lot of distance. What a joy it was to be in this place.

At home, things were still difficult, especially for my mother. Tapiwa had come into the world, while at the same time Joseph Jr's drinking sprees continued to cause heartache. Dad would still spend his days watching over the barbershop and his evenings drinking with his friends, meaning the burden of looking after us all still fell on Mum. She was under immense pressure. One day at school, I was caught talking out of line by my teacher Mr Tekere, and he promised I would suffer the consequences of my ill behaviour. In other words, I would be getting the 'rod' the following day. Back at home my mum was already struggling to keep us disciplined, and I was meant to be the sensible one. This did not sit well with me, so I had to devise a plan: I simply wouldn't go to school the next day. Of course, my parents could not find out about this plan, so the next day I allowed my unsuspecting mother to send me off as usual, though I made sure I left without my siblings. Once out of sight, I took a detour from my usual route and hid until classes commenced.

Once I believed the coast was clear, I allowed myself a walk around the neighbourhood to kill some time, only to then spot my cousin. Though I tried to run away, my little legs were no match for his, and he eventually caught up with me. I was taken home, and so had to draw an excuse from my burgeoning bank of wisdom. I tried to claim that the teacher had not been present, and therefore there had been no point in staying. It didn't wash, and so I was taken straight back to school. Thankfully, when I did eventually show up the rod stayed in Mr Tekere's draw. I had gotten away with it. It was only when I got home later that evening that I suffered the consequences. As I was playing in the backyard, I was felled by a massive slap across my face. I felt dizzy and numb. I was in a state of disbelief and then pain. I had never seen such a display of anger from my Dad. What was he even doing home at this time? Is this how disappointed he was? I would have taken a beating at school anytime over this.

From then onwards, he was intolerant to any sort of mischief. A little later, in grade five, I remember becoming annoyed with a girl at school, who kept claiming I had a girlfriend. It was not a cool thing to do at that age, and so I confronted her. It did not end well. In an effort to stop it all, I hit her. My Dad found out, and he spoke words to me that I was to remember for a long time: 'Don't you know that you never hit a girl, no matter what she has done?' He accompanied this lecture with a heavy slap.

During most of our assemblies, the headmaster would call out the name of a student and ask them to come to the front of the hall. He'd then go on to praise them for their academic progress in front of everyone else, with the intention of motivating us all to keep working hard. On one of these mornings, I found myself listening intently to the words of our headmaster: 'This boy is excelling in all his subjects and this has a lot to do with the choice he has made to participate in a sport that teaches him important lessons: respect, obedience, discipline and so much more,' he said. That was where I needed to get to. I could save myself from the slaps, while having fun playing sport at the same time. I was hugely encouraged, and I was going to make sure to get close to the boy in question: Stuart Matsikenyeri.

When you grow up in a township you have to make do with what you've got. You create your own fun; you make your ball out of nothing. To make our cricket stumps, we'd find bricks with holes in them and put sticks in the holes. For our gymnastics, we used to collect the leftover grass on the fields after the council had cut it. With this we'd form a grassy mound, which would act as our cushion. We'd then collect old car tyres and pile them on top of each other, which would form a trampoline for us. We'd take a run at this loose structure, bounce off it, do a somersault mid-air and then land on this mound of grass. It's only by God's grace that nobody broke their neck.

Gymnastics was not our only use for these disused tyres. Like most other countries in the world, football is the most popular sport in Zimbabwe among children. All you need to do is make a ball and then you are away. In Zimbabwe the milk used to come in plastic bags, and we'd collect these bags once people were done using them. We'd blow up two of these plastic bags, tie them together and put them in a paper bag, which we would twist and cover. In the meantime, we'd also have collected a number of tubes that used to come in car tyres. We would tie all these together, forming a sort of continuous tube. This tube would then be tied all the way round the paper bag. We now had a ball that bounced.

This sort of innovation meant that when it came to organised sport, we often did not have to be taught the basics; we were already well-versed. The same applied for cricket. When we started proper training at school, we were already very comfortable throwing the ball. How? We often spent much of our spare time trying to hit birds with small stones. Our accuracy was honed. You would hardly find a youngster who couldn't throw the ball properly. We'd also create our own traps from disused wire to catch rats – I could still make one to this day. We'd leave our staple food, maize (which is corn) on this carefully-made trap, and wait for the rats to come. Hand-eye coordination wasn't a problem for us kids who had grown up in Highfield, so when it came to cricket the first thing we were taught was how to hold the bat in the correct manner.

In 1992, with the sport still dominated by the white minority, the Zimbabwe Cricket Union (ZCU), as Zimbabwe Cricket was then called, had formed a programme to develop cricket nationwide – especially in high-density schools like ours. Three centres were opened at the Mbizi, Chengu and Chipembere primary schools. Coaches were stationed at these centres to scout for talent in young boys. Cricket was practised as part of Physical Education in the morning and there would be afternoon sessions for those that wanted to take the sport more seriously.

Stephen Mangongo, Bruce Makova and Walter Chawaguta were the coaches assigned to these three centres. During one of these sessions, Mr Mangongo asked me to attend a practice at the neighbouring Mbizi Primary school in the afternoons; they had a concrete pitch and we did not. I had learnt that Stuart – the boy who had been singled out in assembly and was becoming a close friend of mine – was playing cricket, so it was not a tough decision for me to say yes, even if football was my first love. I quickly learnt that practice was compulsory every afternoon, and that ill-discipline would simply not be tolerated.

Mr Mangongo was at the centre of this strict regime. Mangongo, or Steve as we used to address him, was an interesting character. He had an ability to instil a love for the game in you. When he knew he had you hooked, he changed, becoming a stern disciplinarian. We feared him once he took this turn, but he was a very effective coach all the same. Punctuality was non-negotiable; alertness crucial. Failure to meet these criteria would result in hefty punishments, which included a lot of running and beatings. Coach Bruce Makova was an even harder man. He was always serious, invariably spoke in English – not our first language as children – and demanded very high levels of behaviour. Boys generally preferred the other two coaches, as this man was an intimidating figure. He was a big fan of Sachin Tendulkar and Brian Lara, so his coaching was generally modelled around them. Coach Walter Chawaguta was the most likable. He was a very gentle, understanding man. Spotting talent was not his strength but once he had something to work with he was brilliant, a real favourite of the boys.

Steve used to beat us and today it would be understandably unacceptable. For me, though – at this specific time – it probably straightened me out. I'm actually happy I got them. Maybe I look it at that way because I came from a home where my dad would use the same method of punishment. The way I interpreted it was that they both wanted me to do well – they would beat me because I had made a mistake. If they didn't want me to make that mistake again, they hit me. I saw it as good for me. When I talk to my kids about Steve, I tell them that he was a person who really cared about my cricket, and when I talk about my dad, I say that it wasn't for those beatings I wouldn't be where I am today. In some ways, it makes even more sense to me now than it did then, though I would never act in the way they did as a coach or as a parent.

Stuart and I soon developed a close friendship. We spent most of our time together at school, cricket training and at home, often with bat and ball in hand. His dad was a police officer with the Zimbabwe Republic Police, and so they had accommodation within the camp. His mum was barely around – she spent a lot of time in their rural home in Chimanimani, which is in the east of Zimbabwe. For us, cricket became something close to an obsession. 'Eat, sleep, drink cricket' was coach Steve's mantra, and so we did.

Sadly, Stuart's dad passed away in 1994. It was an extremely difficult time for him and his family, especially as they could no longer stay in the police camp. Thankfully Stuart and his brother were taken in by a kind relative, Janet Matikiti, which at least enabled them to go through primary education without having to move schools. It wasn't far away from where I lived, so we still saw each other regularly.

I was constantly playing cricket, but soccer was still my first love. Though I knew it wouldn't please my cricket coaches – who did not believe in sharing cricket with anything else other than education – I wanted to explore my talents, and so in 1993, aged ten, I joined a local team named Zimbabwe Crackers. I soon caught the eye of the club manager, Zozo, who like Steve told me that I was a natural and wanted to see me at more practices. It was nice to hear that from a coach who was well respected in the community. The only thing I didn't like about soccer was the general attitude of the players: my soccer friends were rowdy and disrespectful, while my cricket friends were quieter and calmer. As long as I was staying out of trouble, Mum didn't mind which sport I was trying my hand at, or which one I was more devoted to. Anything to keep me occupied and away from the 'bridge boys' – a ghetto term used for boys who had nothing else to do but to sit by the road and cause mischief – was a good thing in her eyes. My parents had learnt plenty from their experiences with Joe. He had almost achieved a scholarship at a young age for his talents over 100 metres, but apart from that he had not achieved anything else and didn't benefit from that positive influence sport can provide. In the end he had to start helping at the barbershop.

Though Stuart liked soccer, and was good at it, he was not a fan of me playing it – to him cricket was the number one, and nothing else could compare to it. It had to be cricket and cricket alone. For a while it compromised our friendship, until eventually he devised a plan to save me from the mistake I was making. He knew that coach Steve had a serious hold over me, as he did over him. He told me that Steve had demanded that I come back to cricket without fail. It was a lie, but it scared me so much that without a second thought I gave soccer up. From that moment on it was almost exclusively cricket.

Soon enough, I was making headline news. The ZCU, pleased at how their programme was taking shape, produced an article about the progress taking place in the various centres. The article appeared in the country's biggest newspaper, *The Herald*. Alongside the article was an image of me in my batting stance. Such a magnificent picture, I thought. Because cricket was such a white-dominated sport at the time, the article was very important in breaking down the elitist image that surrounded it. Though the article did not speak about me as an individual, my mum was extremely proud of it. She would carry the newspaper cutting in her handbag, showing all of her friends, including the ones I had started becoming acquainted with at church. My dad, on the other hand, was unmoved.

The programme started by the ZCU was proving extremely fruitful. There were a number of talented players, many of us who went on to play representative cricket at some stage, either at school or professionally. Lovemore Mbwembwe, Alester Maregwede, Norbert Manyande, Vusi Sibanda, Hamilton Masakadza,

Blessing Mahwire, Stuart and I all progressed through the system at different stages, a system which created a lot of interest in the neighbourhood.

As a school we generally played games against other schools from the high-density suburbs, such as Mbizi and Chengu. Later we would travel to face other teams from neighbouring suburbs, teams who we would usually dominate, before we were eventually invited to play against private schools. Our first game was against a Harare private school called Hellenic Primary. On arrival, I was amazed by what I saw. Given where we were coming from, this school was out of this world. The fields seemed bright green, without the vast areas of dust which we were used to seeing at our school, and everything looked so neat and immaculate. The Hellenic team met us in the car park to welcome us, all of them dressed in sparkling cricket whites and blue blazers. Most of our white clothing was more cream than white. It had done a few years' service, and it showed. They walked us over to the ground, where more new experiences awaited us. This was the first time we had come across a grass pitch, proper wooden stumps and bails. Added to that, the boys that were showing us around this field were wearing spiked shoes.

When we got to the ground we felt very inferior. We'd be singing together on the bus, but when we arrived at the car park there was complete silence. There were beautiful cars everywhere, and then we took one look at the field – you couldn't falter a thing. It was quite intimidating. Some of our players wouldn't even have socks or white shoes because they simply couldn't afford them. We even had a boundary marked out for us: back at Chipembere we'd use any old measurements to signal a boundary: posts, trees, concrete walls, you name it. We had one kitbag between the team, while each of their team had their full complement of brand-new gear. How would we compete?

But then I started to observe the respective warm-ups. We were very organised. We organised our bags straightaway and waited for our coach to call us over. When he did, we were straight into our warm-up drills. We knew what we were meant to be doing: fielding practice, then stretching. We knew our roles off by heart, but it was clear our opposition didn't. I could hear them asking questions like, 'Coach, where am I batting?' That's when I knew we would be fine.

By the first over, we knew we were going to smash them. We scored a couple of fours, which at that age were not so easy to come by. We thought we'd done well to post a score of 116. That was until Steve showed up in the dressing room. Our target had been 125, and we'd failed to reach it. Our punishment was no tea.

One of the opposition parents came in and told us it was time to eat – they had made cakes for us – but all we could do was look at her. We had to obey our coach. We missed tea and then went and bowled them out for eight runs. My contribution alone with the bat had been sixteen runs, and I hadn't had a bowl. Our opening bowlers, Lovemore Mbwembwe and Vusi Sibanda, the latter of whom would play international cricket with me, accounted for their whole side. We had never played with a leather ball before this game. I laugh when I think about it now.

As a youngster, it was cricket that allowed me to mix with white children, and cricket that made me aware of the fundamental inequality that still existed in our society. Many of my friends from the township simply wouldn't meet white people, whereas we'd regularly head out to white-owned farms to play games. It didn't take much to work out who all that land belonged to. But even during these days, I think I was able to differentiate between decisions made politically and decisions made by human beings. I think because of the innocence of being a little child, I concentrated more on people – I realised that many of these people I encountered were good people, no matter how different their lives were to ours.

Needless to say, the Hellenic parents were stunned by the quality of cricket they had witnessed from a team where some of the boys played barefoot. One parent was so impressed that he asked if his son could join our practices in future. Coming from a white parent, this was a particularly bold move. The boy's name was Andrew Stone, and from that day on he joined in with our sessions. He had entered a world of dusty fields, concrete pitches and bins for stumps. Andrew and his parents fitted in immediately, and in time he started to play as well as us, if not better. Andrew's success encouraged another rich parent to bring his child along to our practices. Mohammed Sirdar was an Asian boy who went to Sharon school, and he too settled into the group quickly. As they learnt from us, we learnt from them. Among other things, our spoken English began to improve, because we constantly had to communicate with them. Our first language was Shona, the dialect of Shona people, the largest ethnic group in Zimbabwe. We also learnt about general cricketing etiquette from Andrew and Mohammed. We became better boys as they became better cricketers.

More games were organised for our school side around Harare, and we continued to win. It was hard to know if we won because we were good, well-drilled cricketers, or simply because we feared losing so much. We were so dominant in our own city that a trip to neighbouring South Africa was arranged for us. Our squad consisted mostly of boys from Highfield, as well as Andrew and Mohammed, and a boy named Daniel Hondo from Cranborne. We had to raise funds for the trip, and one of our jobs was to sell cricket magazines to the crowd during national-team matches. Quite frankly, we did a terrible job. We would constantly get caught watching the game itself, dreaming one day of representing our country. I remember watching the great Pakistani batsman Inzamam-ul-Haq one afternoon, turning to Stuey and saying, 'Wouldn't it be nice to play together on this ground one day?'

You have to remember, we watched no cricket on television as children. The rich people had DStv, which was satellite television, so they'd have more channels and more access to games. Subscription to DStv was $50 a month, so there was barely a soul in the township with access to it. Instead we had two channels – ZBC and Joy TV – both which didn't show cricket. We didn't watch cricket, we were taught it. The first bit of cricket I ever watched on television was when our coach Bill Flower showed us a video called The Third Umpire. It was a video of all the brilliant run-outs that had been referred upstairs to the third umpire. I remember how excited I was when he put it on. Later, I had a friend named Patrick, and he was obsessed with the great West Indian teams of the past. He had a VHS cassette and a documentary about the legendary Sir Viv Richards, and I somehow ended up in possession of this video. That was the only other bit of cricket I watched as a child, apart from when I went to see a live game.

The first thing I had to do for the tour of South Africa was sort out a passport. I was only eleven years old and had never been out of the country before. We spent long afternoons waiting in the passport offices, and I would arrive home tired, without having eaten or studied. Soon we set off for Johannesburg in two minibuses dressed in our blazers and ties, extremely proud of ourselves. The journey was long, and we stayed in our blazers for a long time, fearful that we'd look untidy without them. Thankfully coach Bruce noticed this, and we were eventually allowed to cool off. We did not act like ordinary eleven-year-olds: we were very aware of our actions and knew that if we stepped out of line we'd be punished.

The first meal we had upon our arrival in Johannesburg was particularly spicy, so much so that we struggled to eat it. Our coaches reminded us that it was rude to reject food from our hosts, so we soldiered on with tears in our eyes. Later on, we went to meet our host families, which was a big deal in itself. We were to stay with a white family, which was a completely new experience for us. They had a different culture and a different way of living to our households back home. We lived with an old man named Mr Klink, who lived with his grandson Vincent, a boy we immediately got on with. They also had a huge dog, who we were told never to go outside with. Once we saw it, we were more than happy to stay indoors.

In our only warm-up game, we bowled the opposition out for 31, reversed our own batting order and still won by nine wickets. In the first proper tour game, Stuart and I walked out to open the batting. Given we both barely stood taller than the stumps, I think people thought it was some sort of joke. That did not deter us, though, and we won comfortably. We won our other games easily as well, before we faced Soweto one last time before the end of the tour. We had been scheduled to visit the Gold Reef City theme park to end our trip, but Soweto had been so shocked by their original loss that they demanded a rematch. Cricket came first, of course.

We batted first, and at tea we were surprised to learn that we had only made 89. Alester had top-scored with 66, so to us this didn't add up. With all our other batsmen plus extras, we had surely mustered more runs than this. Coach Steve was enraged and took his frustrations out on us. With tears in his eyes he called us into the changing rooms, and one by one he called us up to receive a beating on the head with a cricket bat. Andrew was sitting between me and Stuey and looked absolutely terrified. But just as he stepped up to receive his punishment, Mangongo shouted, 'And where do you think you're going? You and Mo go outside, now.' Andrew and Mohammed were exempt from the beating. They were stunned to see us in good spirits when we came back out for Soweto's innings. We calmly explained that getting upset would not help anything – we still had a game to win. Stuey – who was a rare bowler at that age by virtue of being able to spin the ball – was the key as we shocked everyone and secured another victory.

We had arrived in South Africa in 1994, not long after the sporting boycott of the country due to the regime of Apartheid had ended. The ICC had only lifted their ban on South Africa playing international cricket in 1991. As countries we were neighbours, but we had very different recent pasts. However, both their international cricket team and ours remained dominated by whites. I would captain Zimbabwe before South Africa had their first non-white captain in Ashwell Prince in July 2006.

Our school team was made up predominantly of black players (there were no white children at our school), but given our age we didn't really consider this much at the time. We were too young to realise the significance of touring a country that had only just left Apartheid behind. I was too focused as a child to dwell on these finer points anyway, but Stuey remembers one incident on that tour. We arrived at the ground for one of our matches, only to find we had not been allocated a changing room. They claimed that the groundsman had left, and that they did not have the keys to open it up for us. However, the team we were playing against – from a white school – had access to one. Mangongo was furious. If it was true and they did not have access to our changing room, why couldn't they as hosts change outside? Instead we were left to change under a tree. It was only when we got back to Zimbabwe and started discussing the incident with others that we began to realise why that had happened. Over time we would start to listen more intently to the conversations our parents and older siblings were having on issues such as this, and incidents like that started to make sense. At the time we understood nothing.

Stephen Mangongo's impact as a coach was not just limited to school cricket – he was equally important in the club scene. At the start of the 1990s, Mangongo took over a team originally named Bionics Cricket club, who played their home matches on the northern edge of Harare. He quickly changed the club's name to *Hungwe*, the Shona word for the national bird that adorns Zimbabwe's flag, before they moved to the grounds of Churchill High School on the condition that they changed their name to Old Winstonians. This was perfect for my generation of cricketers, as we lived a lot closer to the high school than we did the old ground. Eventually, our name was changed to Takashinga, which translates as 'we are brave'. The management felt the name would help the club align more with the community it represented.

I represented Takashinga in my teenage years. In 1998 the club reached the second tier of Zimbabwean club cricket, and in the 1999/2000 season we were promoted to the national first division. There were no age group teams at Takashinga to prepare you for men's cricket; you just went straight in when you were ready. When you were close to being ready, you were invited to train with the seniors – which we considered to be an honour – with the aim of being fast-tracked to the first XI. Me, Stuey and two other boys who had benefitted directly from the development programme – Hamilton Masakadza and Vusi Sibanda – all knew from a young age that we would eventually make the Takashinga first team. Despite being a few months younger than me Hamilton made it first because of his height advantage, but I was quick to follow him.

Like with the school system in Highfield, Mangongo was the key man behind all of this. Again, it was all about cricket for him; about winning at all costs. He got the club to be where it's at now. If you knew he was around, you would not miss a practice. There were consequences if you did. Once you were at practice, you weren't going to mess around. His initial drive was to make Takashinga the first all-black team to appear in the first division, and he was successful in his goal. Many of Zimbabwe's most recognisable players – many of whom are black – passed through the club's doors before playing international cricket. At the time, I wasn't aware just how great an impact the team was having. I was just an innocent boy hoping to see his dream come true. Things were happening at a rapid pace, and I was loving every minute of it.

Another key moment in Takashinga's history was Andy Flower moving to the club from Old Georgians at the end of the 1990s. It was a period when racial tensions were high in the country and in cricket too, so to have a white player of such standing captain a predominantly black team was quite something. Along with his father Bill, who was a mentor to many of us, Andy also became involved in the campaign to get our team a ground in Highfield. The club eventually settled on a site called the Zimbabwe Grounds, a place where Mugabe had delivered his first post-independence speech to a record crowd. The pitch was sorted, a pavilion was built and the crowds started to come.

It was Bill who sold the vision of the club to Andy. He had been working with what we called 'the squad of excellence', and when he explained our plans to Andy, Andy liked what he heard. Andy played a big part in the season we won our promotion to the first division. It was of no surprise that he contributed heavily with the bat – he had been in Zimbabwe's Test side since 1992 – but for me his main impact lay elsewhere; it was the talks you had with him while watching events unfold that made a difference to you as a player. We would constantly discuss the game in detail.

I remember sitting in the pavilion alongside him one afternoon having just been dismissed for five runs. He took a chair, came and sat close to me and said, 'Tatenda, what were you trying to do there?' I'd been clean bowled. 'I tried to hit him over the top,' I replied. I and many others on our team were natural strikers of a cricket ball, so it was almost a sign of disrespect to us when the bowler bowled with mid-on and mid-off up. Our mantra was, 'You must bowl with them on the boundary, otherwise I'll hit you over the top.' I'd tried to do exactly that and had been clean bowled. 'What were you trying to do?' Andy repeated, and so I gave him the same response as before.

'You do know he's knocking on the door of the national team?' he asked.

'Yes, I know.'

'And you're trying to hit him over the top.'

'Yeah, he's got mid-on and mid-off up.' I was adamant.

'You're batting at number three, and he's got the new ball.'

'But he's got mid-on and mid-off up!'

'You don't know how the wicket is playing, you don't know how much the ball is swinging, you've only faced ten balls and you're hitting him over the top?' We left the conversation there.

He was batting at five, and so when another wicket fell, in he went. He scored 40-odd not out to win us the game at a canter. He came back in, came straight to me and said, 'Look, that's what I was talking about. There was no need for me to hit the ball in the air because we were only chasing a low score.' He was Zimbabwe's greatest batsman, and he was just knocking the ball around, giving the opposition no chance. I adopted his method. The very next game I scored 63*, having done exactly what he'd told me. I was now implementing the finer details. I improved so much in that year with Andy that I started to leave the other guys in the team behind.

I have never come across a coach who has been to Zimbabwe, visited the townships and subsequently spoken of a lack of natural talent. The talent is always there. As kids we used to spend ten months of the year outdoors. In the townships, no one had enough money to buy all the gadgets that kids today have. What else were we going to do but go outside and play sport? If you go to the townships as a coach you don't start by teaching children how to run and throw, you teach them how to bat and bowl. It really is a case of harnessing the talent that is there. Though our coaches weren't bad on the technical aspects of the game, a lot of what we implemented in our batting was self-taught. Obviously, making contact is the first thing you know you have to do as a batsman. Without doing this, you won't score any runs, so we devised ways of trying to hit the ball cleanly and consistently. We'd play a game with no wickets where you are given out as soon as you miss the ball. Still, we'd struggle to get each other out, so we'd take it even further; only playing with the edge of the bat, or only playing with a stump. Our next step would be to get the little cock from inside a leather ball and use that. I remember it once taking us a whole afternoon to get my brother Kudzai out, and he was only using a stump. It makes sense that if you're batting well with a stump, you'll do okay with a bat.

South Africa are one of the better cricketing nations in the world, a team playing at a far higher level than Zimbabwe, but throughout age group cricket we used to match them. I remember on our first tour of South Africa playing against a side coached by Jimmy Cook, who is the father of the South African opening batsman, Stephen Cook. Ryan McLaren and the great Hashim Amla were two players we played against from Under-14s to Under-19s, and we'd often have more success than them, but when schools cricket came to an end they'd start to pull away from us and reach the next level.

Once you reach the end of your teenage years in Zimbabwe, there is no high-performance pathway to enrol in – that age group is simply not catered for. We don't have universities that specialise in cricket development, we have few colleges that play cricket, and we don't have many academies to cater for the obvious talent we have. There is therefore pressure on these talented kids from the townships to go out and earn a living as soon as they have finished school, rather than risking their future on cricket. If a player is lucky enough to come from a family that does have a bit of money, they may often travel further afield, going to university in South Africa, Australia or England.

Part of the problem is getting the parents of the youngster to understand what their child might be capable of achieving in the game. If you want to keep them playing cricket in Zimbabwe, what do you tell these parents, and where do you place these players in the set-up? I remember once coming home and trying to explain to the rest of my family that I had just scored 150 in a game, and what that meant. Only Kudzai – the only other member of my family to play cricket – could really understand what I talking about. Getting the parents of kids from the townships to understand what cricket can do for their child is difficult without a proper system in place – they are too busy trying to make ends meet in life, and who can blame them? As a young boy with stacks of ambition, my attentions would soon turn to getting a scholarship that would allow me to pursue my cricketing dream.

3
The Man of the House

DAD'S HEALTH WAS DETERIORATING DUE TO EXCESSIVE DRINKING. He had developed cirrhosis of the liver. While I was making my first serious steps in cricket, the pressure was mounting on my mother, who had to run the barbershop, look after her sick husband and raise the children who looked to her for guidance. Even though I would still go and play soccer secretly, my silent prayer was to get a scholarship to a good school through cricket. That would ease the burden of education expenses on my family. My dad didn't have a medical aid scheme, and so his hospital bills were being taken care of by the money coming in from the barbershop. These were very difficult times.

Frustrated and depressed by the situation at home, I was pleased to learn that there was a soccer match taking place at the Circle Cement Grounds one afternoon, which gave me a break from the misery of watching Dad in agony for a few hours. As I was walking home after the game, I met two boys who were clearly trying to tell me something, but I couldn't gauge exactly what the message was. As I continued to walk through the neighbourhood I came across a lady who was disliked by most of the young boys, as hardly a kind word ever came out of her mouth. To my surprise this woman greeted me cheerfully and asked to talk to me. I wondered why she was showing me so much warmth, given how she usually acted. Once she had me sat down she said, 'Be brave for your Mum. Don't let her see you cry because you will just make it worse for her – your dad just passed on.' I didn't know what to say. The message the boys had been trying to get to me now made sense.

I walked straight home, and when I got there, people were gathered around the house, as is tradition in Zimbabwean culture when somebody dies. The men were sat outside on stools around a fire while the women sat inside the house singing hymns and preparing food for everyone. Other women would be going around imitating how the deceased used to carry himself, in order to collect funds to help with the burial and so on. I was a boy who didn't want sympathy, so I thought I would sneak inside and avoid people. I then went straight behind my dad's car and wept for him. I wondered how my mum was feeling, and I longed to see her face. I went inside to see she had been crying, her eyes all swollen red. My heart was torn to pieces. I couldn't refrain from crying, despite the words of the lady on the street.

Life was never the same without Dad. He was incredibly tough on me, yet I appreciated his discipline. I remember how he used to take me on drives and have heart-to-heart conversations with me, and I knew his toughness was not hate. He wanted me to do well. He was just preparing me for the world.

The days flew past, the mourners went back to their houses and the house felt empty. I resorted to cricket for comfort, and a big moment was closing in on us – scholarship trials to get into a high school that prioritised cricket. There were only four places up for grabs, and there was stacks of competition. I had quickly realised after Dad's death that I was the only boy Mum could turn to. Without him, there was a question of whether I would be able to continue my education at all. The income generated from Dad's barbershop would have generated enough money to send us to one of the local high schools, but without that we were struggling. A scholarship at a cricket-playing school would alleviate any worries about my future.

I quickly realised after Dad's death that I was the only boy Mum could turn to. If I showed any signs of weakness, that was going to affect her. At the age of twelve, I had to quickly forget my own feelings. It taught me to be mature. Mum used to say, 'If I die, what happens to Tapiwa?' I would tell her not to worry. I would make mature decisions, rather than just play the typical teenager.

I began to realise that if I played cricket professionally I could earn a lot of money and support my whole family. In the townships, at any given time, we had two or three extra relatives to stay. Culturally, this is still normal today. And so, an extra pressure was placed on achieving a scholarship, knowing there would be only four places at the Harare Sports Club.

During a net session ahead of our trials I picked up a hand injury after a rare fight with one of my teammates. The boy's father was the caretaker at our school, and so he was therefore trusted with locking the gate when we finished practising late each evening. For some reason, he demanded we left early that night, and after an argument I struck him. On reflection, the pressure I was putting myself under got the better of me. It meant handling the bat was a simple task that I could not perform as effectively as I'd have liked. I couldn't pull out though, and there were no excuses. The type of coach we are talking about here used to say, 'If it's raining outside your house, that doesn't mean it's raining at school. Still come for practice. If you are dead, come for practice.' I had to go.

Needless to say, I performed badly on the day. My season's performances might still have been able to carry me, but unfortunately, Farai Mukahiwa, from the suburb of Glen Norah, put up a performance that simply could not be ignored. I had not done enough to earn a scholarship. It was a huge blow; I really needed this badly to help ease Mum's financial commitments. I couldn't bring myself to tell her. With the reputation I had built up for myself, it was obvious in her eyes – and in the eyes of many others – that I would get the scholarship.

I kept hoping and trusting that something somewhere would happen for me to end up getting one, and miraculously it did. Upon hearing the results of the scholarship trials, Mr Sirdar, Mohammed's dad, decided to offer a full scholarship, paid from his own company, to Stuart on the condition that the Zimbabwean Cricket Union offered the one reserved for him to me. Mr Sirdar had seen me play many times before, and word about my injury had started to spread. I was therefore fortunate enough to be the recipient of a scholarship, and that was the best news I could possibly give Mum. Given the depth of talent on show four scholarships was a pretty small number, but at least it provided a few youngsters with an invaluable opportunity to forge a career in the professional game. It got better soon after that, with more scholarships made available and half-scholarships offered in some cases. Today the programme is dead; there are no scholarships available, and they have not been replaced by academies. So much talent in Zimbabwe is lost nowadays.

I was to start a new life at Churchill Boys High, together with my closest mates. I had every reason to be happy. At home though, Mum was still struggling to hold the family together. Over the years, Dad had worked hard for us to have three cars and a house of our own which we did not have to rent. All of us had been through the education system as well. But soon enough we had to sell two of these cars, and the third was stolen when my older brother, a new driver, was ambushed by thieves. While things couldn't be going much better for me personally, everything else seemed to be falling apart. One night Mum started crying uncontrollably, seemingly without a reason. She gathered us all round for a prayer and then sent us all off to sleep. That never usually happened. I did not realise quite how bad the situation was until the day we had to buy new school uniforms. After walking many miles from shop to shop to compare prices, Kudzai and I were very tired. We went into one particular shop and tried some more clothes on, only to leave with nothing again. This time though, Mum had a plan.

Somehow, she had managed to devise a ruse with one of the assistants in the shop. She had obviously indicated to them when we had tried on the correct size, only to tell the owner of the store that we were not going to purchase anything. Later on that day, this member of staff met us near the store during their break and handed us a bag full of uniform. Mum gave them some money, but it was just a token amount. I knew what she had done. I never mentioned it, but I was certain that our financial situation was out of control.

'I'm really proud of you for taking the burden off my shoulders by getting a scholarship,' she said to me. 'When you start boarding, work hard, you hear me?' I was unhappy about the uniform situation but seeing her smile when I had become accustomed to a grieving face was priceless, so I smiled back.

The first day of boarding school was an exciting experience, but that excitement soon faded when we were shown around and informed that we had a week to learn the names of the teachers, the prefects, the playing field and the school's war cries. That was just the beginning. Hostel life was built under strict rules of seniority. No matter how wide a door or a gate was, we were always supposed to give way to a senior, and we had to lift our cap in the process. If a senior – anyone in a higher year than yours – was five metres behind, we had to stop, stand on the side and let him pass. A cap was to be worn at all times, unless inside. First year boys were called sprogs, which meant 'a worthless piece of garbage who waits to be told what to do.' As sprogs, we were in charge of the hostel bell, which we first sounded at 5.30am and then 6.15. By 6.20 we all had to be standing in lines of three, ready for uniform inspection. If we were not turned out immaculately, we were severely punished by a teacher or one of the prefects.

Dinner was at 5.30pm, and after that we'd have an hour and a half of study. During this time, the hostel would be deadly silent, resembling a graveyard. At 8pm the television was put on for an hour, before we were allowed to retire to our rooms at 9pm, unless we wished to continue studying. At least I was used to this sort of system at Chipembere. It was sad to see others who had no experience of this routine bursting into tears every night at the start. I guess Churchill played a big part in keeping me on a straight and narrow path. The school was named after the British wartime leader Winston Churchill, one of the hostels was named Winston, and the British bulldog was the school emblem. I was also lucky that I had friends alongside me. Stuey, Hamilton Masakadza and Vusi Sibanda – all boys I had played cricket with before youth level – had all received scholarships as well.

We were introduced to our new cricket coach, Peter Sharples, who was around sixty years old. Mr Sharples was different from my early coaches in every way possible. He was Caucasian, very tall, calm and gently spoken. He believed in trying to understand what the player was attempting to do. He was far more of a father figure to me than my previous coaches had been, and I had not come across this sort of method before. I think all the players, myself included, appreciated the way he went about things. If you weren't driven from within, he wouldn't try and push you, which meant some of their players lost their way in cricketing terms. He wanted the players to understand what it was he was trying to do and why he was doing it. The player could have his say as well. He was particularly receptive to that, the opposite of Mangongo. His style had been, 'I'll tell you what to do and you do it.'

I embraced his methods and adapted swiftly. He thought my technique meant I was suited to opening the batting, primarily because of how technically sound I was. He wanted me to bat from start to finish, to make use of all the overs available to me. He made sure I played for all the teams: when I was in form one I played for the Under-16's, and when the first team had an easy game I played for them. He didn't just get me to bat at seven or eight, he pushed me and got me to open, but he was soft in his approach.

Mr Sharples didn't like soccer and wanted us to play either hockey or rugby in the winter. He believed rugby to be a hooligan's sport played by gentlemen, and soccer a gentleman's game played by hooligans. I chose rugby. I had also mistakenly qualified for the cross-country team after an impressive trial run, and so I was under pressure from the headmaster, Mr Mutsekwa, to represent the school in that as well. He knew about my soccer talents, but all I wanted to do at this stage was to play cricket. I skipped cross-country training, and subsequently received six whippings from the coach. When it came to rugby, I had to get my older sister to buy my kit, as she had now started work and I knew of Mum's financial difficulties.

Stuey and I hardly went home during exit weekends – instead we used the time to study and practise our cricket more. When I did go home during the holidays, I realised I was no longer acting like other boys of my age. I preferred helping Mum at the barbershop. I had changed a lot, and there was plenty of gossip going around that I was missing my teenage years just as I had entered them. Word would go around that one kid was now smoking marijuana, another was pregnant, someone else had dropped out of school. I remembered Mum's words about working hard, and that's exactly what I did. All of a sudden, the conversations I had with friends back home started to change. To me they now seemed quite childish. I felt I was more focused with a clearer sense of direction, whereas they seemed to be drifting through life.

It was great to see my siblings, and they were doing well, but the house was always noisy, and all of a sudden this began to irritate me. I wanted to be either working at my game or closed off studying, which proved difficult. I had no one to talk cricket with either: Kudzai was the only one who understood the game, but he was going in a different direction. One morning I woke to find a young lady in our lounge. Before I had even asked who it was, Mum came and told me that Joseph had made her pregnant, and hence preparations were under way for marriage. Miriam was a very nice lady, humble and meek in spirit. The two didn't match at all, but she was now no longer able to go to university, and my mum had another mouth to feed.

Going home acted as a reminder for me that I needed to work tirelessly. Financial hardships were becoming even more obvious. It was at this point I decided that I simply had to be a professional cricketer. I was already well aware that it was a serious career option for me when I secured my scholarship, but I now decided that it was the only option. Nothing else would do. I would practise more than other boys of my age. I started asking questions about how professional cricketers practised, how much time they put into individual training. I would do exactly as I was told. I was ready to feel the fear. I told myself that life's difficulties vanish when faced boldly.

It didn't take long for me to start experiencing the fruits of my labour, as I found myself selected to represent Zimbabwe Under-14's on a tour of South Africa. I had made many big contributions for the school team during the season, including a partnership of 386 with Stuey in one game – he ended on 201*, while I made 156. Also in the school team were Mohammed and Andrew, so it was a lot of fun. On tour Stuey and I found ourselves batting together again, but not at the top of the order this time, instead down at seven and eight. That presented a problem for us, as we only owned one bat between us. Andrew, who usually helped us out by lending us a spare, was not on this tour. This could have been rather embarrassing, but thankfully a teammate of ours named Bruce Henwood came to the rescue. By the end of the tour, Stuey had been promoted to open and I was batting at three. On the way back, a lot of the richer players made their own way home, so it was left to four of us to eat all the food that had been budgeted for.

Around this time, I started to play in an annual cricket tournament called Strugglers Week, which was organised by Bill Flower. On one day of this tournament a wicketkeeper failed to turn up for one of the games, so I filled in for him. I took to the task well, and very soon keeping became a more permanent job for me. During one of these games, every player in the field stopped suddenly and started to stare towards the pavilion. Andy Flower had turned up to give his dad something. Later on, when Bill asked for Andy's opinion on my makeshift keeping, he remarked that I had a natural pair of catching hands. This was before I had played with Andy for Takashinga, and I was naturally delighted. I was even more thrilled when he promised his dad that he would give me his old cricket equipment, which I received later on.

Around this period Zimbabwe was mired in political turmoil. In the late 1990s, the Zimbabwe Congress of Trade Unions (ZCTU), led by Morgan Tsvangirai, who would later challenge Robert Mugabe for the presidency of the country, had become the most powerful opposition to the government and since December 1997 had called a number of strikes. Their demands during this period were that tax rises should be reversed, prices of bread and petrol should be reduced, Zimbabwe should withdraw from the war in DR Congo and that government 'lawlessness' should end.

On this particular day when Andy showed up there was another strike taking place, and so shops were closed, no businesses were running and there were people demonstrating out on the streets. A commuter bus had been burnt and there was lots of violence. Despite this crisis we just wanted to play cricket, and Bill Flower was more than happy to oblige – he never stopped for anything. His first thought was how Stuart, Hamilton and I were going to get to the game, and so he came and picked us up individually. At the game itself there were no problems. We were playing at the CFX academy, a venue that was surrounded by houses and set away from the main roads. The journey back home was a different story.

Given the climate Bill was worried for our safety, and so decided to drop us home as well. It was dangerous for a Caucasian man to be seen in certain areas of the city and the country in general, but there was only one route he could take and it was through the most unsafe area of the capital. Massive rocks were blocking the other roads home. We had to travel straight through the Mbare township, the poorest township of Harare and the most dangerous. People say that you can get anything you want in Mbare. They also say that if you go to Mbare looking for a car wheel, be sure that they don't sell you the wheel of the car you've got with you already.

As we drove home, men with iron bars approached the car and ordered Bill to pull over. He whispered to the four of us with him to put our heads down and slowed down as the men approached. He then pretended to open the window, and just as they came close he sped off, somehow avoiding the rocks designed to stop cars getting through. Stones were thrown at us from behind, but we managed to escape unscathed thanks to Bill's bravery. He was prepared to put his own safety at risk during times of political and racial tension just to make sure we could play a game of cricket and get home in one piece. If you mention his name anywhere in Zimbabwe, he is well respected. He played such a massive role in the development of young Zimbabwean cricketers. I have since returned to Zimbabwe to launch the Bill Flower Academy in his honour. That gesture to take us back to Highfield that day speaks volumes about him as a man, and he did an awful lot for me.

As a young boy, experiencing situations like that from an early age prepares you for many things later on in life. Though what was happening was clearly frightening to us as boys, we never questioned whether we would play or not. As long as we could get there, there was only one answer. Growing up in a tough environment moulded me into someone who didn't scare easily. Even after such a close shave, it didn't cross my mind that we shouldn't have played that day. In fact, if someone had asked me if I wanted to play the next day as well, I would have agreed straight away. Things quickly go back to normal.

Growing up where we did, our parents rarely tried to shelter us from things that we probably shouldn't have seen. I remember a particular incident when a young girl my older sister Jean used to walk to school with took her own life. I was still a young kid when this happened, but my mum did not shelter me from what had happened. I even remember going to the house with her and seeing the girl in her room. It just becomes another part of life.

4
A Boy in a Man's World

AT SCHOOL MY CRICKET CONTINUED TO DEVELOP AT A RAPID RATE, so much so that at the age of fourteen, I trialled for the Under-16 national team. During the trials I batted and kept extremely well, which meant I was the only underage player to be selected for the squad, who were coached by Bill Flower. There was no guarantee I was going to be selected in the final XI, but it was a great experience nonetheless. I was very much the baby of the team and didn't have anyone to hang out with, so I spent most of the time with Bill. I felt a little uncomfortable in that environment, but I was selected for the third game of our tour as an opening batsman, and after that I kept my position at the top of the order and as wicketkeeper for the remaining games. At one stage during the series Bill even managed to persuade me to do a TV interview in English, a language I wasn't particularly fluent in at the time. At the end of the interview I was commended by the commentator, who was impressed that I was prepared to answer questions in a straightforward manner, something a lot of athletes seem uncomfortable doing. Even then I wasn't afraid of speaking my mind.

As soon as we returned from that tour I heard that I had been selected, as a fifteen-year-old, to go on tour to Namibia as part of the Zone Six development team. This was a men's team and I was going to be the only boy. For the first time I would not be staying with a friend or with a family, but I'd be sharing a room with a teammate I didn't know. I was given far more responsibility and had to look after my own wellbeing.

On the cricket field, I didn't feel intimidated in the slightest. My only problem is that I perhaps wasn't of a strong enough build. I had the technique, but I wasn't yet able to score at the rate required for a 50-over game at that level. But I didn't feel intimidated. My cricketing career so far had prepared me for this moment. Like many professional sportsmen, I grew up playing with people older than me, even at primary school. If you're good enough, you will find yourself playing with the seniors. In our final year of primary school we were already training with the senior team at Takashinga. Playing with elders was considered the norm.

I was shocked, if anything, by what the players got up to off the field. I soon found most of the squad were completely irresponsible. I thought we were there to play cricket and win, and you'd expect most people to carry themselves in a professional manner if they are aspiring to have a career in the game, but I saw things on that tour that a young man should not see, and I was hurt by it. The guys were always out drinking during the evenings, and I often heard chatter with female voices in the hotel corridors while I was inside watching movies. I had a roommate who I didn't see for most of the time, because he was often out until I went to sleep, and sometimes he did not return at all. This disgusted me. What made things more awkward was that my former primary school coaches were part of this team as players. They had been my coaches at club level, but they were now my teammates. Despite my age they tried to get me to drink, but I made it clear that I wasn't up for it and they failed to convince me otherwise.

I do think part of the reason cricket has a culture of drinking is because it's such a mental game. I also believe that the mental strain it places on you is why many players have suffered from mental health problems. The game pushes you to the limits mentally, and it can become extreme. You are tested both mentally and physically, and the two combined can be overwhelming. You have to win the game in your mind before you can win it out on the field. I have played with and seen many players at both recreational and international level who have the talent, but they fear failure too much to succeed. They struggle to win the battle going on in their mind, which means their game naturally suffers, whatever level they are playing at.

I think that in whatever profession, if a person is really determined to really go out there and be the best there are certain things that they have to be prepared to sacrifice, otherwise you just end up being like everyone else. I like to believe there is a certain mindset that one must have if they're going to achieve great things and be counted in the world. That mindset certainly did not seem to prevalent among the players on that tour.

Following that trip, there were rumours flying around that I was to captain the

Under-16 team on a tour of South Africa. Despite what I would go on to achieve in Zimbabwean cricket, at this stage I wasn't ready for all the responsibility that comes with being captain. Every time I heard the rumour, I was quick to dismiss it. When the time came for the announcement, I put my head down and prayed that I would not be the named called out. A huge grin spread across my face when I heard the announcer say Andrew Stone from St John's College was to be skipper.

This was the best age group team I was involved in. I had a lot of friends in the side, and with Bill Flower as the coach we were confident of beating most of the teams we encountered. In our warm-up game, we had to play a Durban side including Hashim Amla. He managed a fifty, but so did three of our players, including myself, and the game ended in a draw. We played brilliantly on that trip, winning every game we played.

I had set myself the goal of playing in the national team as soon as I left high school, and I still had two years to achieve my goal. After my O Level exams, I was called to join the Zimbabwean Under-19 World Cup team. Though again I was not guaranteed my place in the team I was happy, as I knew it would increase my exposure to top-level cricket. I aimed to utilise every opportunity that came my way, and tried to be as disciplined as ever, just like Dad had raised me. My mother was still having it tough, so there was no room for failure, and I spent no time messing around. Any other boy would be having the time of their life travelling and exploring, but I really had no time for that. My vision of a comfortable life was playing international cricket – I wasn't an average teenager who wanted to spend their money on clothes or taking girls out. My life was different, and I had to be responsible.

Before we left for the World Cup in Sri Lanka, we stopped off in South Africa for a few warm-up games. A lot of players were struggling against the spin, but I managed to apply myself well at number seven and made enough of an impression on coach Iain Butchart for him to move me up to number three. Given that I was also keeping, I had a lot of responsibility in the team. Paul Strang took over from Butchart before the start of the tournament, but my role in the side did not change. Paul, who himself was working his way back into the national team, was very impressed with my fitness levels, and I used to try and compete with him in the gym. I felt this way I could gauge whether I was up to the required levels for international cricket.

During that World Cup I scored two fifties, which at the age of sixteen I considered to be a success. I had gone as a reserve player but ended up batting at number three and keeping wicket. Importantly, Paul Strang gave me a good report to the ZCU, suggesting that if they needed an understudy to Andy Flower in the years to come, I should be the one that they should turn to first. When I returned home, I soon discovered Steve Mangongo was not so impressed with my efforts. He believed I was good enough to have made three centuries, and so dropped me to Takashinga's second team. I was shocked, but all I could do was prove myself all over again. Luckily, when I turned up at the meeting point for our game that weekend, some of the other players had not arrived on time. Mangongo had zero time for poor time management, and so I was back in the first team straight away.

We were playing against a full-strength Georgians side who had the likes of Craig Evans, Trevor Gripper, Grant Flower, Craig Wishart and Travis Friend in their squad. Mangongo was still on my case about my supposed failure at the World Cup, and so moved me down to number seven. Our top order struggled to score freely, and I ended up making 38 quick runs late on to help us to a total of 230, giving us a chance to defend what we had. In the dressing room, Mangongo moaned about the score we had made. He wasn't the only unhappy one – I was not impressed at where I'd been asked to bat.

I would often bowl my medium pacers when we defended low totals, as batsmen often struggled to get me away for runs in pressure situations. My type of bowler – slow but accurate – is often particularly successful in club cricket, where batsmen don't have the same power or ingenuity as those at the very highest level. My captain, Walter Chawaguta had wanted to bring me on to stem the flow of runs, but I point-blank refused to bowl. I had the ability to move the ball both ways and he needed that to give us a fighting chance, but I had also grown tired of being pushed around by my coach. My friends agreed with my sentiments, and so they backed me out on the field. It was a touch of teenage angst kicking in. Needless to say we lost the game, and I knew what was waiting for us in the changing rooms. There was dead silence when we walked in – the calm before the storm. Then it started. A lot of words were thrown my way, and not very kind ones either. Stuart and Hamilton were included in this barrage because they had backed me, but as far as we were concerned it had been a necessary measure. The club leadership hadn't realised that we were starting to become adults, and that they needed to show us a little bit more understanding. We were becoming adults but still being treated as children.

Practice continued to be demanding at Takashinga, who were still called Old Winstonians at this stage. During one of these gruelling sessions, I overheard Mangongo talking with the other coaches, and the topic of discussion was me making my provincial debut for Mashonaland, one of Zimbabwe's five first-class outfits. At the end of the session I went up to him to confirm what I had heard, and he told me that it was true. In fact, he was surprised that I hadn't been given the news myself. When I got home I asked everyone whether there had been a call for me from the management team, but no one had heard anything. I was confused. The game was supposed to be the following day. What was I meant to do? I sat at the telephone until 9pm, but still nothing. I didn't know how I was going to get to the ground the next morning, as I didn't know where we were playing, and we no longer had a family car. I asked my sister if one of her friends would drop me off at the Harare Sports Club first thing, so I could find out where the match was being played. Viola Muza, who used to run the ZCU office pretty much alone, informed me at 8am that the game was being played at the country club, so again I got my sister's friend to rush back.

When I arrived, the teams had already concluded their warm-ups and the toss. Clearly, I wasn't playing. The manager looked shocked to see me, and unhappy to say the least. He shouted at me for not arriving at the ground on time, despite the fact that I had been given absolutely no details about the fixture. I had always known that there would be opposition to me making my way in the game, but I never knew it would be this strong. I was glad my sister had not stayed to witness this. He had not advised me of anything at all; I was there on hearsay. This is how he treated me? Instead of making my debut, I was made to do the drinks for the game. This was the first time I came face to face with opposition that bordered along the lines of racism. It was the way the coach spoke to me, the way he shouted at me. There have been people over the years who have spoken strongly about the way they feel to me, but not in the way that he did that day. I don't remember the exact words, but I remember him saying something along the lines of, 'That's how it is with you people.' I was thinking, 'You people? Which people?' That did not sit well with me at all. I do not believe myself to be the sort of person who quickly turns something into a racial matter, but to this day I believe my judgement to be correct on this one. I was yet to turn twenty years old.

Thankfully, my upbringing had prepared me for injustices such as this. I did not react to his provocation and was instead very apologetic – even though I knew that he was in the wrong. I just wanted to break into the national team, and nothing or no one was going to stand in my way. Even if it meant being harassed, I didn't care, all I wanted to do was to accomplish my goal. Mangongo had heard what had gone on and made his way to the ground. He managed to get me away from twelfth man duties, so I could play for Takashinga on Saturday and Sunday instead. Even though he could be tough, Mangongo always used to look out for me. I got runs in both matches, just as the selectors were getting a squad together for the tour of the West Indies.

Straight after that second game I played with Takashinga, I received a call from Dave Ellman-Brown, who was then chief executive of the Zimbabwe Cricket Union, as it was still called at the time. Right away he asked me to meet him at his offices with a passport. When I put the phone down in the dressing room, I found my teammates all staring at me in anticipation. What was the news? I told them, and one of them just shouted, 'Passport! What for?' I didn't know, so I just shrugged my shoulders.

I was nervous to meet him. I didn't have a wide range of clothes to choose from – I only had two sets of casual clothes besides my cricket gear, which I had been given for free. I just picked up what was available and left the house very early in the morning. I certainly wasn't going to be late, in fact I was around two hours early for our 10am meeting. What he told me was simply unbelievable. He wanted me to leave the passport with him and meet him at the ZCU offices the following day with the vice-president, Peter Chingoka. The selectors had made the decision for me to go and join the national team in the Caribbean. I felt numb all over. I was biting my nails to make sure I wasn't dreaming. Only two days earlier, I had been humiliated by a bigoted coach, and subsequently not made my first-class debut. Now I was joining up with the national squad. Brown continued, telling me that I was going there as an understudy to Andy Flower. I could barely even register what he was telling me. All I knew was that I was going to the Caribbean to watch Andy, and that I would try to learn as much as I could.

My mum and my sister Jackie were present at the meeting the next day. None of us had any idea what was in store. When we got there, she was told about me joining the team, and the money that I would be getting. Instantly her face brightened and her eyes began to glow. She couldn't fathom the amounts that were being mentioned. They were figures that we never thought we'd be discussing. It's hard to recall the exact figures involved, but say my mum was getting around

$500 per month from the barbershop, I would be making around six times that for this trip, around $3,000 dollars. That was just the basic wage as well; it didn't include extras such as match fees and allowances. The meeting was concluded with a smile on my mum's poor face. She never realised that cricket could take me to these heights, and yet this was only the beginning. When we got back, my mum and sister immediately started discussing what they would do with my earnings, which I marvelled at. It was too soon to be talking about all that. I thought about all the games I had played ever since I started playing cricket, all the games that nobody had been bothered about watching. My mum only came to watch me once throughout my whole career, and that was when I was on the verge of national team-selection. Now, because of the money being mentioned, everyone in the family was interested.

Within a few weeks I had my visa and was prepared to travel. Mr Chingoka met me at the airport and offered me some inspirational words as he handed me my air tickets and passport: 'Young man, a cricket ball moves the same way everywhere in the world; it comes from the bowler's hand and towards the bat. In England, it might swing a bit more, in India it might bounce low, and in Australia you may be faced with steep bounce. The main point is that it comes the same way, therefore, just bat the same way as you do in Zimbabwe and you will be guaranteed great results.' On punctuality, he said, 'It's better to be fifteen minutes early than a second late.' With those words of wisdom, I was on my way.

Things were happening faster than I had anticipated. Joining the national team was something I had targeted at the age of eighteen, and now here I was all alone in business class on a 24-hour flight to the home of some of the legends of the game. Although I was excited to join the team, I was also nervous. I had no idea what it would be like. It's funny how I didn't know, or at least didn't pay any attention to what was happening. At home, one newspaper's headline was 'Taibu makes history', with the accompanying text:

The Churchill High School boy was named as one of the players who will replace the four to be dropped after two Tests against the West Indies. Those four players will return home after this current Test finishes. The series should prove a big leap for Taibu, a form four student, who is being tipped to eventually replace Andy Flower, the team skipper, as wicketkeeper. Strang described Taibu as a promising player, both as a batsman and as a wicketkeeper, and said the Churchill schoolboy only needed to be exposed to more first-class cricket to develop into a good cricketer. The son of the late barber in Highfield, cricket seems to be changing Taibu's life and his mere selection into the senior team is quite an achievement.

When I arrived, an immigration officer said to me, 'Young boy, what's your name and where are you going?' I told him that I was joining the Zimbabwe national cricket team. He tutted and went, 'You, playing cricket for that national team? Who's the fastest bowler you've faced man?' I named a Kenyan player, and I talked about Henry Olonga and Heath Streak. He tutted again and said, 'Boy, I'm talking about real fast bowling! You mean to tell me that you can face Curtly Ambrose, Courtney Walsh and Franklyn Rose? Look at yourself!' He had a really good laugh and told me that my country had sent me on a suicide mission. This gentleman put a real fear in me before I had left the airport, though I tried to comfort myself by reminding myself that I was only going as an understudy to Andy. All I was going to do was watch and learn.

After that encounter, the liaison officer took me to our hotel. The team had already gone for practice, but when I went to meet them I was given a very warm reception. It was once a fantasy, now it was a reality. That reality soon hit home when I got into the nets for the first time. If I'm not mistaken, I ducked the first six balls that I faced. It was bouncer after bouncer after bouncer. All of a sudden, I had to put my favourite shots into my pocket, because at that pace I couldn't hook the ball. I could only cover drive and cut. I wouldn't get a lot to drive, but I got plenty to cut.

As I was a young black Zimbabwean – or a young black African in the West Indies – I was big news back home when I was selected. Though black players had played for Zimbabwe before me, I was the first one to have come through the ZCU development programme in the townships. I found myself on the radio or in the paper every other day. I remember going on to field as a substitute during one match. A ball was played out to me on the boundary, and I remember going for a one-handed pick up and missing it completely. Henry Olonga later said it was the first time he ever saw the crowd applaud a misfield. Normally you would be jeered for such a silly mistake, but I had them on their feet clapping. Even when I came off the field, the whole crowd was up and clapping for me. That was nice. I think to a great extent that support gave me a sense of belonging, and all those fears began to vanish little by little.

There were some surreal moments, including encounters with the former wicketkeeping great Jeff Dujon, and the star of the West Indian team, Brian Lara, one of the finest batsmen to ever play the game. Brian was kind enough to give me some of his time and advice. He had got into the Windies team at the age of 21, and he told me that all he did at first was cut and pull the ball. Curtly Ambrose, who stood at 6ft 7in and was coming towards the end of an international career in which he took 630 international wickets, was sitting next to him when he said it. He turned to Brian and said, 'Boy, hook and cut who? Who did you used to hook and cut?' Later on, I remember Ambrose walking past with Lara while I was in the nets and saying, 'This boy can bat man.' It was comments like this that helped me to feel at home and more relaxed.

I was a very shy individual at this stage, and the older boys would always be laughing at me because I was attracting the attention of girls of a similar age. Many would show an interest in me, but I didn't respond to it. I was now setting myself a new goal and I really didn't want any distractions. In terms of catching the signs of a girl showing interest, I wasn't very streetwise. I vowed that I would not go the usual route of boys my age, who were beginning to experiment in terms of drinking, smoking, partying and dating.

I noticed that Andy and Henry were two of the most respected players within the team; Andy because of his general leadership qualities, his ability to play the game and his leadership posture; Henry because of his conversion to Christianity. I went to the two of them and told them I didn't want any peer pressure because I may give in. I asked them to tell the other players off if they tried. I wanted them to act as my voice.

I spent a lot of time with Andy on this tour, and we became good friends. It seemed to me that he found it hard to trust anyone, so when he felt under pressure with his game, he would come and talk to me. I was just a little innocent boy with no words of wisdom to share, but I was someone who would listen to him. When he stayed for extra practice, he'd asked me to stay with him. It was during these times that we spoke a lot. He acted as a big brother to me. He told me that if I was to do well at an international level, I shouldn't trust anyone in the team, particularly the board members. He believed that as an organisation we were content with being mediocre. Shortly before the tour to the Caribbean, during a national-team practice session, Andy called me over and said, 'Tiba, you see all these guys?

What do you think about them?'

'Well they're quite good, they're playing for the national team,' I responded.

'Well I don't think that way. I think they're quite average.' I was shocked. These were international cricketers he was talking about. Average?

'They're good in our local competitions and when we're practising,' he said, 'but when it really matters, when the fight is really on against tough opposition – against Pakistan, against West Indies, against England – they put their tails between their legs. They're weak. If they ask you to emulate them or try to coach you, don't listen. If you're going to emulate your game on someone, pick Aravinda de Silva or Sachin Tendulkar, because of your height. I would not advise you to pick Lara. His technique is awkward.'

Andy never fully explained to me why I shouldn't trust these people, instead telling me I'd understand later. He then went on to ask what I was doing with the money that the federation was paying me. I told him that I was keeping it with them, so he advised me to take it out and open my own account as soon I got home. We discussed ways of investing money wisely.

He always asked me what I was thinking. He had a tremendous way of finding out if I had something burning in my heart. Although he was a great player with so much ability, he would seek my opinion in different situations, which to me was one of the reasons he was so good. I was very shy, and my English wasn't very strong, but he was very clever. He would take me away from people and ask me my thoughts in confidence. If he thought my point was a valid one, he'd present it in front of the team himself. He'd test me, asking me what I hoped to achieve from a practice session. I knew I had to really plan my sessions now, just so I had an answer for him.

Towards the end of the tour, our coach, Dave Houghton, sorted me a sponsorship deal with Gray Nichols, which allowed me to get some proper new kit. I then finally made my first-class debut. It was an odd sensation, making my first-class cricketing debut on a tour with the national team. It was against the West Indies President's XI, and I was unbeaten on eleven runs when the rain arrived. Overall, we didn't too badly as a team on that tour, but there were moments we wished to forget as well. We lost the two-Test series 2-0 but had a golden opportunity to earn a draw. Chasing just 99 runs for victory in the first Test match, we were bowled out for 63 on the final day. Ambrose was the star man for the West Indies, rolling back the years.

The tour came to an end, and as players we all had the choice whether we wanted to go home for a couple of days before the tour of England, or whether we wanted to go straight there. The married guys went to see their families, while myself and five others made our way straight to our next destination.

A week later and all of us were together again, and our first warm-up game was against Hampshire. Stuart Carlisle advised me to Test my new bats in the nets against the old balls before I used them in the middle. Having all this equipment was still so new to me, and I was learning all the time. In the game against Hampshire Alistair Campbell made an impressive century, but that seemed to be somewhat overshadowed by me making 36. Once again, I seemed to be all over the newspapers. With me still just being sixteen years of age, the English media had their story. One journalist wrote, 'Young Taibu looks one for the future. Put the name Tatenda Taibu in your diaries as one to remember. In the absence of Andy Flower he looked neat and tidy, with a very good pair of hands.'

I was just happy to be playing, but there were a couple of issues that those already established in the squad were not happy about, issues that needed to be addressed as quickly as possible. The first issue was concerning Dave Houghton: some players were not happy with him as coach, and were not keen on the idea of playing for him any longer. Luckily for them, they would not have to. On 21 April, six days before the game against Hampshire, it was announced his contract as coach would not go beyond April. Dave himself had asked for an early release from his contract, and was replaced in the post by the Convenor of the Selection Committee, Andy Pycroft, for the tour of England. The other issue was our match fees, which led to the players signing a petition, and there was a question of whether we would take to the field at Lord's at all. If we were not given our proper dues, we would refuse to play. The boys wanted a pay increase, so they were closer to the level of what other international players earned around the world. Some of the senior players had been talking to one of the coach drivers who was taking us around the UK, and they soon realised he was getting paid more than we were. Andy was not amused. He spoke to a lawyer, who went and did some investigating, and he returned with the information that as players we were only getting around a 3.5 percent cut of all the revenue flowing into Zimbabwean cricket. This percentage figure was significantly lower than the cut players from other nations were taking, and my teammates deserved and wanted better.

I had asked Andy if I needed to get involved in either of these matters – I felt that given my age I had little opinion to offer. He allowed me to stay away from the Dave Houghton issue, but wanted me to sign the petition. He assured me that I would not be targeted by the board, because they would know that the senior players were behind everything. His theory was this: if you want to go fast, go alone, but if you want to go far, you go together.

Andy told me that it was very difficult to strike in Zimbabwe, because the hierarchy would use divide and rule tactics against us, eventually making us fight with each other instead of them. But now we were here in England, we could just decide not to play at Lord's. They couldn't target anyone, because we were all in one place as a team.

Peter Chingoka arrived in England a few days after we had signed the petition to discuss the concerns we had over it. He walked into our changing room after one practice session holding a copy of *The Herald*, which had a picture of me keeping on the front page. I guess it was a clever way to break the ice, with rumours going around that we weren't prepared to take to the field. I admired the way he spoke so confidently. He started by mentioning how rare it was for a sportsman to be on the front page making headlines – that honour was usually reserved for the president. He then got the issue of finance. I didn't understand what was being discussed at all, but an agreement was made, and we were to take to the field of play.

Everything seemed to go to plan to me. We were promised a fair share of the total income, although I didn't know what that really meant because I had not yet received any money at all. I really did not care much about what had transpired at the time. Growing up in a humble family had moulded me into someone who did not care much about money. I had grown up seeing my father and mother giving out food to those in need, so much so that my father had earned the nickname 'Doctor cash' for his reputation of giving out food to anyone in need in our neighbourhood, even the little kids in the street if he was in a good mood. I was in a different situation to all the other players, though, who needed the money to put food on the tables for their families.

Andy still wasn't happy. 'Tatenda, remember what I've told you about this group. When I get home, someone is going to stab me in the back.' I was taken aback – I thought we had all agreed; we had all signed the petition. I soon found out he was right. When Andy returned home later on, I went to pick up some bats that he had promised me. The headlines in the papers were that he had been replaced as captain. 'Tatenda, do you remember what I told you? That's exactly what has happened.' Later on that year, Heath Streak replaced Andy as our skipper.

We played the Test match at Lord's. I had only seen the beautiful ground on television before, but to think I was now walking on that very grass was exciting. The changing rooms were immaculate. I knew that I wasn't good enough to be playing in the team at this stage, but the feeling of walking on the Lord's field made me not want to miss it the next time we played here. I had heard stories of players not being able to find their way from the changing rooms to the field, and that soon became me when I went to take the drinks out. We lost the Test match inside three days. We made a paltry 83 in our first innings, and in response both Graeme Hick and Alec Stewart made centuries in England's total of 415. We did pass the hundred-mark as a team in our second innings, but our total of 123 meant the margin of defeat was a massive innings and 209 runs. Most of the team were playing at Lord's for the first time, and we seemed affected by nerves. The famous Lord's slope also played on the minds of our players, and it was too much for the team to handle.

It seemed that we could not deal with what the English pace attack threw at us, which was strange – we had fared a lot better against the likes of Courtney Walsh and Curtly Ambrose. For the two days after the Lord's Test, we tried to find answers as a team. Andy was now in temporary charge, because Dave Houghton had resigned with immediate effect, leaving us without a coach. While all the players were quiet, Andy turned to me and said, 'Tiba, what do you think?' I just stared at him. I really wanted to say something, but I was unable to get my words out.

He picked up the baton and took me to one side. We left the whole team watching, and he asked me to free myself up and say what I wanted to say. I didn't have the right vocabulary to express what it was that I had noticed, so I took a pen and paper from the table and began to draw. He didn't stop me, and I didn't feel embarrassed in front of him. I drew a batsman and a bowler, and wrote 22 yards in between them, and started to put my point across. The simple message I was trying to convey was that with the exception of Andy himself and Murray Goodwin, all the batsmen were still moving their heads as the ball was being delivered, thereby not giving themselves enough time to watch the ball before deciding on a shot to play. I was so humbled to see Andy go back to the group, switch the television off and explain my point to the rest of the team. Obviously, he spoke with far more authority than I could have done, and he asked the team to implement it in practice. Andy wanted me to think about the game. During one net session he got me to bat first, then called all the players around to come and watch me. I don't know what they talked about, and I never had the guts to ask him.

I had first started learning English when we had been taken as youngsters to play cricket against the all-white schools, and I had continued to learn when I enrolled at high school. I could understand it perfectly well, but I had grown up speaking Shona, so to actually say what I thought in any detail in English was still really difficult for me, and that was the number one language in the dressing room. There were other black players in the squad – Mpumelelo Mbangwa, Henry Olonga, Mluleki Nkala – but they all had very different upbringings to me. I was still really the first player in the Zimbabwean team to have come from the 'ghetto'.

During these tours I hardly called home at all, except to Stuey. When we arrived at one of our hotels one day, though, I had a message from Norbert Manyande, a boy who I had played cricket with and against in primary and secondary school. I wasn't as close to Norbert as I was to Stuey, Hamilton and Vusi, but he was a friend nonetheless. I called him back in excitement, only for him to bring me some deeply troubling news. My mother had been sick ever since I had left for the Caribbean and had been getting worse every day. By the time Norbert called me she had already been admitted to hospital on a couple of occasions, and most people were fearing for her life. Norbert, upon hearing this news, had been to visit her. He had become disturbed when he asked my family if I knew the condition she was in, only to find that she had got them all to promise not to tell me while I was on tour. She did not want me distracted by anything, and felt she had to correct a lot of wrongs by giving me the best opportunity to do well on tour.

In all the years I had been playing, she had never watched me once. I didn't mind – cricket is a time-consuming sport, and she had seven children to raise. She did so well to buy me all the clothes required for me to be presentable, despite them mostly being out of her reach financially. Now, not a week would pass without me being in the newspaper, but she had no idea just how well I was doing because of her condition.

The few times I had spoken to her while I was in the Caribbean and the UK, she had pretended to be absolutely fine. My sister Jackie, who was the main one looking after her, did very well to keep it a secret from me. As Norbert revealed my mum's state to me, tears filled my eyes. Why would they do this to me? I got so angry that I could not finish the conversation. I really needed some fresh air; it was as if I could not breathe properly. I took an aimless walk, which did not help much. I needed answers and they had to come right away. I called Jackie, who I thought would be able to provide answers, but she just repeated what Norbert had already told me. The explanations they gave did not satisfy me. Why had they hidden it?

I decided to find comfort in bed. Talking to people wasn't making me feel any better, so I tried to sleep the pain away. I was awoken a little later by the phone ringing. It was the team manager, asking my thoughts on whether I was ready to play the next Test. I did not really digest what he was saying, because I was feeling a little bleary-eyed. Then all of a sudden it hit me – play what? I needed someone to talk to, so I called Jackie back again.

'Tatenda, that's great news!'

'Great news? Do you know how old I am?'

'Anyway, what does she know about cricket?' I thought to myself. I needed to speak to someone who understood the game. I called Andy to ask if he was free for a chat. He left the door open for me and asked me to speak freely.

'Did you hear? They want me to play the next game and they want me to keep wicket,' I asked with my eyes wide open.

'Oh, Tiba, that was actually my decision, you are batting so well in the nets and the warm-up games. I dropped three catches at Lord's, you will do a better job.'

'You really think so?'

'Yes.'

That's all I needed to silence my conscience. As I walked out he said, 'Tiba, in the next warm-up game against Yorkshire you will bat at four, so you can spend some more time in the middle.'

I was roommates with Mluleki Nkala. Mululeki was well spoken – he had gone to one of the best private schools in the country and was earmarked to be Zimbabwe's first black captain. On his debut, when he was just eighteen years old, he had dismissed Sachin Tendulkar. He had settled quickly in the national team, and he liked to go out at night. One morning I woke up to see the bag he had left on his bed the previous night still in the same position. He had not come back. I didn't know what to do: if I told the management team I could land him in serious hot water. Should I keep it to myself, or should I let someone know? I decided I would pack his bags, leave out his travelling clothes, pay for his room and keep my fingers crossed that he would appear soon.

Having breakfast at the team hotel at this time was never a particularly pleasant experience for me, as the conversations were invariably focused on girls and beer, neither of which interested me much. Hardly anyone seemed concerned about Mluleki's whereabouts. We had to travel to Yorkshire, and time was ticking faster than I had ever seen before. I had no choice but to tell someone. I decided to tell Neil Johnson, who I knew Mluleki had really warmed to. Neil asked if I had settled his hotel bill, which I had. Mluleki had not told anyone where he had gone, so it came to a point where we simply had to let the manager know. He made it clear that his passport, bags and tickets were to remain in the hotel, and a note was left for him at reception that he was to go home right away.

There was such silence on the journey up north. Just before we left the bus, the manager addressed the team, giving us a stern warning about our future behaviour. Still, at least the players managed to convince him to overturn his decision on Mluleki, so he joined us later on that day. I was to carry on rooming with him, but he was effectively grounded. He could only go out for breakfast, team meetings, practice and games.

On the first day of our game against Yorkshire, the conditions were overcast, typical for England, and the wicket was favourable for bowling. I was batting at number four. I had two innings before my debut Test match, and I was frankly terrified of failure. I only managed one run in the first innings before getting out to a simple straight ball, and this meant I had one more chance to find form, in what was turning out to be a close game, before my first international appearance. I walked out in the second innings with Matthew Hoggard standing at the top of his mark. At this time he had not represented England, yet I hardly got any loose balls to put away. 'If this guy is making it so difficult for me,' I thought, 'how much more difficult will it be when I face their national team?'

These were some of the questions and feelings making my adrenaline pump. I would try and stick around until he got tired – surely he was going to tire. Just then, a ball bounced unusually and caught me on my right batting glove. I didn't retire hurt despite the obvious pain, as I saw that as a sign of weakness. Instead I continued struggling, pretending everything was fine, and was dismissed not long after. I had scored just four on this occasion. I didn't show the physiotherapist my hand either, as I was worried it would put my Test selection in jeopardy.

Looking back now, I reckon if I had batted at my usual number of six or seven, I would have been fine. But because Andy had such faith in me, I had been pushed up to four on a green track in conditions I was not used to. I think I feared failure so much because of the trust and confidence Andy had in me. I think at the time it actually put more pressure on me. I knew he wanted me to do well but having spoken to him before, it became obvious just how much belief he had in me. I think I got a little bit numb that day, and I didn't move as quickly and smoothly as I usually did at the crease.

While I was keeping wicket, I tried desperately hard to hide the pain I was feeling. I kept well, but that did not aide my recovery. The following morning, I could hardly make a fist. I had no choice but to let the physio, Amato Machikicho, know. I had three days to recover and that was not possible. It could have been possible had I made it known during the game that I had been hit, but I had tried to be brave. By now, the news had started to spread that I was going to play. I tried to catch a few balls the day before, but I was forcing myself. The task of breaking the news to the selection team was left to Amato. I was still just a young boy from Highfield whose heart was breaking.

I was shattered to say the least, but I had a way of keeping my facial expression straight. I started to think clearly, and more maturely. What if the injury had been so bad that I could never play again in my life? I realised I needed to go back to school to finish my education. I had missed the whole of a term already, but I was going to go back anyhow. Henry Olonga had been injured as well and was going home, so I asked the manager if I could join him. I was also missing my family and friends, and I had not told any of the touring group about my mum being very sick.

5
Finding Comfort in Love

THE JOURNEY BACK HOME WAS LONG AND TIRING, BUT AT LEAST I had someone alongside me this time. Henry Olonga had looked after me on tour, making sure I was kept away from the distractions of the world. I had many questions for him, but I didn't know how to ask them.

I wanted to speak about a particular incident on tour that had been playing on my mind. Ever since I had been in the changing room with the national team it had seemed a happy place to be, with everyone always joking around, but one moment upset that tranquil environment. Mluleki Nkala, who I had roomed with on the tour, had several nicknames in the dressing room, one of which was 'Nugget', which was a type of shoe polish in Zimbabwe. Mluleki was given this nickname because of of his dark skin colour. It's not something that he seemed to feel uneasy about, he was called it every day and it wasn't just the white players that used this nickname. On this particular occasion it was Neil Johnson, who Mluleki was particularly close to, that used this nickname, and for some reason it seemed to spark something inside of Henry. He was raging. 'Take your words back,' he said to Neil. Everyone just stood there. 'Take it back, you can't be making fun of someone's colour.'

'You're overreacting Henry,' said Neil, and Murray Goodwin came over and said a similar thing. Neil asked Mluleki if he minded the term, before Henry released his bombshell: 'That's why Mugabe is taking your farms off you.' All hell broke loose. While we had been touring the West Indies, Mugabe's controversial land seizure programme had intensified, with farms being taken from white farmers with increasing violence. On 15 April 2000, just over a month before the Lord's Test, Davis Stevens became the first white farmer to be killed in what would become a bloody and sorry conflict. Tensions were high. Of course, being on tour we did not see what was going on first-hand, but we were seeing pictures and videos from back home with increasing regularity. I remember watching them myself, and it was incredibly sad. We had been watching these videos, seeing the destruction, and so I couldn't believe Henry had said that, that he believed it was a good thing. We had all done well to skate around the subject so far, but this changed the atmosphere. It was very tense from then on.

When I returned to the Zimbabwe, I could tell things had changed – there seemed to be more tension in the air than before. I played a lot of Board XI and Zimbabwe A games during that period, and the changing rooms weren't like they had been before. People seemed to be on edge, and there were a few racial fights that broke out in the changing rooms, which I had never previously seen. I believe that this happened partly due to the racial tensions that had been exacerbated by the political situation in the country, and partly due to the types of characters that were present in the dressing room. There were some individuals in my dressing room, such as Trevor Madondo and David Mutendera, who simply didn't like doing the right things. Brighton Watambwa was another one. They liked to go out partying until the early hours, and on one occasion one of them missed the bus for a game. If you missed the bus you didn't play, and so the individual was replaced. The player in question thought he had been dropped because of his race, although on this particular occasion I didn't think that was the case. However, in general I think that heightened tensions in the country meant that people pointed fingers at each other more readily, and debates on race were played out in the open.

In my previous experiences, cricketers had sledged opposition players to try and get them to lose concentration. The chirping was often intelligent and witty, but it was almost always good-natured. When I returned to Zimbabwe from England, things to me seemed to have changed in the first-class game. The sledging I witnessed now seemed nastier than it had been in the past, more personal. As youngsters, we were often goaded into this by the more senior players.

At the time, the only white friends I had were cricketers. If I wasn't in the national team or playing cricket I was in school, so I wasn't really close to any white people in my personal life. There was tension everywhere, though, and everyone wanted to know your opinion on the matter. I never liked to see anyone struggle in life and have always believed that if you have any power you should try and make someone's life easier. I was of the view that it was unfair that the majority of people did not own the majority of the land in Zimbabwe, and it was undeniable: the white minority still owned most of the farmland in the country. However, I was also aware that the people who had the land had made these farms their home for decades. To forcibly remove them from these homes would not be fair either, and two wrongs don't make a right. 'Surely there is enough room for everyone in Zimbabwe to have land?' I thought. Even today it seems to me as if there is enough land, so surely there was a way it could have been divided.

Robert Mugabe was of the belief that the UK had broken financial commitments made in the 1979 Lancaster House agreement, which had ended white minority rule in our country. Following that agreement Margaret Thatcher's government had largely been interested in protecting the property rights of the white minority – her foreign secretary Lord Carrington insisted the new Zimbabwean constitution agreed in 1979 include a ten-year forcible ban on the redistribution of farms.

Twenty years after Mugabe's rule had started, before the war veterans began seizing land, 6,000 white farmers still occupied half of Zimbabwe's 81 million acres of arable land, with around 85,000 black farmers crammed into the rest. Since independence, only ten percent of arable land had moved legally from white to black farmers. Mugabe's promises to the people were being stymied by the fact that, according to the constitution, white farmers did not legally have to sell, and when they did it was often at inflated prices. When the constitutional bar on compulsory purchase fell away in 1990 the government did pass laws permitting it to forcibly buy up land, but by then a lot of it was given to ruling party officials and army officers by our president. The poor people in need of land would have to wait even longer. Britain, meanwhile, would not provide more funds for legal land reform until Mugabe left office.

My view at the time was that the government should have compulsorily purchased some of the land from those who owned the vast majority (this could have happened as of 1990), allowing them to then distribute it more evenly to the people who needed it. To me, that would have worked for everyone. The ones who had been farming for years could keep some of their land and they could keep their homes, while they could also offer their expertise to the new farmers that the government had distributed the newly-acquired land to. I believe that would have reduced the suffering. In terms of the farms being redistributed, that needed to be done. It was the way it was done that was wrong – it was just one big shedding of blood.

Some people will inevitably say that the only way the government could take the land off those who already had most of it was by force, but I don't go along with that. If the government wanted to reclaim vast swathes of land to redistribute it more evenly among the population, then they had the authority to do so. Sure, some people might not have liked it, but they would have been compensated and in the process, Zimbabwe would have become a fairer society. But the government also had the choice of how they were going to approach this process, and this is where they went about things in completely the wrong manner. It also seems that when Mugabe did start taking some land back in the early 1990s, he didn't distribute it fairly himself, instead giving it to allies in the government and the army. The majority of the country did not see any benefit.

I have friends that tell me stories of what transpired, what happened to their families, and it wasn't pleasant. Black, white or Asian, if they are my friend they are my friend. I can't mention names, because that would not be fair, but I have a friend whose little boy was thrown against the wall by these soldiers, the people Mugabe got to carry out his dirty work. At first my friend feared her son might be dead, given how motionless he was on the ground. It was at that time that they knew they had to get out of Zimbabwe. The war had come to them, and it became impossible for them to stay. Despite it being their home for many years, they knew it was no longer worth staying, so they took off and left.

I had another friend whose daughter was raped while the fighters took over their farm. They were tea farmers, and we still remain close to them now. To see what was happening to these people was heartbreaking.

Still, despite this, I did not feel conflicted representing my country, because I believed sport could be a unifying factor in times of such strife. Sport is entertainment at the end of the day, not too serious, but around that time I think we took it beyond that as a team, and I thought we had the power to bring people together.

Because I was travelling so much, I saw how the conflict was reported both at home and abroad. In Zimbabwe, a lot of the media was government-owned, and so they were not impartial, but I do believe that western countries exaggerated what was happening too far the other way. In truth, I don't think there was any media outlet that covered both sides fairly.

When I finally got home, I couldn't believe the condition Mum was in. She had lost so much weight. I wanted to cry when I hugged her, but I knew that I had to stay strong so I restrained myself. We got inside and I started distributing the little presents I had got on tour to my siblings. I still didn't discuss how things had gone in terms of my cricket, because I knew none of them would understand apart from Kudzai.

Instead, I shared stories that weren't related to cricket. I told Mum about my tour Mum, a woman who worked at one of the hotels we had been staying in. She had seen me as one of her own sons and would give me free lunch and supper every day while she asked what was going on at home. She tried to make me feel as comfortable as possible. Since the political ructions had started Zimbabwe was in the news all over the world, and so she was concerned for me. 'Son, if you ever want to get out of your country, remember you have a mother here,' she used to say. The media plays a big role in how these stories are portrayed, and they made it sound like no one was safe living in Zimbabwe during these times.

It was not long before Mum asked for the money I had made. I gave her the dollars which I had left over in my pocket, but I could see in her reaction that she had wanted me to give her more. She still had that initial meeting with Peter Chingoka in her mind, when I had first been called up to the national team. She started talking about plans to build a cottage and more. I was not interested in all of that; I simply wanted to sit down and have a conversation with her about life. I wasn't going to be home for long. She broke my heart by continually talking about money. I thought the best thing was to go and visit Stephen Mangongo and Amos Maungwa down at the club to tell them about the tour, as all of my school friends were away. When I told her I was going out, she got angry. I could not understand why this was, so I carried on walking away.

Seeing Amos, a club member at Takashinga, was nice. He said something to me that day which I have kept in my heart since: 'Tiba, when you make decisions, don't make them because somebody else has told you, make a decision because that's what you want to do. If you make a decision because of someone else and it goes wrong, that person won't be there to make it right, and if it comes out right that person will then take all the credit.' When I saw Mangongo he was not so happy to see me, and I could not figure out why. The atmosphere turned cold, and I quickly made an excuse to leave. It hadn't been the welcome home I'd expected or hoped for.

I felt really sad and dreaded going back home. Was anyone happy to see me? I looked skywards: 'God, is this why I came back? Was it not better to have stayed on tour?' There was no answer. I passed by the Gwanzura Stadium close to my house, where I would go for my individual fitness sessions. I sat against the wall with my head in my hands, my elbows supported by my knees. I couldn't believe that I was the same person who was on top of the world just a few days earlier, about to become one of the youngest players ever to play Test cricket. I had been in a five-star hotel and now I was sat with my back against the dirty walls of the Gwanzura. Whoever said there was no place like home surely didn't have me in mind.

I was trying really hard to think beyond my playing days already. I knew the attention you got when you weren't doing well was not the same attention you got when you were doing well. Not only that, I knew that I was the same person that no one had cared about just a year before. Only a few people were bothered about me then. I was now in the paper, on the television and on the radio, and all of a sudden people pretended to care about my interests. That's why when I speak about Bill Flower and Steve Mangongo, I speak with so much respect and reverence, because they did care about me before I got famous.

There was suddenly talk of me quitting school to play full-time. The CFX Academy had just opened its doors. The team was to effectively act as the Zimbabwean national side's academy, and they competed in the country's domestic competition for the first time in the 1999/2000 season. The guy who ran the academy wanted me to be the poster boy for it, and he had started coming to Highfield to take my mum for coffee. She had been taken in by what he was telling her. 'Tatenda,' she said. 'People go to school so they can get a job and earn money. You are already earning money and so you don't need to go back.'

She had already signed the forms he had given her, and he was now just waiting for me to sign. I remember saying to her, 'If it wasn't for the fact that my name was going to be tied to this academy, which brings in a lot of money and sponsors, he wouldn't be here taking you out.' But she couldn't see that. I tried to make her understand that if I broke my leg tomorrow, none of these people would be around anymore. I tried to make her understand what had happened when I thought I was making my first-class debut, how I had been treated. I thought that by speaking to her she would understand, but she kept pushing for me to leave school so I could play for this academy. I went against her wishes, bought my own uniform, and stored some money away. I wanted to continue my education.

Everything had gotten out of hand very quickly. 'Mum, I'm not going to be giving you all the money,' I revealed. 'You are very sick and the only sane boy you have is me. Your first-born Joseph is an excessive drinker and in no condition to look after Tapiwa if you die. For me to be able to look after someone else, I must have a solid base, and so I'm going to save some money and buy myself a house.' She just looked at me with a sad face, as if to say I was useless.

I didn't just buy myself a uniform, I also purchased a cell phone and a bicycle. The bicycle was for fitness purposes. The following day, I went straight back to school – I didn't even want to wait for Monday to come around. I wanted to study accountancy, business and maths. In the end, I chose art over maths, because I saw how much further my classmates were along with the latter when I returned. I was glad to be back in school, living life by the bell. Going back to school felt different. The sun was still shining the same way, and the wind was still blowing like it had done before, the only difference was that many people now knew who I was. I was now widely respected by all those who were aware of my achievements, and world spread so quickly that even those without any cricketing knowledge also held me in greater esteem. I was still the same boy with the same blood, hair and skin, but I was amazed to note the difference in the way I was looked at because I had been mentioned in the media.

It was going to be a tough year. I would be at school an average of one day a week less than everyone else, as the ZCU did not want me to stop playing competitive cricket. They asked my headmaster if he could grant me time off to allow me to travel with the Board XI for some games against South African sides, and they would pay for extra lessons for me to have during the holidays when I was less busy. When we had a game, we would travel on the Monday evening, play from the Tuesday until the Friday and then travel back on the Saturday. I would only have the Sunday and the Monday to catch up with the other students. They were the days where the others had time to relax, time they used to try and catch a glimpse of their girlfriends. Dating was the last thing on my mind. Just like my thoughts about others who had started to latch on to me, I wondered whether a girl would fall for me or my money. Regardless of how many records I broke and how well I played, there was always going to come a time where I had to hang up my boots. Would they still be there for me after that?

My art teacher was very understanding of my situation, allowing me to use his lessons to catch up on my other work. Even then, I still found myself behind the eight ball, and just as the Board XI games drew to a close, the school cricket season began, and expectations were high. I simply wasn't allowed to fail. When I batted, it became very dangerous for me to be struck on the pads, because the opposition umpires were keen to dismiss me. I became the victim of some atrocious LBW decisions. The only way to counter this was to start doing my individual practices without my front pad on, to get into the habit of using the bat at all costs.

I had always avoided being a leader, because I did not speak well in front of people, but I could no longer avoid it. Luckily for me, captaining our school was a fairly easy task: we had six particularly strong players, and we won virtually every game we played. Only two or three of us needed us to play well for us to win. I was playing well personally, but failed to convert many fifties into hundreds, while Hamilton was the one making the big scores. We all knew that it wouldn't be long before he'd be called up to the national team, but whether or not he knew it I was not entirely sure; he was a character who never seemed to take anything particularly seriously.

One cold Saturday afternoon, when I was walking into town after watching a school rugby game, I received a call from one of my sisters, Jackie, to tell me that Mum had just been admitted to hospital. I stopped and looked up to feel the air brush against my face – the trees were covering the skies in an arc like a beautiful tunnel. I walked a few steps then stopped again in order to try to think clearly. It was very similar moment to when Dad had passed away a few years before. Just as I was strolling at a snail-like speed, the cell phone rang again. Before Jackie even had the chance to say anything, I knew that Mum had passed on.

It was devastating. You hear about parents living to an old age, about their little ones looking after them. I remember sitting there and thinking, 'That's not going to be the case with me.' When Dad passed away, I would sometimes take comfort in the fact that I still had Mum. Now she was no longer there. As children we used to fight a lot, and I wondered how we were going to manage.

Many thoughts travelled in and out of my little brain, and my heart was not big enough to come to terms with the emotion. 'Whatever bad anyone does to you, whatever differences you have with them, it will count for nothing when they are gone.' That was my initial thought when I heard the news. My last few moments in Mum's company had not been the best. We had spent those moments arguing about my future and about money. All these events played around in my head until I came to a halt in the street, like I was sinking in quicksand. My eyes were watery, and I looked up to the skies once more in search of answers to the questions

I asked of myself. 'God, who is going to look after Tapiwa?' The boy was just too young to be without a parent for guidance. I felt I was the only member of my family who could look after him well, to give him a fair chance to do well in life, but how was I going to do that when I was still just in school?

I finally gathered myself together and headed for home. Word had reached the others there already, and as is the custom for funerals in Zimbabwe, the lounge was cleared to make space for the mourning family to sit while people came by to pass on their condolences. I did not hide like I had done when Dad had passed on. Instead I was up and about, making sure proceedings ran smoothly. On the second day of mourning, my spirits were trampled further when I was called into a meeting by the elders, who were in charge of collecting the funds for the proceedings. They informed me that they didn't have enough money. I was just a seventeen-year-old boy, and it felt unfair that I was being involved in all of this. There were four family members there who were older than me. I just sat and listened as they spoke, not offering an answer.

There were some ZCU representatives that came to show their support at the funeral, and among them were two men I respected highly, Peter Chingoka and Max Ebrahim, the latter of whom upon seeing me called me over to offer some comforting words. I appreciated that so much: not because of the words he said, but what they meant to me. I was given a significant contribution towards the funeral funds, which along with the money I withdrew from my own account, covered us. Before passing away Mum had told Jackie to copy her signature and withdraw all her funds so that we would have somewhere to start from in her absence.

On the way to church, Jackie asked me whether I would say a few words. 'I hope you have something prepared, because you will have to speak. You are way stronger than all of us – I will hardly even start, because I will break down right away.' I agreed with her and jotted down a few points. Later on, the MC asked the final speaker to be a family member. Only Jackie and I knew at the time that I was going to take responsibility. I got up, walked slowly to the coffin, and asked those who knew the words to sing a hymn with me that my mum had liked. It was a song she used to sing while doing her chores. I began to sing and slowly others joined in. Tears were rolling down my cheeks, but I managed to keep my composure. I had to refrain from weeping to finish the speech. What I said must have been particularly emotional, because when I started others began to cry. It meant

I couldn't finish myself, and so I went to where my other siblings were sat and sought comfort.

For three or four days, you have company at the house; different people from different walks of life to talk to. After the burial, though, people go back to their own houses and you have to start dealing with what has happened. It's at this point that it becomes hard to deal with, when you start to face the reality of the situation. We were kids, and we had to run the business. We had a shop to run, and some of us had to return to school.

I never was someone who liked sympathy, but I knew I would be getting plenty of it when I returned to Churchill. I wanted to shut it all out, so I quickly returned to the things I was focusing on before. I knew we needed to look after Tapiwa. While I finished my studies and before I got my first property, my older brother Joseph, who had just moved to a new city, looked after him.

When I did return to school, I tried to joke around a lot to avoid thinking or talking about what had just happened to me. I even started trying to date, which went horribly wrong after I met a girl who lied to me about her age. If there was one thing I could not stand it was lying. She tried to make it right, but I called it quits anyway. My joking around did not last long, and I soon reverted to the Tatenda that hid away, sitting in my little corner in the prefect's study, listening to all the latest gossip without offering my piece of mind.

One day, I found myself listening in on some gossip about a beautiful girl at our neighbouring sister school. Most of the boys involved in this conversation were saying she was a bad girl, but without really providing any evidence to back up their point. In African culture, women going to parties and getting drunk is seen as a shameful thing, and that is what they were alleging she was doing. I just couldn't see how it could be possible. As I was listening, I could tell that there was a missing piece to this puzzle.

I was known by the other boys for being quiet, but when I did ask to talk they would invariably pay attention. 'May I say a word?' I asked, as everyone fixed their gazes upon me. 'I perceive that you are lying about this girl. I don't know her, but if you can give me a few days I will prove to you what I am talking about.' There was uproar from the rest of the boys. The only way I could make my case was to speak to her myself.

I asked Nyasha Mushunjie, the head boy of the school with whom I shared a mutual respect with, if I could be given outside gate duties for a time. He usually wanted me on corridor duty so I could deal with the troublesome form three and four pupils, but thankfully he allowed me to swap jobs for a while, just until I could prove my point.

The girl in question, named Loveness, had developed a habit of arriving to school either very early or very late so she could avoid passing through the human tunnel the boys used to make for the girls coming from the east side. On this particular day, I waited for a long time, hoping she had not arrived early. I soon spotted her, so I walked up, greeted her and started firing questions. I knew that I didn't have much time, so I asked as many as possible, hoping that I would learn something useful sooner or later. It wasn't long before she started talking about the Bible, and it was then I knew I had my answer. The rumour-mongers would not enjoy hearing about this: Loveness reading the Bible would not fit in with their preconceptions about her. I was satisfied that I had my evidence. Over the course of the conversation I actually found that I was attracted to her as well. I asked to walk with her again in the afternoon, to which she agreed.

When I met the others in the prefects' study at break time, I reported my findings: 'I told you, she is a good girl.' As they listened intently, I proceeded to tell them how the conversation had gone. I finished what I had to say, and then left them open-mouthed as I revealed I would be walking home with her in the afternoon as well.

I was glad to receive further confirmation of her good character as we walked together in the afternoon. Her home was a fair distance from school, but we barely noticed the time as we chatted away happily. As we approached her house she began to slow down, her body language suggesting that it was time for me to turn and go – it was taboo in Zimbabwean culture for a girl to bring a friend of the opposite sex home with them. I didn't take any notice of these norms; all I wanted was her family members to know that I was a gentleman, and so I wanted to introduce myself to them. At this point in time she was staying with her brother, so introducing myself to him was my first port of call.

The first person she introduced me to was her brother Reverend Gezi, who was sitting in his outside study. He turned around and said just one word: 'Afternoon.' He looked me down from head to toe, and then resumed to study for the sermon he was to preach on Sunday. I waited outside while Loveness went to change into her casual clothing. We continued to chat for the evening, and all those who passed by commented on how well suited we seemed to each other.

Eventually it was time for me to take the long walk back to the boarding hostel, but it felt so short, as I continued to play the conversations with Loveness over in my mind. Boys will be boys, and they were very excited when I returned, having missed my dinner. Time had escaped us.

6

Tough at the Top

IT WAS 2001, AND A LOT HAD BEEN HAPPENING IN ZIMBABWEAN politics over the previous two years. The economic crisis engulfing the country had been worsened by our involvement in the DR Congo civil war in 1998. Mugabe's decision to go into Congo had not proved a popular one with Zimbabwean citizens, and in the same year the Movement for Democratic Change (MDC) was formed by a broad coalition of civil society groups and individuals. At this stage the MDC's main political purpose was to campaign for a 'No' vote in the 2000 constitutional referendum, as Mugabe sought to give the government more powers to seize farmland off white farmers. The MDC were successful in their goal – Mugabe lost the vote – but squatters seized hundreds of white-owned farms anyway, in a violent campaign supported by the government.

In June of the same year, Mugabe's ZANU-PF party narrowly fought off Morgan Tsvangirai's MDC party in parliamentary elections but he lost his power to change the constitution. The land reform programme continued at pace, and the fallout of it started to filter through to the game of cricket as well, though as a youngster I decided to stay totally away from the media, and therefore did not have much of a firm grasp of specific events. That's not to say I wasn't aware of what was going on.

The situation eventually got so bad the Finance Minister of Mugabe's government, a man named Simba Makoni, acknowledged the country's economic crisis, saying that foreign reserves had run out. He warned of serious food shortages, and most western donors, including the World Bank and the IMF, had cut aid because of the president's land seizure programme and the presence of his army in Congo. Makoni's original budget in 2000 was realistic, but it offered little to repair confidence in the country's broken economy – inflation was up to sixty percent, and unemployment had rocketed to fifty percent, by far the largest figure since independence. Makoni often seemed at odds with his party and his president, and in 2002 he was axed in Mugabe's first reshuffle for two years.

I met Makoni on a couple of occasions, and he would later run for president in 2008.

I remember meeting him when we had a match in Bulawayo; he was giving a speech at the hotel we were staying in. I listened to him and he talked a lot of sense. Not only was he talking about the problems in our economy, but he was offering solutions to them. He knew what he was talking about.

I would see Makoni again at the same hotel on a different day, and on this occasion his team asked me if I would pose for a picture with him. I had no problem with this, but the Zimbabwe team manager did. He had a discussion with Makoni's team, which was rather serious-looking. I asked him what it had all been about, and he said to me, 'That picture must never come out.' I asked him why, to which he replied, 'He's running for president and Robert is a patron of our cricket.' I couldn't believe it; it was only a picture. It gives you an indication of how politics often is in Zimbabwe, and also how it intertwines with sport.

During this period, it wasn't just hard for opposition parties and political figures to fight back against the incumbent government – it was also very hard for the people of Zimbabwe, who had practically nothing. In fact, it was almost impossible. Zimbabweans by nature are peaceful people, and they persevere. Fighting is seen as a last resort to them. We try by all means necessary not to cause commotion or conflict, instead just hoping that things will change for the better. When you see a crowd of people demonstrating in Zimbabwe, you know things are bad, because it's not their first port of call, it's their last resort.

Those who did fight back often suffered the consequences. There were all sorts of rumours about what the police did to people, and often these rumours would be confirmed as true when you spoke to a family member or friend whom these things had happened to. A friend of mine had to take his cousin to hospital after he had been whipped by police – the boy had been struck so badly that he couldn't physically sit down, so he had to kneel in the car on the way to the station. These things were happening all the time.

Another demonstration of the brutality of Mugabe's government came a few years later with a programme named 'Operation Murambatsvina' – a Shona word meaning 'drive out the rubbish' – which commenced in 2005. The operation, termed by officials as a 'cleanup of illegal slums and black-market vendors', was a brutal programme which saw the government abruptly demolishing shanties and roadside markets in the big cities. Thousands of people were evicted, and homes were either burnt or bulldozed to the ground. Mugabe wanted to uproot the very poorest city dwellers, around 1.5 million people, who had become some of his most hardened opponents in the years before as unemployment levels rose to record highs. The UN estimated after three weeks that the campaign had left 200,000 people and 30,000 vendors homeless, though human rights and civic leaders said the numbers could have been seven times that.

If Mugabe wanted to clean up the country, then that was up to him, but once again, it was the sheer brutality and manner he went about it that made it so awful. What I had a problem with was the fact that there was no plan for the people who made their livelihoods from these markets. If you're going to destroy someone's house, where are they going to live the following day? It would have made sense, surely, to warn people in advance of this crackdown. They could have told them what they were doing was illegal, and that they planned to stop it over time, but in the meantime, they were going to provide refuge. I can understand that people were building where they were not meant to build, and that he wanted that to stop. But at least build some temporary shelter for these people, while you work out how these people are now going to make a living. Where is a person going to go after you have destroyed their house? Perhaps Mugabe didn't care. Perhaps he was destroying the lives of people posing a threat to his government.

Because I was so intent on avoiding the media in 2001, I had missed the news that Andy Flower had picked up an injury and would be undergoing treatment for three weeks. Meanwhile, Stuart, Hamilton and I had been selected to play for the A side against India in a warm-up game, which was to be played the day before the triangular series against the West Indies started. I batted terribly.

After being dismissed I went and sat beside some of the spectators near the dressing room. One of them was Dean du Plessis, the well-known cricket commentator who has no sight. Dean instead relies on his acute sense of hearing and other cues and is able to work out what is going on from that. At this point,

I had no idea how a blind man could know what was going on without being told. To me it was like the wind: we do not see it, yet we are aware of the effect it gives.

Dean's cousin, Gary Brent, one of the nicest people I have come across in the game, was sat next to him, flipping through the pages of one of the daily newspapers. I soon saw my own face on one of these pages, with the accompanying headline confirming my selection for the national team the following day. I was already angry at my performance, and instead of this news soothing my heart, it made me angrier. 'Why is it that I'm always the last to find out what's happening to me?' I thought. I wondered whether our coach might be waiting until the end of the day's play.

We lost the game, and as I walked away from the changing room with Stuey I told him what I had seen. He was so excited for me and couldn't understand why I was so down. I felt unwanted, and if there was one thing that I really struggled with it was the feeling of being at a place where my presence was not welcomed. I had felt exactly the same way when I was meant to have made my first-class debut a while before. When we arrived back at the hostel Stuey, being the good man that he is, simply told the sports master to arrange transport for me early in the morning to make sure everything was in order. I went to get some rest. I made sure I arrived at the ground early the next day, giving myself a chance to familiarise myself with the national-team dressing room before everyone else arrived. I was soon hit with another shock when I opened the door: every other player was already in, and they all had their gazes fixed upon me. Was I late? Was I not supposed to be there? In truth, I didn't have a clue what was going on. There had clearly been some sort of team meeting going on, but once I walked in there wasn't another word uttered.

Henry Olonga rose from his seat, came straight over to me and said, 'Tibs, this meeting was not about you.' I liked Henry, and generally took notice of what he said to me, but how could I possibly believe him in this instance? The next player I saw was Donald Campbell – brother of fellow international Alistair – who like me was also a wicketkeeper. Instantly he started packing his bags before walking out of the changing rooms. He had all his shirts there prepared for him, whereas I had nothing. It was clear that there had been an argument about me and Donald, but I didn't have any idea as to what it had been about. Donald would never play an international game for Zimbabwe in his career. There was room in my head for plenty of speculation about what had gone on, but it was hard not to believe that race had played a role in the discussion I had not been privy to.

Amid all this commotion I was supposed to be making my international debut. It felt like all the odds were stacked against me. I had to make up my mind: was I going to let this situation destroy me or shape me? I kept telling myself over and over again that I couldn't change what had happened, but I could map my own destiny.

The warm-up passed so quickly that I hardly noticed anything around me. My heart was beating so quickly that I thought it was going to burst out of my chest. As seconds turned to minutes and minutes to hours, I started to feel more comfortable. It wasn't long until I got my first international dismissal: a stumping to get rid of West Indian batsman Darren Ganga off the bowling of Brian Murphy. I batted down the order at number ten, which meant I could not really influence the game much. I scored 1* off a single delivery as we failed to chase down our target of 267 in 50 overs, falling around 25 runs short.

I felt that I coped with a difficult situation well. Because I was so focused as an individual, and still am, all I saw was what was in front of me. People often talk about the crowds and the noise, but I never really had a problem like that throughout my career, as I was so glued to what I wanted to achieve from a game or a tour. Everything else became blinded to me; outside noise. I think because I had been in the squad before, it was expected that I would make the side soon enough, which maybe took some of the shine off it when it actually happened. For me, it almost didn't feel like I had made my debut.

Stuey made sure that Loveness came to watch, though I didn't even get a chance to notice her in the crowd as everything was moving too quickly. As soon as this game was over we had to start thinking about the next day's fixture against India, the other team involved in that tri-series. It meant three matches in as many days. Prior to the game, my spirits were lifted a little when I heard Andy's voice in the commentary box. He suggested it was a chance for the coach to promote me up the order, to see what I was capable of. We were not batting well as a team anyway, and it wouldn't hurt for the team to take a step back or two in order to give me the necessary exposure so that we could hopefully win more games in the future.

I remained at number ten, and sure enough our top order failed to deliver again – I walked in with the score 102-8. I was facing up to Harbhajan Singh straight away, one of the greatest spinners in the world. You could not compare my stature, height or the quality of my bat and pads to anyone in my own team, let alone the Indian players. Yet at the end of my little innings I was 19* as we were bowled out for 133. Only opening batsman Dion Ibrahim had scored more runs than me. India lost just one wicket in their chase of the total. My little cameo made an impact, though, and I was soon sent through some new gear through by the Indian cricket manufacturer SG. It had been sorted out for me by the great Sunil Gavaskar.

Despite the quality of the opposition, I did not feel overawed at all, and I didn't have any specific plans to deal with the threat of Harbhajan. That would come later on in my career, and only against extraordinary bowlers: against Muttiah Muralitharan you had to have a set plan, and against other spinners such as Pakistan's Saqlain Mushtaq and India's Anil Kumble. Against the spinners you have to be able to pick up the stock ball and the variation. Murali was especially difficult; it was so hard to pick up on his subtle differences. Before you had a chance to adjust to them, you would often find yourself back in the dressing room. I knew what I was meant to be looking for, but I didn't spend enough time in the middle to pick it up.

At one stage in Sri Lanka when I wasn't picking Murali's variations, I scored three ducks in a row. I decided to approach Younis Khan, the great Pakistani batsman who was so used to playing spin bowling. I asked him how he managed to spend enough time at the crease to be able to pick up the necessary cues. I knew that for Murali's off-spinner you had to look for him releasing the ball from the side of his hand. If you saw the back of his hand with the thumb sticking out, that was the doosra, which spins in the opposite direction from the conventional off-break he bowled most often. If you didn't see the thumb but saw the ball coming out of the back of the hand, that was the ball that went straight on. You had three variations to deal with.

I still had no idea how I was going to spend enough time out there to pick him. Younis said that in practice he used to get someone to throw fast off-spinners at him on an even bit of grass, but not on an actual wicket – perhaps the outfield. In this drill he would make sure to get his bat straight and would then try and read the spin off the pitch, without paying much attention to his foot movement. This was all just so he didn't get out in the early stages of his innings, and once he worked out how the ball was behaving off the pitch, he was able to study the bowler's hand more closely. Once he had that sorted, he started to feel more free at the crease and could therefore dominate the bowler. I took this advice on board, and it worked for me almost instantly.

That's the difficulty of international cricket in a nutshell. Some will give up before they have really got going, but the ones who keep working hard at these aspects tend to survive longer. Bowlers are also human, and they come up with ways to counter what you are doing. They create new deliveries; find different angles on the crease from which to bowl at. Those who survive in international cricket are the ones who keep on learning.

Pace was never such an issue for me, and I always felt comfortable taking on the likes of Shoaib Akhtar and Brett Lee, the quickest bowlers in the game at the time. Because of the adrenaline coursing through your body, your reflexes become sharper. There's less than a second to think, and the ball can be swinging or reversing, but once you grow accustomed to it you grow in confidence, and you tend to only be dismissed by your own errors. I remember my adrenaline pumping particularly when I faced Shoaib, as his aim was to hit you and hurt you. It was like reaching the final level of a video game; you have built up to this moment and this is as difficult as it will get.

At the very top level, the game is about who adapts the best. For me, there are two types of batsman: a significant amount see the ball, but only the very best watch the ball closely. The ones that have a still head are able to pick the length quicker, because they are so focused on one thing – watching the ball. When you watch the ball, you can actually see the seam and which way it is going; when you see the ball all you see is a red thing coming towards you. It's the same when facing spin bowling: if you watch the ball, you can see how many revs are on it, how much it is going to turn and which way it is going to turn.

You can only watch the ball that intently if your balance is good in the first place. Balance is all in your feet; your feet are your base. When the ball is about to be bowled, a lot of batsmen get too eager to play and go searching for it. Instead you need to wait for it to come to you. Balance is a very hard thing to practise. You have to try and get the weight of your body on the middle of your feet or your heels, without going back too far. You should never apply the weight on the balls of your foot, because that leads to your head being in the wrong position, causing you to fall over.

Coaches have an important role to play, but the most important thing to a team is the individuals that make it up. You need a team full of self-driven individuals to make a successful side. A coach should be a guide to the players, offering support when needed, rather than someone who tells them what to do. All the minor details, all the gameplans still need to be carried out by those on the pitch. If you have a coach telling the players what they do, it means the players are coasting. They have done enough to make the side, they will attempt to implement the gameplan they have been presented with, but they don't go the extra mile. They won't practise that little bit more; they don't devise their own solutions or come up with their own plans if the current one is not working. They won't go beyond the sound barrier of the game. They push themselves to a point and then say, 'That's enough. Cricket is my occupation, I can just carry on playing.' But the ones who set themselves goals and landmarks, they become the leaders in the side and achieve more.

Those who ask more of their teammates become more respected in the side. When they ask more of you, you can't help but want to give them it. The more players you have like this in your side, the more successful you will be, and the easier it becomes for the coach.

We did not qualify for the tri-series final, and so our attentions turned to our Test series with the West Indies. To me, Test cricket remains more important than one day international cricket, a view still held by most in the game, I think. We flew to Bulawayo, where I would make my debut in the longest form of the game. At this point I believed my keeping to be more natural than my batting, although I still viewed myself as a batsman who could keep. When it came to keeping I wasn't too nervous taking to the field. I kept neatly throughout the match, and my first dismissal was Carl Hooper, standing up to the stumps off the bowling of Bryan Strang. Unfortunately, Hooper had already made 149, with the Windies scoring 559-6 declared in response to our 155 all out.

Walking in to bat was different. With fielding there is comfort in numbers, and I was constantly learning on the job. When you make a mistake out there as a wicketkeeper you have a chance to rectify it immediately. When you make a mistake batting you're straight back in the dressing room, and all you can do is look on and clap your teammates, while left to ponder where you have gone wrong yourself.

I was welcomed to Test cricket with several bouncers, one of which I hooked for a boundary to record my first runs in the game. That was off the bowling of the pace bowler Colin Stuart, but overall, I found it hard to adapt to Test cricket straightaway. The ball was coming at a speed I had never experienced before –

I had played barely any first-class cricket at this stage still – and the reverse swing didn't make it any easier. I was soon dismissed by Stuart after making just six runs. I had been batting at nine in the first innings, unable to make any real impact, but our number three Stuart Carlisle injured his finger while fielding, so the line-up had to be changed for our second innings. When the question was asked as to who wanted to take his place at number three, I put my hand up without hesitation. Earlier in that Test match I had asked senior batsman Alistair Campbell how someone could score a Test century against bowlers of such devastating speed, but despite my doubts about my own game I was still willing to test myself. I had grown up in the tough camp of Stephen Mangongo, where the only way you can't succeed is by failing to try at all. Throwing the towel in was not an option for me.

I walked in to bat in the second innings with Stuart, the bowler who had dismissed me in the first innings, standing at the top of his run. Just my luck. He had been bowling with a nice rhythm, and I was soon back in the pavilion, having made just four. At least I had given it a crack. The West Indies won the game by an innings and 176 runs.

Carlisle's injury brought about a little change ahead of the second Test in Harare; my school mate Hamilton Masakadza was to make his debut. I had witnessed Hamilton's talent up close for a long time, and a year earlier he had become the youngest ever Zimbabwean to hit a first-class century. Here he created more history, scoring a brilliant second innings hundred as we mounted a stirring comeback in a game that ended as a draw. With it he became the youngest player to score a Test century on his debut (17 years and 254 days old) and Zimbabwe's first black player to make a Test hundred, becoming our Tenth Test centurion in total. The atmosphere when he reached the landmark was absolutely electric. I remember seeing one stand full of kids in purple blazers singing our school songs. I was so glad for Hammy, and that innings inspired me and many others who watched it. His presence in the team meant I was once again down the order, and once again I was dismissed twice by Stuart without having scored many runs.

As usual, there were problems bubbling under the surface in Zimbabwean cricket. Just before we were about to play our opening match of the tri-series tournament against the West Indies, Heath Streak announced his resignation as captain. Heath cited communication problems with the selection panel after he and coach Carl Rackemann had been left off the original six-man committee. Just a couple of hours later, after a meeting with Peter Chingoka and other ZCU officials, he was back as captain, saying that the problems had now been resolved and he had been asked to continue. Both he and Rackemann had been reinstated on the panel.

The main issue surrounded race and the introduction of more non-white players into the team. A number of existing squad members believed that there was too much political interference in team selection, and that going down this road meant that players would not be selected on merit, and therefore Zimbabwe would not be selecting their strongest possible XI. It was reported at the time that Heath and Carl disagreed with the selection panel over the selection of three players ahead of the game against the West Indies, two of whom were actually white. The problem was averted in the short term, but it was an issue that did not go away in the following years, and I would soon assume an important role.

Around a month later three non-white selectors resigned because the racial balance of the selection panel had been upset when Streak and Rackemann had returned. They would all later return when Heath's father Dennis resigned from the panel due to a conflict of interests. Meanwhile, there had been a row over representation at the Mashonaland Cricket Association's annual meeting in Harare. A breakaway league, with ten teams comprising of black or Asian players, was to be formed unless the ZCU could diffuse the situation. My coach and mentor Stephen Mangongo was acting as a spokesman for the aggrieved clubs, and he was saying that the white members had used their 26-22 numerical advantage at the meeting to vote black nominees out of office.

Andy Flower had recently given a speech in which he said that there were no racial problems among the players themselves, saying the team did not see colour and that it could act as an example to the country at a time of racial, social and political conflict. From my little experience of the dressing room at that time what Andy was saying appeared to me to be true – these outside issues were hardly discussed at all, only a few whispers here and there. However, those comments did not go down well with Peter Chingoka, who repeated that reform needed to continue in the national side. After the Test series had concluded Andy was fit again, and he took over as wicketkeeper again for the time being. Hamilton continued in the team after his hundred and deserved to do so. I returned to school, studying for the exams to come.

Returning to school meant I got to spend more time with Loveness again. I tried killing two birds with one stone – mixing hard work and pleasure – by setting up a study group consisting of just me and her. We studied a couple of similar subjects, and so we would do our homework together after I had walked her home. After studies, we would chat away until it was time for me to go back to my hostel. I would miss supper most of the time.

One day we got so carried away in conversation that we lost track of time. It was deep into the night. Reverend Gezi did not mind, as long as we were safe at home. When I saw the time, I panicked – the main gate at my hostel would be shut by now. I would have to do what I had previously declared I'd never do: I'd have to scale the Churchill fence. That task was usually reserved for the troublesome boys drinking alcohol. I actually had two fences to deal with before I reached the window, where one of the other boys would be able to help me in.

I got that far, but as I was halfway through the window, one of the other boys whispered 'Chips', which was a warning. Everyone vanished, and I was left hanging like a rotten tomato. Mr Mabohyi, the hostel matron (as we called the housemaster), stood facing me. 'Good evening sir,' I said. 'May you please open the gate for me to enter?' I was very polite.

'You are already half in Taibu, just get in,' came the calm reply. I wish I had been dreaming, but I wasn't. I went straight to bed, wondering what Mr Mabhoyi was going to do about what had transpired. I was a prefect, not usually known for my mischief. Luckily for me, I wasn't reported to the higher authorities at the school, but I had learnt my lesson.

Loveness was very understanding, and we decided to limit how much we saw each other for the time being. Soon enough, Loveness herself was sent to board by her mother. She was not happy about it. I understood what her mother was trying to achieve, but what she didn't realise was Loveness was not a character who could be controlled by the bell like some of us. This further disturbed our communication, and the only way we could speak to each other was via letter, delivered by her friend Esther.

I cherished any time I spent with her greatly, though we found ourselves in further trouble when we were caught kissing by a schoolteacher as we said our goodbyes. News of this did not reach the school yard, but Loveness's mother found out, and she was not amused. I always prided myself on being a gentleman who owned up when he was wrong, so I had a tough phone call to make.

'Hello?' came the voice at the other end of the line.

'It's Tatenda,' I replied. There was silence for around three seconds, but it felt like a whole minute. 'I'm really sorry for what happened between Loveness and me. I'm sure you won't enjoy hearing people talking about it. All I want to say is I'm really sorry.'

There was silence again for a while until she said, 'It's okay.' I was so relieved. I didn't know what else to say, so I just cut the phone. I cursed myself for that.

I was so excited to finish my A-Levels, after two tough years of balancing my school work and my cricket. I had been touring with the Board XI team that visited South Africa on an almost weekly basis, where we would face provincial sides. Permission to do this had been granted by the headmaster, Mr Mutsekwa, who loved the game intensely. I thought now I would be able to see Loveness more. Little did I know that the following night I was to join the national team on their tour of Sri Lanka. How was I going to break the news to her? I didn't want to send another letter through Esther, so I asked permission from her mother to release her from school, so I could at least spend one day with her. Fortunately, she said yes.

7

Life in the Fast Lane

AS I WAS SAYING MY GOODBYES AT THE AIRPORT, I HEARD A SCREAM. I quickly realised it was Loveness, and I rushed to her as she started to break down and cry. I hugged her in my arms. I was going to miss Loveness immensely, and at the same time I knew I wasn't really ready for the tour ahead in Sri Lanka. There was also the small matter of Muttiah Muralitharan to think about.

Instead of going to the hotel from the airport, I headed straight to the ground to watch a warm-up game. Our batsmen were not going well. Andy walked by me and said, 'Get ready to play tomorrow.' I had so much respect for him that I didn't raise my concerns: the jet lag, the lack of practice. I had only time for one training session. Still, I received a boost a little while after when he walked by again and said, 'Nothing to worry about, you can't do any worse than this.' He would regularly say that sort of thing to me.

In the warm-up game I batted well at number six, making 42 runs. It was the highest score on our team, and it meant we would be defending a low total when we came back out. Our backs were against the wall. Before I knew it, Andy told me that I would be bowling the next over. I was taken aback: Andy had seen me bowl before in club cricket back in Zimbabwe, but I doubt any of the others knew I could bowl at all. I suddenly needed to go the toilet. I bowled four good overs before I started cramping up in my legs and arms as the long flight started to take its toll. My performance on the day meant I would be in the side once the tri-series came around a few days later. We would be facing Sri Lanka and the West Indies, and I would be playing only as a batsman.

It was tradition the day before the start of a tournament or a big series for us to have dinner together. On this occasion, the team management decided that it would be lunch rather than supper, so that we'd have plenty of time to rest up ahead of the game with Sri Lanka in Colombo. Around halfway through the meal, as jokes flew around the table, one senior player summoned me to help a girl who had asked for directions to the business centre of the hotel. As I began to tell her, I was told that it'd be better if I took her there myself. Everyone round the table was laughing, but as a junior member of the side I simply had to do as I was told. She spoke English very well and made it clear how much she loved the game, so I helped arrange tickets for her for our game.

She asked me if she could have the telephone number for my room, and later rang me to thank me for the tickets. As a thank you she invited me to hers for dinner with her parents, an invitation which I gladly accepted. The food was wonderful, and her parents were accommodating and very knowledgeable about the game of cricket. After the food she gave me a tour of her mansion, with her bedroom being the last stop. She shut the door behind us, and an awkward silence followed. Eventually she picked up her pink lip gloss, put some on, and asked me if I wanted to try some myself. I laughed nervously and decided to make my excuses, telling her that it was way past my bedtime. I was very naïve. She gave me photos of herself to keep as we said our goodbyes, and the driver took me back to my hotel.

'What a fool you are, Tatenda,' I thought to myself when I got back. 'Why did you not just yield and kiss her?' I had a very faithful girlfriend back home in Harare, but I was playing different scenarios over and over in my head. In the end, my feelings for Loveness had won the battle.

On the cricket field, things could not have gone much worse for me. I played and batted in our first three matches of the series, but failed to score a single run, facing a total of just four balls. In the first game, I batted at number seven and was LBW to the left-arm swing bowler Chaminda Vaas for a golden duck. On the day he picked up staggering figures of 8-19 – which remain the best figures in ODI history – as we were bowled out for a pathetic 38. This at the time was the lowest ODI total of all time, since beaten by Zimbabwe again when we were bowled out for 35 against the same opposition under my captaincy in 2004. I remained at number seven for the second game against the West Indies, which we won, but on this occasion, I was dismissed on my second ball by Carl Hooper. In my third game

Murali had me for another golden duck. I had not yet had my chat with Younis Khan about how to play him. Mercifully, I was not selected for our fourth and final game of the series. Andy had said at the start of the tour that I couldn't do much worse than the current crop of players, but I think it was fair to say that I had proved him wrong.

After I had been dismissed for a third successive duck, I actually contemplated quitting the sport altogether. In fact, I felt like no one was going to convince me otherwise. I could get the team manager to arrange my flight back to Zimbabwe, and I'd be done for good. As these thoughts swirled around my head on the way back to our dressing room, a strange thing happened. A man in the crowd shouted, 'Don't worry young man, it doesn't matter how many times you fall, what counts is the number of times you get up and fight again.' That did me the world of good. I had no idea who had said it, but the words really resonated with me at the time.

I think thoughts of quitting entered my head in the first place because of how much pressure I placed on myself. There was a big difference in how I viewed myself as a player and the ability I believed I had, and the statistics I was actually producing. It wasn't adding up. I had made my debut, gone away to finish my A-Levels, and then rejoined the team for this triangular series. I no longer saw myself as a beginner; I had a higher opinion of myself. I believed that I could make the side purely as a batsman, and I had to because Andy was going to be the wicketkeeper for a number of years yet. I had to push myself, and I had done that, and yet here I was failing in such spectacular fashion. That's why giving in seemed like such an appealing prospect.

As well as the encouragement from the unknown figure in the stands, I spoke to Loveness on the phone that evening. I usually only wore my cricket gear on tour, as that's all I thought I needed. Loveness thought otherwise, though, and instructed me go shopping for some new clothes. I wanted to save my funds to the last cent, so I could own a house at a young age and settle down, but she persuaded to part with some money for once. At this moment, I was convinced that I was going to marry Loveness. I just knew it.

For the first Test against Sri Lanka, which started just two days after Christmas, Hamilton joined the squad, and it was nice to have a familiar face around. While I missed out on selection in Colombo he opened the batting, though we ended up losing by an innings and 166 runs. After that, me and Hamilton packed our bags ready to head to the Under-19 World Cup. The Sri Lankans would go on and win the second Test by an innings and 94 runs, and the third Test by 315 runs. The series was undoubtedly a step in the wrong direction for the side. In my first series – a 1-0 defeat to the West Indies – we had been battered in one game but drawn the other after a good batting display. The same had happened in the following series against South Africa, which I played no part in: one heavy loss, one draw. We had then proceeded to beat Bangladesh 1-0 in a two-match series. Though we were still one of the weaker teams in international cricket, getting thrashed in three games in a row was not usual.

When we lost we often lost heavily, but we'd also get into plenty of winning positions as well, and against the better sides we'd often just fail to get over the line. Far from discouraging us, I believe this actually kept us going. We knew that we had only been playing international cricket for around ten years and were continuing to improve. There were plenty of things we could work on. It was later on when I was captain, after the mass exodus of senior players, where I didn't feel like we were going anywhere, but I didn't feel like that at this stage.

At the Under-19 World Cup in New Zealand, I was to captain a unique team, with a good mixture of youngsters with some experience – myself, Stuey, Hamilton, Charles Coventry, Sean Irvine and Conan Brewer – and a very talented group of younger, more inexperienced players including Brendan Taylor, Elton Chigumbura, Stanley Marisa, Waddington Mwayenga and Alfred Mbwembwe. The younger squad players had so much talent, but also had so little experience, which made it particularly challenging for me as skipper.

We were introduced to our new coach, Steve Rhodes, whom we called 'Bumpy.' Rhodes, who was recently the coach of English county outfit Worcestershire, was an impressive man, and funny to go with it too. For me, there was the advantage that he had been a wicketkeeper himself as a player, playing in eleven Test matches and nine ODIs for England. I learnt a lot from him. Before long, he had also spotted my ability to swing the ball both ways.

Stephen Mangongo was also there on this tour, and for me that was brilliant. He had a unique way of getting us to play hard and tough, but he acted in a very mellow manner on this particular tour. He also tipped Bumpy off about my bowling abilities, having seen me rise to the occasion a few times during club games in Zimbabwe for Takashinga. Together they formulated a gameplan, which involved me taking my pads fifteen overs into a fifty-over game so I could bowl in the middle overs, before I would put them on again for the last ten.

In the end, we did not make the quarter-finals of the main competition, but I ended up winning man of the tournament for my performances as we entered the plate section and emerged victorious. My bowling was a particular revelation: across seven games I took twelve wickets, including figures of 3-14, 4-30 and 3-8. I also scored 65 not out in our plate final against Nepal. My performances led to me being called up to the main national team again, where I was joined by Charles Coventry.

Overall, I still felt disappointed. When I arrived at the tournament, I believed we were good enough to challenge for the trophy. I had played international cricket and Hamilton had played international cricket, while Stuey and Sean Irvine had represented the A side. Charles Coventry was on the fringes of the senior team. We had five players in and around the national-team squad, whereas with some of the bigger nations that number was zero, and they would only have one or two players each that had played any first-class cricket at all. I thought we should be one of the teams competing. At the end of the tour, I was slightly disappointed with my own stats, especially with my batting – I was hoping to win the team more games with my runs. Against New Zealand and Sri Lanka, the two toughest opponents we faced, I made just 30 runs across two innings.

I was clearly one of the bright young talents in world cricket for my age – my selection for Zimbabwe's senior side had confirmed that – but as a keen student of the game, I was also aware of the realities of representing one of international cricket's smaller nations. I knew that on average we were playing around seven Test matches a year, and in years where we played a lot of cricket, we would play around 20 ODIs. When you compare the amount of games we played with the amount other countries played, it was not a lot. Take the year in question, 2002. In that year, we had six scheduled Test matches compared to with India's fourteen. Excluding the ICC Champions Trophy in September, we had thirteen scheduled ODIs across 2002. India had 32.

Even if at the Under-19 World Cup I was one of the most exciting prospects, the likelihood was that many of the players behind me ability-wise would end up overtaking me in a few years' time if they played for one of the bigger cricketing nations, due to sheer exposure alone. The more you play against other players at the top level, the more you are going to get better. It's not a difficult concept to understand. The challenge was how to keep up with these players when playing about half the amount of international cricket they were. I certainly had to keep hammering the bowling machine, while domestic cricket in other countries was also an option.

Between 2005 and 2011 Zimbabwe would not play a single Test match at all. That hiatus, coupled with the internal problems I had with ZC over the years, helped to prevent me achieving what I wanted in the game. I had ambitions to be the world number one, and I was ranked 27 in the ICC batsmen rankings when our own cricket board voluntarily suspended our Test status in 2005, a move that was encouraged by the ICC. It was big news when I had taken over India's Sourav Ganguly in the rankings shortly before that, because he was captain and I was captain. He was around thirty years old at the time, in his prime.

Our last series before this indefinite break came in September 2005 against India in Zimbabwe. I was captain of a sinking ship but managed to score 71 not out and 52 in the first Test match in Bulawayo as we succumbed to another heavy defeat. In the second and last Test match in Harare, I scored nought and one as we lost by ten wickets. It neatly encapsulated where we were as a cricketing nation compared with the big sides, and the gap was only going to get bigger in the intervening period. I was 22 years old and wouldn't play another Test match until our one-off encounter with Bangladesh in August 2011, by which point I was 28. I only played five Test matches after that.

In between the Under-19 World Cup and the upcoming tour of India, I had a couple of weeks back at home in the dusty streets of Highfield, which was becoming a rare occurrence. I planned to spend some more quality time with Loveness. We'd spend each day of the two weeks either at my house or hers, and gossip about us started spreading like wildfire in the neighbourhood. Some were saying we were too young to be starting a relationship, others started spreading rumours that we both had other relationships outside of ours. It didn't really bother us, and we continued to see each other every time we got the chance.

I started to get to know her siblings, and she became acquainted with mine as well. As a result of spending so much time with Loveness, I stopped practising quite as much. Stuart, my practice partner and my closest friend, was very understanding about this.

Two weeks in Zimbabwe, and it was time to head to the airport again. Loveness went back to locking herself in her room, which I was told she did regularly when I left. It reached a point where her Mum was relieved when I was around, because she had become so anti-social when I was not.

I soon arrived in India to play two Tests and five ODIs. This was my first time in the country, though I had been told how much different it was to anywhere else in the world. In India we were treated like royalty. The whole squad and everyone around us were held in very high esteem – it seemed as if everyone knew who you were. There were scores of staring eyes everywhere we went.

We constantly had cameras in our faces, and the speed at which everything happened was much quicker than anywhere else I had been in the world. Everything was hurried, and it was only when we got on the team bus that things would calm down. I would look out of the window, trying to catch a glimpse of the real India, of what was happening out on the streets. Coming from the high-density suburb of Highfield, I thought I had an idea of what poverty meant, but what I saw through the window here completely changed my perspective. I had always felt empathy for others, and what I saw here completely broke my heart. There were so many mothers carrying their babies on their backs, gesturing to motorists to give them food. When I saw a similar situation in Zimbabwe I would give away any coins I had in my pocket, but here we were on a heavily-guarded bus.

In Zimbabwe, a lot of people who live in poverty live in the rural areas. They don't have electricity, and they have to travel to get their water from dens, but they at least have something. They can do their own sustenance farming and therefore get a little bit of food for their family. They tend to have enough land to at least farm for their families. In the 1970s, when Zimbabwe was still Rhodesia, there was a big move to improve sanitation in the rural areas. The Blair Research Laboratory – an institution named after Dr Dyson Blair, the former Secretary of Health, and renamed the National Institute of Health Research in 2011 – developed the Blair toilet in this era, which helped revolutionise sanitation in many African countries. This toilet – also known as a pit latrine – was deployed *en masse* in the rural areas of Zimbabwe. It was designed to make use of air currents. There was a septic tank-like pit, over which was an upper structure with an open, light-trap entrance and ventilation pipe from the bottom pit with a fine wire grate that kept out and trapped flies. Flies could not spread diseases from faecal matter, and gases produced by the waste were redirected outside.

When looking at people in India living on the side of the road, my first thought was, 'Where are they going to bathe?' I remember looking out the window – this time from the five-star hotel we were staying in – and the first thing I'd see were people bathing in a den. There didn't seem to be any toilets around. India is so immensely populated that it makes it especially difficult for parents to provide for their children. It's no start at all really. It broke my heart. Where were they to bathe? Where were they to go to the toilet? Perhaps it was the sheer number of people living in poverty – Zimbabwe has a population of less than twenty million, India has a population of over one billion – that meant I was so taken aback despite what I had seen back home on a daily basis.

At our hotel we were warmly welcomed with some traditional dancing, and everything was given to us on a silver platter. It was in India that I perfected my signature, with fans constantly asking me to sign bats and photos. Some would even ask me to scribble on their skin.

Still, when I retreated to my hotel room the world felt like a very lonely place. I was so far away from home. I could almost hear the four walls speaking to me, creating doubts in my mind. Yes, I had been awarded the best player award at the Under-19 World Cup, but that was in a tournament full of kids with limited first-class experience. Here I was up against tried and tested professionals at the very top of their game. Sachin Tendulkar, Sourav Ganguly, Rahul Dravid, Zaheer Khan, Harbhajan Singh and Anil Kumble were some of the names I'd be facing up to in the weeks to come. How was I going to score any runs?

On one particular evening, when I was struggling to clear the demons from my head – the four walls never seemed to give me any positive answers – I was distracted by a sound coming from my door. Someone had slipped a letter through. It was from one of the newly-recruited board members, Ozias Bvute, and it read, 'To my younger brother Taibu. Believe in yourself, you are good enough.' Who would have thought that a few words from a person I had met only one previously would have such an uplifting effect? I would get to know Ozias a lot better in the years to come.

We ended up losing 2-0 in the two-Test series. In the first Test in Nagpur we were easily defeated, by an innings and 101 runs, but in the second Test in Delhi we only lost by four wickets. They were chasing 126 to win in the final innings, and we had them 105-6, but in the end they got home. My wicketkeeping was fine in this series, but my batting left a lot to be desired. My problems against spin that had reared their head in Sri Lanka just wouldn't go away. I had not yet found a method of how to start my innings against this type of bowler, and I couldn't get any sort of start. In my first innings in Nagpur, batting at number eight, I was clean bowled by the leg-spin of Kumble for one run off sixteen deliveries. In the second innings it was the off-spin of Harbhajan that accounted for me. I had failed to score a run off ten deliveries. In total in the first Test I had scored one run off 26 balls. In Delhi I at least managed to get going somewhat, scoring thirteen runs in my first knock before being trapped LBW by Kumble. In the second innings, Kumble got me again for ten. I had scored 24 runs in my last seven international innings over two formats.

There was a lot of noise in the grounds during the Test matches, but that was nothing compared to the atmosphere we were greeted with for the ODIs. I felt more comfortable about my game in this format, but I was batting in a position where I could not really affect the game at all – either at nine or ten. In the first ODI, I was privileged to be batting alongside Dougie Marillier as he hit an astonishing 56* off 24 balls batting at the lowly position of ten to send us to a miraculous victory. Dougie – who had been left wheelchair-bound for three months by a car crash when he was sixteen – had made a bit of a name for himself as a big hitter and had become famous for walking across to his off stump against the fast bowler and flicking the ball over the wicketkeeper's head. This was long before innovations like this were the norm like they are now in the age of Twenty20 cricket. We went 2-1 up in the series with two games to play, giving us a fantastic opportunity of an unlikely victory. In one game I made a stumping off Ganguly off the bowling of Marillier, which soon became famous in India. I was not aware that one piece of work could gain such notoriety, but here was different to everywhere else.

For me, keeping wasn't so much about having a set technique, it was more about adapting to the conditions you found yourself in. If I went to Australia, I used to study how the keepers moved, because their wickets behaved differently to how ours did back home. Generally, I would have a preconception about how their keepers liked to keep. Watching their technique allowed me to work out how the ball behaved in their conditions. The same was true in India. In Australia they move their feet freely, because the ball carries more. You tend to catch the ball above your knees, so you can dance around. Then you go to India, and you realise that they almost catch the ball with flat hands – they do not create a ball-like shape with their hands to catch it. It's almost as if they clap on the ball to catch it. The same can be said for Pakistani keepers, who face similar conditions. The ball does not carry as much, so they stand closer. They are taking most things below their knees at home.

One thing you are struck by when you visit different countries is the uniformity of players' technique. A lot of this is governed by the conditions you play in on a regular basis, but players are also copying those they have grown up watching. MS Dhoni keeps in a certain way, and young Indian wicketkeepers are likely to study and copy that technique. When playing in Sri Lanka recently, I noticed how many of the young batsmen in the country blocked the right-arm off-spinners in exactly the same way that Mahela Jayawardene did for so many years at the top level. It's natural to copy your icons.

English keepers like to catch on their knees. When they catch the ball, they tend to do it with their fingers pointing up, and then they fall onto their knees. Alec Stewart used to do this a lot. This is because the ball tends to wobble after it has passed the batsman and the stumps. If you catch like this, with your fingers pointing up, you are in a better position to change your hands quickly than you are if you are if you use the Australian or subcontinental method. England was particularly difficult: in a Test match at Chester-le-Street in 2003, I conceded fourteen byes in one innings as they scored 416. Later, on a tour of Sri Lanka in 2004, I conceded no byes at all as the opposition racked up 713-3. At the time, it was the highest innings total in Test match cricket history without the wicketkeeper conceding a bye, a record since eclipsed by Sri Lanka's Prassanna Jayawardene in 2009.

I used to copy what the home wicketkeepers did in each country, tailoring my technique one tour at a time. I never broke any fingers keeping, whereas most of the other wicketkeepers I have spoken to have. I believed in my hand-eye coordination, so I was happy to try and replicate what others did.

I also had pretty unshakeable belief, which helped me immensely when I dropped a catch behind the stumps. I was able to put any mistake to the back of my mind because I used to leave no stone unturned in my preparation for the game. If I knew I had prepared to the best of my abilities, and given full concentration when I was out there, how could I blame myself? You will see that there are hardly any pictures of me keeping with sunglasses on. I was always sponsored, but I always used to have my sunglasses on my cap. I didn't want to leave any excuses; I didn't want to blame a mistake on anything. That way I was able to forget any error quickly. If you have something to blame it on, the mistake tends to linger. I left no room for that. My warm-up was always the same.

Full concentration when the bowler is running in, everything else blinded. I had to deal with any mistakes myself.

There was always a large crowd standing outside our hotel in India – despite the heat – waiting to catch a glimpse of us. On one occasion, our team manager Mr Merman asked me to go to the fence to sign a few autographs. One fan asked me for a handshake, and I obliged, but that soon turned out to be a grave mistake. There was such a push from the people that the fence ripped, and we had to rush back inside as the police restored order. Going shopping was a mission as well, and we had to have armed police with us at all times. When we entered the shops, the doors would be closed and locked. We'd get great discounts, but word soon got around the mall that we were there and people flocked to us. I loved the Indian people. They reminded me of the people back home a lot: when they love you, they love you with all their heart.

We ended up losing the final two games, and therefore the series. This was due to the introduction of Yuvraj Singh, who scored 80* and 75 to snatch things from our grasp. While we were busy with games outside of Zimbabwe, more comments concerning race started to filter into the dressing room. People were talking more and more about what was going on back home. In the very early stages of my career I had tried to block any comments I heard out of my mind. Now I found it more difficult to shut them out. The dressing room was definitely tenser than it had been previously.

There was one comment in particular that stuck with me. We had just lost a game, and I was going around the dressing room collecting kits off people. In India you got everything for free, so I used to go and collect all the unwanted kit off players so I could give it to kids back in Zimbabwe. I made an announcement asking the guys not to throw away anything they didn't want. I was happy to pay for the excess luggage on the plane. One of the players responded by saying, 'I wouldn't give my kit to a bunch of racists.' I believe the player in question was referring to Takashinga, the team I often represented back home. In recent times Takashinga had gained a reputation for bad behaviour on the field, characterised by a game in early 2002 where Gift Makoni had vehemently opposed being given out LBW by an umpire, causing the matched to be delayed. Makoni had initially refused to leave the field, and when he did he took the stumps with him, throwing them on top of the balcony in protest. It was an ugly moment, and with Zimbabwean cricket sliding into political turmoil, Takashinga – the first predominantly black team in the first division of our club cricket system – were not viewed kindly by some. This was indicative of just how divided a society we were representing. Andy Flower had said previously that the players themselves did not see colour, and Andy himself had intermittently captained Takashinga, but events back home and how the government was acting was causing previously unseen friction and disharmony.

I got along with the player in question, so later that evening I went to his hotel room. I explained to him that the kits were going to kids at Takashinga Cricket Club. I told him I had heard what he had said, and that I thought it was unfair to label everyone in one community as racist. There were those with racist views where I came from, but the kit was going to kids. Some of these kids did not even have shoes, and the player who had passed the comment was actually the favourite of a lot of them. I told him that he had just put them in a category they didn't belong in. He apologised and seemed genuinely remorseful.

I understood the problems with Takashinga, and I understood that the hierarchy at the club were seen as loyal to the regime, but I tried to separate those people from the club itself. I was in Takashinga, I was part of Takashinga, I was right in the middle of Takashinga. I tried to think about the good that the club represented, all the youngsters that came from the houses in Highfield to play the sport they had grown to love. To me, that was the real Takashinga, and if you were to go back there even to this day, you would be treated to a wonderful reception by the kids that still play there.

Still, to play for the club you had to put up with a lot of nonsense from those above you which as youngsters we did. However, when I heard the news that Henry Olonga had joined the club a short while later – in a role that would see him mentor the likes of me, Hamilton and Elton Chigumbura – I knew that it was a disaster waiting to happen. Knowing Henry as I did, I knew he wouldn't stand for the nonsense that we did as young players. Though Henry was black, I don't think he was viewed as 'one of us' by the hierarchy, due to his more privileged upbringing. Henry's first language was not Shona. His arrival coincided with the club becoming more militant and more embroiled in conflict as tensions in the country heightened, and therefore it was a relationship that was unlikely to last.

I started to learn to drive. I knew it wasn't going to be very long before I got my first car. I wasn't planning on buying one, as I was very confident I would soon get a good national-team contract. A car was usually part of that package. Being a quick learner, I was pretty quick to master the concept of driving. Time did not permit me to take my driving test, though, as this time I was on my way to the UK.

Steve Rhodes, who had been one of our coaches at the Under-19 World Cup, had organised for me to play some club cricket with a team called Worcester Norton Taverners. I would be spending time in a different environment, playing in different conditions, thousands of miles from home with no one I knew around. This was going to be so hard for Loveness and me. We had hardly spent any time together, and here I was packing my bag again. Not for a month or two, but for six.

Steve had mentioned that I would play cricket and work part-time. What did I know about working? Ever since I was a boy, all I knew of was hitting and catching the ball.

On arrival in the UK, I was welcomed by the club chairman, Roger Weston, who took me for a cup of tea and then to the house I would be staying in, with a couple called Richard and Kate. Everyone at the club was so nice to me. I appreciated them taking a stranger into their home. They were from a different culture and had a different way of living. I thought I would be able to adapt well to the English way of living, but I wondered how it would be for a couple to adapt to the way I lived.

I was soon down at the cricket ground, introducing myself to my new teammates. It was a life that was so foreign to me: I didn't like drinking alcohol, and I didn't like being in pubs. Most English club cricketers liked both. I enjoy good conversation, of course, but not with others speaking and music playing in the background. But that was the order of club cricket, and so I had to adapt.

I started well in my first game, scoring a half-century, which was a promising sign for the season. However, I never really fulfilled that promise, and for the rest of the campaign I failed to really click into gear. I scored fifties every now and then, but in the main it was just a string of ordinary scores. I didn't live up to the expectations people had of me, and that contributed to me being homesick.

The job I had been offered was to help the ground staff with their duties, but in the end I turned it down. The thought behind having a job was the extra cash, but I was not money-orientated. Because I didn't drink or go out, my weekly allowance was more than enough. I was so convinced that I was going to have a long and successful international career that I did not believe I needed it anyway. The money would eventually come. Instead I continued to work hard at my game and my fitness levels, knowing that I'd likely be rejoining the national team when I returned home. The season was becoming monotonous, so anything that happened outside the club felt like an added bonus to me. A little excitement came when Worcestershire County Cricket Club had a couple of injuries while the Second XI were playing away from home, and so Steve Rhodes called me in to help with twelfth man duties. I would learn from England internationals Graeme Hick and Vikram Solanki, as well as Australian pace bowler Andy Bichel, among others. I always believed that chatting to other players would help me as my career progressed. It wasn't long before I warmed the hearts of the attentive Worcestershire faithful, and I was soon nicknamed 'Tiger' for my fielding efforts.

Andy Flower was over in the UK as Essex's overseas player, and so we had a chance to squeeze in a catch-up over the course of this game. I'd never say much in our conversations but believed that simply spending time with one of the greats of the game would prove beneficial. Andy was not the only high-class player around, and I also witnessed Hick score a triple hundred for the third time in his career against Durham. Until he reached his double century, he barely hit a ball in the air.

The dressing room-environment was different in England. They used to have the television on when England were playing as well, and players would pop in from the balcony from time to time to check the score. On one particular occasion, Gareth Batty – an off-spinner who would soon represent his country – had been dismissed. Gareth was primarily a bowler, but he took his batting very seriously. As he walked back to the pavilion after getting out, the lads made the wise decision to leave the changing room, where they had been watching England take on India. Everyone except me. I soon realised why they had all vanished. He stormed in and turned the whole dressing room upside down. Cricket bats were sent flying and so was all his equipment, while he went on a foul-mouthed rant at no one in particular. I had never seen such a temper in all my life.

That England away series was not until the summer of 2003, and before that we had a Cricket World Cup on home soil. To prepare ourselves for that, we had two Test matches and five ODIs against Pakistan scheduled at the end of 2002, before we then faced Kenya in a three-match ODI series to end the year. My early failures in the international arena meant I wasn't getting too far ahead of myself.

I started to improve drastically, but I stayed humble every time I did do well. My batting was now starting to reach the level of my wicketkeeping, though I continued to be more consistent in games with the gloves. I was so comfortable in that department that I would even stand up to the stumps to Heath Streak on occasion, our most dangerous bowler who usually reached a speed of above eighty miles per hour.

Playing against Pakistan was no easy task, especially at home, because our only chance of winning was if we produced a green surface that would assist our pace bowlers. We could not outdo them in the spin department – we did not have anyone of the class of Saqlain Mushtaq. The problem was, they also possessed a fearsome pace attack: Waqar Younis was still in the team, and they had the raw pace of Shoaib Akhtar and Mohammad Sami backing him up. Stuey and I were selected to play in the warm-up game. Sami was at the top of his run. I knew he was going to attempt a yorker first up; he had cleaned up my friend Stuey in that fashion just a few balls before. I scored six painful runs and left the crease with my body full of bruises. If that was how quick Sami was, what about Shoaib?

A couple of days before the first Test began, I picked up the new balls I had purchased from India and called Vusi Sibanda. He had the strongest arm of all my peers, so I asked him to assist me with my personal practice. I asked him to stand eighteen yards away from me as opposed to the usual 22, and got him to throw it as fast as he could at me. At first, I hardly picked a thing up, but as time went on I became more accustomed to the pace. I knew I was ready for the challenge ahead.

We were 93-5 when I walked into bat in the first Test in Harare. Pakistan had made 285. I walked out to face Shoaib, who was the fastest bowler in the world. In a few months' time at the World Cup, he would be the first bowler to ever be clocked at 100 miles per hour. The adrenaline was pumping, and a hint of fear was tapping away at the back of my mind, but I had a simple plan. I would play what needed to be played and leave anything that wasn't hitting the stumps. My team were in a spot of bother, so I didn't need to be taking the game to the opposition. Like always, he bowled quickly. I was batting with Andy, and I remember us taking it in turns to cop it from the 'Rawalpindi Express', as he was known. We both received plenty of blows. I prided myself on getting in line with the rockets he was unleashing, which led me to receive a nasty blow in the ribs at one stage. I was in immense pain, and just wanted to drop to the ground. I could barely breathe. But I knew that would be a moral victory for him, so I stood my ground. I gathered myself, stood up tall and let out a scream. I wasn't about to show any signs of weakness.

Andy came over, gave the naughty smile he used to reveal and said, 'Tiba, was that nice?' I just smiled. What else could I say? The following ball was another vicious bouncer and struck me on the right bicep. The big man followed it up with a chirp. In response I did one of the silliest things ever: I gave him some back. Who in their right mind chirps Shoaib? His run-up got longer, and the chin music continued. One Andy left, and another Andy joined me at the crease, Blignaut this time. The battle continued with Shoaib later on and became so fierce that Andy pleaded with me to stop giving it back to him. Backing down was never part of my make up, so I carried on. I knew that my partner was right, but my adrenaline was pumping, and I couldn't get out of the state I was in. He ran in harder and bowled quicker. He bowled me one bouncer that only didn't hit me because I remained completely motionless; there simply wasn't enough time to get out the way.

I ended the innings on 51*, my highest Test score and my first half-century. Andy Blignaut had also scored a fifty, but in different circumstances – he made his at a strike rate of 131.57, while my strike rate at the end of the innings was 43.22. I had proved to everyone I could grind it out. In the second innings I made 28 before falling LBW to Waqar Younis. We ended up losing that game by over 100 runs, and the second Test by ten wickets, but I had shown my batting to be good enough for the highest level of the game. I only scored 15 and 37 in Bulawayo, but I was getting much more accustomed to occupying the crease.

In the ODI series that followed, which would act as more direct practice for the World Cup to come, I averaged thirty across my five innings. The problem was, as a team we did not look good enough to compete with the best. We were on home soil but suffered a 5-0 thrashing. In the first game we came within seven runs of victory but were comfortably beaten in the remaining four. Our bowling was a problem; Pakistan batted first on four occasions out of five and made at least 300 every time they did.

The series against Kenya did not prove to be quite as difficult. The first game was affected by weather, and the in the next two we cruised home. I was not needed with the bat in any of the games. The World Cup was next.

8
World Cup of Woe

THE 2003 WORLD CUP WAS TO BE CO-HOSTED BY SOUTH AFRICA, Kenya and Zimbabwe. It was the most prestigious event in cricket, and it was a brilliant opportunity for us as a team and as a nation. The first World Cup had been in 1975, and it was England who hosted the first three editions. In following tournaments, host duties were usually shared between countries. In 1987 it was India and Pakistan, in 1992 it was Australia and New Zealand, in 1996 it was back to the subcontinent and to India, Pakistan and Sri Lanka, and in 1999 England and Wales. Now it was our turn.

In 1983 Zimbabwe had taken part in our first-ever World Cup, stunning everyone by beating Australia at Trent Bridge in what was our first international cricket match. We also competed at the 1987 and 1992 World Cups, before playing our first Test match in 1992.

Cricket had begun to seep into the consciousness of ordinary people in Zimbabwe, so co-hosting the World Cup was a massive deal. We had been making steady progress as a cricketing nation, and I believe that if we had continued on the path that we were on in 2003, cricket would have overtaken football as the main sport in the country. Things were starting to change. Whereas you previously saw kids playing football in the streets, now you saw them playing cricket. I remember going back to Highfield around this time, and on several occasions, I parked my car on the side of the road and went to join the kids playing in the street. It was a common sight. The game of cricket had been brought alive in our country. As it transpired, things did not go exactly to plan.

Our first group match was to be played against Namibia at the Harare Sports Club on 10 February. Before this, though, there had been debate all over the world about whether we should be hosting any games at all, given the political situation in our country. The government-sanctioned land invasions of the white farms, which had begun in 2000, were still continuing and had led to several deaths. In 2002, Mugabe had won another presidential election with 56.2 percent of the vote, and though the Organisation of African Unity had described the election as 'transparent, credible, free and fair', the validity of the results had been questioned and condemned by many, including Zimbabwean opposition figures and western governments.

The opposition leader Morgan Tsvangirai was on trial for treason, a trial which was due to start a week before the tournament began. He had been charged with apparently plotting to kill president Mugabe and seize power, though he was later cleared in 2004.

England, who we were due to face in Harare, three days after the Namibia game, had been deliberating whether they would fulfil the fixture in Zimbabwe. The England players and cricket board had been worried about the social unrest and political situation in Zimbabwe in the lead-up to the tournament, and those fears were heightened when they received a message from a militant organisation named the Sons and Daughters of Zimbabwe – an organisation known by Interpol – which read: 'Come to Harare and you will die.'

However, the Deputy National Commissioner of the South African Police, Andre Pruis, had looked into the threat and concluded that it was probably the work of one individual, and that the letter's author had 'no capacity to carry out a threat'.

Pruis, South Africa's second most senior police officer, said he had consulted the country's crime intelligence division and the secret service: 'They indicated no knowledge of the Sons and Daughters of Zimbabwe. It has been sent by a person with the purpose of disrupting the World Cup. This person or persons have no capacity to carry out a threat and should be treated as propaganda and not as a direct threat'.

The media always seemed to enjoy asking me and Andy Flower questions together, and on the eve of the tournament I was asked to attend one of these press conferences with my closest confidant. The reporters always used to ask Andy a question first, and then would follow up with a very similar question for me. We usually had a similar view on things, but his first answer in this conference caught me off guard. Andy was asked if he thought England should fulfil their fixture in Zimbabwe, and he answered no. I never actually heard his explanation, as I was too busy trying to process what I had just heard. Had he made a mistake with his answer? What was he saying? On the eve of the first World Cup game to be played in Zimbabwe, he was suggesting one of our opponents should not show up in the country at all? When it was my turn to answer, I said, 'I am a professional cricketer. I get paid when I play. If there is no opposition to play against, I don't get paid.'

They turned back to Andy, who said that politics and sport always run hand in hand, even if we tried to ignore that fact. I had never heard him mention this before or speak like this, so I left the conference wondering exactly what was going on. A while later we were released from our media duties for the day. I asked Andy what was going on. 'Nothing for you to worry about Tiba,' he said. 'You are playing well and working hard, and you should pay the littlest attention to this and what is to come for the next few days, especially tomorrow. That's all I can say for now, Tiba.'

As I said before, I had seen how the political situation in Zimbabwe had been covered by both our own media and western media, and I believed that neither told the full story and gave fair coverage. I could understand where the England players were coming from and the concerns that they had. It's also the case that they might not have had the true picture of what was going on in the country. I also had to think of my career. If other countries followed England's path and decided against coming to Zimbabwe, how would I make a living? I'm a professional cricketer who relies on having opposition to play against. If they don't come, another team doesn't come. Where do I end up?

If sport is being disturbed, then tourism is being disturbed as well, and that affects everyone, not just the government. At the same time, I believe that more pressure could have been put on our government internally. The government's actions have a knock-on effect on matters such as sport, and in this case one of the world's biggest cricket teams did not want to enter the country as we hosted the sport's global showpiece. Their decision was heavily influenced by the actions of our government.

On arrival at the Harare Sports Club for our opening game against Namibia, I noticed the media presence was unusually heavy. Obviously, we were one of the

World Cup hosts and this was our first game of the tournament, but the amount of interest and attention still seemed strange. Namibia were not a household name in international cricket. The reason for such attention soon became clear, as did Andy's comments to me the day before. Just prior to the game, Andy, who was still our most famous and successful cricketer, and Henry Olonga, who was Zimbabwe's first black cricketer at international level, had released a joint statement to the media in which they had denounced the 'death of democracy' in our land. Their aim was to shine a light on the social, political and economic problems facing Zimbabwe and the oppressive regime of Robert Mugabe, and they had chosen our opening game of our tournament to make the stand. Both Andy and Henry donned black armbands for the day to symbolise their stand, which would soon become cricket's most famous political protest.

Being young and oblivious, I had no idea what was going on until about midway through our batting innings. There had been a few murmurs of something happening in the dressing room, and there may have been talks at which I was not present, but I knew nothing until I saw Henry sitting on our balcony wearing this armband. I immediately assumed he must be mourning the death of someone he knew. Little did I know that this person was our own country. I asked our Australian coach, Geoff Marsh, who had died, and it was only then that I became aware of the gravity of the situation. The feeling I got was that most of the senior players were already aware of what was going on, and I did wonder why nobody had told me anything.

With Andy, there was a sense that he had nothing to lose – he had already announced that he was retiring from international cricket after the tournament's conclusion. Henry, though, had really put his neck on the line. He was 26 years old and was reaching the peak of his powers. He was a historic figure in Zimbabwean cricket and had established himself as one of our key bowlers. Now he was effectively putting an end to his international career; with the government we had at the time, there was effectively no coming back from what he did, which neatly demonstrated the point he and Andy were making. There was no room for political protest under this Zimbabwean government. The fact that the stand had been taken by one white man and one black man was deeply significant and meant that it would be difficult for the government or our sporting institutions to claim that race was the primary motivator of the protest.

Though it seemed of little importance, we ended up winning the game against

Namibia. Craig Wishart made a brutal 172* off just 151 balls as we piled up 340-2 from our fifty overs. Andy himself showed little sign of his mind being elsewhere, as he made 39 off 29 deliveries. Namibia had reached 104-5 in their chase before rain intervened. I took a catch behind the stumps off the first ball of their innings as Riaan Walters edged a Heath Streak delivery. Heath was our captain that day and gave Henry three overs as our first change bowler. It was a good day for us in cricketing terms, but during most of our time spent out on the field I could not help but wonder whether Henry and Andy would be safe. Andy in particular had been like a brother to me and I was worried for him. The Zimbabwean government was a government known for making people disappear. We had all heard stories of people that had protested in our newspapers, and it was never usually good news. I also didn't think Andy and Henry's actions would bear fruit.

Their fight was a little different to the one I took on when I was captain later on in my career – my fight was sport-related, their fight had consequences more far-reaching. They capitalised on the publicity that comes through cricket to make a statement focused on politics. I wasn't sure how that was going to play out. In my time I have had plenty of fights concerning cricket matters with the Zimbabwe hierarchy, many of which I have lost, but politics is another matter. It was brave of them to do what they did, 100 percent. Massively brave. However, I must admit I found it difficult to see the connection between sport and politics in the way that they did. There was nothing relating to sport in the statement they made.

You still get it in Zimbabwean sport to this day. Many cricketing administrators eventually get involved in politics, often running to be members of parliament in their constituency. Most of the time they are not doing it for the good of the country, they are doing it so they get the necessary support from other politicians for what they are doing in cricket. They are jumping into someone else's ring for personal gain.

Andy thought differently, and I fully understand his viewpoint that sport and politics are interlinked, especially after my experiences. But I still maintain that he and Henry should not have done it. African politics has its own rules, and what they did wasn't going to change that fact – with all the best intentions, I'm not sure how it would have changed the political landscape – so I think they should have just left it. If they wanted to make a point about politics, they could have made it any stage in the previous three years. They could have just come out and said it, nothing was stopping them. Instead they waited to the eve of our first World Cup game in our own country.

I believe Andy came at if from an emotional point of view, and it was undoubtedly an emotional subject. Andy was just like the rest of us; he would have had a friend, a friend's friend or a relative who would have told him a story about their devastating experiences at the hands of our government. We all heard many emotional, provocative things during this time. The stories often involved children. Of course, you think, 'Who in their right mind would do such awful things?' Andy and Henry will have heard the same stories and we all did and decided enough was enough. Their decision to do so was fuelled by emotion. Often the best decisions you make are when you remove the emotion, even if it's there inside you. If I was to ask them both now whether they'd still do it if they had their time again, I wouldn't be surprised if they said no. But I completely understand the feelings that led to it happening.

Despite everything that had gone on that day, we only talked cricket in the dressing room after the match. It was all cricket. Andy and Henry had made their stand, and that was it. We all just went back to wherever we were staying. It was strange, but we had the rest of the tournament still left to play.

Our next game was supposed to be against England. After deciding they would not travel to Harare, they tried to persuade the ICC to move the game to South Africa. In the end, this request was not accepted by the governing body, and so we were awarded the victory. We then suffered two comfortable defeats on the spin, firstly against India and then Australia. I acquitted myself quite nicely with the bat, though – against India I remained unbeaten and was our top scorer with 29*, and against Australia I made 23 before being dismissed by Glenn McGrath.

In our fifth match of the tournament we thrashed the Netherlands, before our last group fixture against Pakistan was halted by rain, and the shares were spoiled. Had Pakistan beaten us that day they would have qualified ahead of us for the next stage, the so-called Super Sixes. Had England travelled to Harare and beaten us, they would have finished ahead of us as well. As it was, we had made it to the next stage without beating another full member nation. Australia and India finished first and second and joined us in the next round; Pakistan and England had to go home along with the Netherlands and Namibia.

The Super Sixes effectively acted as a quarter-final in the form of a group stage. There were six teams in one group, and four would eventually progress to the semi-finals. We each had three games to play to determine the outcome. I saved my best batting of the tournament for our first game of the round against New Zealand, but it wasn't enough for victory. I made 53 off 79 deliveries, but they still had plenty in reserve when chasing down our target of 253. The ICC had a complicated system whereby you carried points over from the first group stage, and so defeat here meant we were in major trouble. We certainly had to beat Kenya in our next game.

On the morning of the game against the Kenyans, who had surprised everyone by reaching this stage in the first place, I headed down to the hotel reception to wait for the bus with my teammates. For the tournament we had set up some team rules which had to be followed by all. Usually on home or away tours we would have two coaches to travel on. We were never told we had to be on a particular coach, but it often transpired that most of the black players would be on one and most of the white players would be on the other. Maybe it was because of our culture; it just seemed natural at the time. However, because we knew the spotlight was on us during this tournament, we had to make a conscious effort to avoid that. Both buses had to leave at the same time, and we had to make sure we were sat next to someone we might not normally sit beside. Effectively, if you were black you had to go and mingle with one of your white teammates, and vice versa. If one bus was late, the other had to be late as well. We had to wait until both buses were full, and then we would travel together.

It was a policy that had been working quite well until this particular morning. Clearly, some had decided to throw the team rules in the bin. I got on one of the coaches five minutes before we were meant to be departing, and there were only black players on board. It soon became clear that the white players had all already made their way to the ground on the other coach. I knew something was up.

Like with our coach arrangement, throughout the World Cup we had made a point of all going to warm up together as a team, but once again half the squad had taken it upon themselves to break the rules we had set ourselves. I was keeping that day, and so our coach Geoff Marsh asked me to stand next to him while he hit some balls to the players for fielding practice. I started to make some noise to get the lads going, but I got no response. Dead silence.

It was hardly appropriate timing, but I had to find out what was going on. 'Something is not right coach,' I said to Geoff. 'I know, Tatenda,' came the response. Many of the senior players had spent the tournament telling me to ignore everything going on around me, but here was the coach telling me that something wasn't right on the day of our biggest game of the competition so far. Instead of telling me not to pay attention, he asked me a direct question: 'Who would you have picked today? Dion Ebrahim or Sean Irvine?'

'Sean,' I replied. It was a question that had a pretty obvious answer as far as I could tell.

'Would you believe that the selectors have gone with Dion?'

'That's weird.'

'After the way he batted in the last game?' After I had consolidated our innings with a measured fifty against New Zealand, Streak and Irvine had had some fun at the end, with Irvine scoring 31* off just fourteen balls. Though we lost the game, Sean had hit some magnificent shots. For this game he had now been left out and Dion, who had made a golden duck in the same match, was staying in the side. I thought they had got it wrong and had made the selection based on race. Dion was Asian. Quite frankly, there was no way he should have been in the team ahead of Sean at that stage. It was unfair on the pair of them; unfair on Sean because he deserved to be in the team, and unfair on Dion because he had not selected himself. The way Dion was being treated by virtually everyone in the side was not fair. It was not as if he was going to go up to the selectors and say, 'Sorry, I don't want to play.' No one would have done the same thing, but the rest of the players were looking at him as if it were his fault. That wasn't fair.

The atmosphere that day was absolutely horrible. Despite Andy and Henry's protest at the start of the tournament and the fear of the repercussions that might bring, the mood in the camp had remained positive. That all changed on this day. I tried to create a buzz on the field, but hardly anyone else uttered a word. There was the odd bit of encouragement from Dougie Marillier and from Grant Flower, but that was it. Apart from that, it was dead.

We started the game knowing we could still potentially qualify for the semi-finals of a World Cup if things went our way but hope soon faded. The team was effectively protesting, and we were bowled out for a pitiful 133. I made just three. Andy, reliable as ever in his penultimate international innings for Zimbabwe, made 63, nearly half of our team's total. Kenya chased down the score with plenty to spare, and our journey was over in bitter fashion.

Most cricketers are able to perform when the pressure is off; only the best are able to perform regularly when the pressure is on. Zimbabwean cricket was improving all the time, but we still had a lot of ordinary players, players who were only capable of performing when they were not in the spotlight. It seemed that we were simply not up to the task of performing in a high-pressure situation both on and off the field, especially in such a toxic atmosphere.

At the end of the game, Guy Whittall called me to come and sit down next to him. Guy was a reliable all-rounder for us and I liked him a lot. He was one of the most professional cricketers I have ever come across – his throws back to me from the deep were second to none. Guy was like Andy in that he always used to ask me what fielding positions I would have if I were captain. He was clearly getting me to think about the game for later on in my career. On this occasion he asked me nothing of the sort, though, and instead proceeded to tell me about what had happened in the team selection meeting. I already knew the details, because Geoff had told me during the warm-up.

I told him that I still didn't understand why we had let the game slip away so easily, given we still had a slight chance of qualifying for the next stage. However, he wasn't paying much attention to my emotional outpouring. 'Tiba, remember how I always used to ask you what fielding positions you would have if you were captain?' I nodded. 'I always thought you'd lead the country one day,' he continued, 'but I never thought it would be this soon.' I felt like I was about to choke. 'Many things are about to change. I know you are learning fast, but you're going to have to start learning faster.' With that he grabbed his towel and made his way to the shower, before I had gathered my thoughts and asked him exactly what he meant.

Our last game of the tournament was against Sri Lanka, and once again we were beaten comfortably. I made just two, once again dismissed by Murali, but it hardly mattered. We were out anyway, and the end of an era had been signalled. Andy was retiring, and there was seemingly no future for poor Henry. His decision to protest had not gone down well at all.

He was expelled by his club side, Takashinga, and was labelled an 'Uncle Tom' who had a 'black skin and a white mask' by Zimbabwe's information minister Jonathan Moyo. Henry had thought his international career would probably be over, but that he might be able to carry on living in Zimbabwe. He realised that was not possible once he started getting death threats after the World Cup.

Henry had to go into temporary hiding from the government, and the fact that we had to travel to South Africa for our Super Six games actually helped him get away. His actions had led to the government putting out a warrant for his arrest after the last match against Sri Lanka (thankfully in East London, South Africa) on charges of treason, a charge which carries the death penalty in Zimbabwe. He would end up following Andy to England in search of first-class cricket but would soon retire due to a knee injury. He played occasional matches for the Lashings World XI, a team I would later become familiar with myself. He has never since returned to the country he represented in eighty international matches.

The World Cup also proved to be the end of the road for Alistair Campbell and Guy Whittall. With Alistair going at the same time as Andy, we lost a combined 18,000 international runs in one hit. Guy Whittall had scored over 5,000 international runs himself and taken over 100 wickets across both formats. Henry himself had taken over 100 international wickets. The heart of our team had been ripped out.

It was clear that the selection against Kenya had caused some controversy. There was a little bit of hide and seek being played at the time, because the ZCU did not want it to seem as if they were putting in place an official quota system. Officially, they were saying it didn't exist, but that only served to muddy the waters, because that is exactly what they seemed to be implementing. Their view was that it would have been unfair on players like me and Henry to go public with an official quota, because we were in the side purely because we were good enough, no question. Stuart Matsikenyeri was also on the verge of the team, and Hamilton Masakadza had earned his place fairly in the Test set-up. They didn't want it to be thought that we were being picked because of the colour of our skin, when really we were being picked because we were genuinely good enough. That's the primary reason for things transpiring the way they did. It had been a thorny issue for a number of years now.

In July 2001, Hamilton had become the first black player to score a Test century for Zimbabwe. In March of the same year, ZC had set up an Integration Task Force as part of 'an aggressive campaign to eliminate racial discrimination within cricket at all levels', in response to a number of incidents in previous years. The task force was facilitated by an American consultant named Dr Richard Zackrison and his presence as an outsider unsettled some of the senior white players in the Zimbabwean set-up. Aggressive targets were set, including for the number of black players in the team, but the key point was that these were just targets, not official quotas.

Nonetheless, not everyone was happy. Alistair Campbell, who had decided to finish his career at the end of the World Cup, was one of those who walked out when the findings were presented soon after. The task force was to find ways to ensure 'the full, equitable, and sustainable nationwide integration of Zimbabwe cricket in the shortest possible time with the least possible reduction in individual and team performance'. It was hoped that this 'rapid evolution' – and its goals and strategies – would be completed by 1 January 2004.

Part of the problem was that there were not enough senior black players to speak up on the issue at the time because of the imbalance in the side. I for one was not experienced enough; I did not know anything about these issues. Andy Pycroft, a former white Zimbabwean international who worked on the task force at the time, later admitted that there was a certain element of the white community that did not want change and a certain element of the black community 'that was prepared to ride over everything regardless, a sort of "we don't care" attitude'.

In South African cricket there has long been a quota system, but in my opinion, Zimbabwe was a slightly different case. Around this time there were many programmes – including the one I had been part of – that were designed to get players from the majority black population playing cricket, and the results were starting to show. At school, we were playing against the top white players from the area; there wasn't any segregation as such.

I believed in a natural process. Nature teaches us that if you try to break a shell with a chick still inside it, you kill the chick, but if you let nature take its course then the chick will find a way out and live. I think a lot of the hard work had been done with the development programme, which is why Hamilton and I had already emerged, with Stuey and Vusi on the verge of doing so. I think if we had let things take their own course, we'd be talking about a Zimbabwe side today that is better than the one we had in 2003, not worse.

What I am convinced of is that if there were people on both sides of the argument with the right intentions, then Zimbabwean Cricket would not be in the state it is in today. Definitely not. Perhaps the situation we find ourselves in now as a cricketing nation illustrates just how much fault there was on both sides at the time.

I'm not sure South Africa is a good comparison. You only have to look at the situation now. In South African cricket today, the national team has to have an average of six non-white players in the team per match over the course of a year. Transformation has been a rocky road at times, and there has often been resistance from some to the recommendations made by Cricket South Africa. Though similar debates exist in Zimbabwean cricketing discourse, as a nation we have found it easier than South Africa to integrate players of colour into the side since the turn of the century.

What is for sure is that the World Cup was a missed opportunity for Zimbabwean cricket. Everything was set up for us to capture the imagination and continue to progress as a cricketing nation. Kids were playing in the streets, and the inevitable next step is they start putting pressure on their school to play it more. I remember during that time many schools requesting cricket equipment, but we failed to capitalise on its sudden popularity. Two years down the line, and we had been exiled from the Test arena altogether. In many ways the World Cup was the catalyst.

9
A Baptism of Fire

DESPITE OUR SUPER SIXES EXIT IN SOUTH AFRICA AND OUR DEFEAT to Kenya, we were greeted by great crowds at the airport upon our return to Zimbabwe. However, we were missing two of our most senior players. Following their protest, Andy and Henry had decided that it was not safe for them to return to the country, and instead headed for England. I think it was a smart move.

Despite the political issues engulfing the team, cricket's popularity was definitely on the rise in Zimbabwe. Several billboards appeared, with me – the little boy from Highfield – the main attraction on them. Football, I believed, was losing its grip as the number one sport in the country. Cricket was taking over. Before youngsters had kicked plastic footballs around trying to emulate our all-time top scorer Peter Ndlovu; now there were logs and tennis balls on the streets as kids tried to emulate Tatenda Taibu.

At our next practice session, there were a lot of new faces and an absence of many familiar ones. Guy Whittall, Alistair Campbell, Andy Flower and Henry Olonga's international careers had all come to an end. It was a new era, and new contracts were issued to reflect that. I became one of the highest-paid players in the squad, and with it was I was announced as the new vice-captain. I was just nineteen years of age. All of a sudden, it wasn't just about going to practice and playing games. I had to be involved in some selection meetings, and I was also invited to sit on some board meetings, which I never enjoyed. I had never heard people speak to each other in such a way in all my life. Such experiences made me wish I had never been given the job in the first place.

I will never forget the first one of the meetings I attended. I remember sitting there thinking, 'I shouldn't be here.' I couldn't handle it. I also thought, 'How are you people going to be able to speak to each other after this?' I didn't like it at all.

I remembered a conversation about Sean Irvine, who was apparently considering ending his international career to go and play county cricket in England. I can't remember if his comments were directed at Heath Streak or Geoff Marsh, but Ozias Bvute, the chairman of the Integration Task Force, was furious; shouting across the table. I had never seen such anger between adults, and it made me feel very uncomfortable.

On most occasions I asked Heath, who was still the captain of the side, to represent me at these meetings. I still had a lot to work on with regards to my own game, and these meetings were taking up a lot of my time. I had been doing so well at balancing my career and my love life, but meetings were starting to get in the way. Loveness often used to say that she had to share me with the world, and at first I didn't know what she meant. I soon realised. The corporate world and the media were constantly on my tail. All of a sudden, I'd have to look in my diary to fix a date with her.

The first series after the World Cup was the Sharjah Cup in the United Arab Emirates, where we would face Pakistan, Sri Lanka and Kenya. Despite the lack of experience in our ranks we acquitted ourselves well, and after an opening defeat to Pakistan we beat both Kenya and Sri Lanka, helping us to qualify for the final. By the end of the tournament Geoff Marsh had decided to hand me responsibility with the bat, and in the final against Pakistan I batted at number five. I took the added responsibility well, scoring 74* in an overall total of just 168. Pakistan chased down the target easily, but I had been named the best fielder of the tournament and was not far off with the bat. It was also here that I received tips on how to play Murali by Younis Khan. Batsmen constantly share information with each other when they can, even if it's with opposition players, knowing that in the long term they all benefit as players.

That tournament in the UAE was a breeze compared with our next tour. My first Test series as vice-captain was to be in England, one of the hardest places in the world to visit. I was still very much in the process of learning my own game, but here I would have to take responsibility for others as well. It was a challenge that I was nonetheless looking forward to. There was a variety of things for me to come to terms with on English shores: the press – who are very different to their Asian and African counterparts – the swinging ball as a batsman and the wobbling ball as a wicketkeeper, and the cold weather. I looked at all these things as experiences rather than stumbling blocks.

The other issue on our minds was the ongoing political situation; just because we weren't playing in our home country didn't mean that the problems just vanished. After all, we were playing against a side who had refused to travel to Zimbabwe for a World Cup fixture just three months earlier. There was plenty of opposition to us touring the country at all. Ninety-four members of parliament in the UK had backed a motion to put pressure on the government to resolve the crisis in Zimbabwe and to not let the tour go ahead. The MPs had even claimed that this was a team picked by the Mugabe regime. Eventually Tim Lamb, who was the Chief Executive of the ECB, rejected this notion and the tour went ahead as planned. I now had so much more on my plate as vice-captain that I did not even know all this was going on in the background, which was probably a good thing.

Heath had been no stranger to the political problems back home; he had perhaps suffered more than anyone else on the team. He had seen his father sent to jail after he refused to give up his farm to the licensed thugs of Mugabe. Still, Heath hadn't made his own political statement at the World Cup. He was of a similar view to me at the time that sport and politics did not mix, and this led to him being labelled the 'anti-Flower' in some quarters. I think that was unfair on him – he was just trying to get on with playing cricket for his country. Heath is fluent in Ndebele. The Ndebele people are a Bantu-speaking ethnic group that make up for around twenty percent of Zimbabwe's population, the second largest ethnic group in the country after Shona people. Heath felt a strong kinship with the Ndebele people, and was well respected in the black community. He was now in charge of his national team at the most challenging time in its short history.

Andy, who had moved to England and played for Essex, came to our defence. In his column in the English newspaper the *Daily Telegraph*, he said that silence of the current squad on all things political should not be mistaken for compliance. He noted that it would be the end of a player's international career if they did speak out, and even advised us not to make a stand, as that would lead to many of the side being eliminated altogether, just as he had been. The MDC, the main opposition party to Mugabe, didn't want us to take that step either.

Andy's column had come just days after another of the UK's leading newspapers, the *Observer*, had run an article detailing how our touring team was politically influenced. The report suggested that the ZCU, as it was still then called, was very much a mouthpiece for the regime and that several of the key individuals in the organisation were directly linked to the ruling ZANU-PF.

The same report also claimed that the team had been vetted, players had been gagged and that a decision had been made after the World Cup to rid the squad of any dissidents.

Board member Ozias Bvute was named as one the key figures, with details stating that he himself had thrown Henry off the bus after his black-armband protest. Also implicated were chairman Peter Chingoka, Ahmed and Max Ebrahim (board members), Babu Meman (team manager) and Vince Hogg (managing director). Not even Heath was spared, and it was alleged that he went along with the official line to ensure his family were left alone. In response, Chingoka asked that the players were allowed to get along with their cricket, while describing the ZCU as an 'apolitical organisation'.

There were many people against us touring – and there were anti-Mugabe protests at our games during the series – but also those who thought it would only cause damage to our team if we were forced to pull out. In an article for the Cricinfo website, cricket writer Martin Williamson offered this opinion:

> Few would try to justify the human rights record of the Mugabe government, but those who remain in the country have serious concerns that the demonstrations, although well-meaning, could actually have the opposite effect to that intended. What is clear is that Mugabe won't be toppled by protests – increasingly his aim appears to be to cling to power at all costs – but they may cause irreparable harm to Zimbabwe cricket. Should cricket embarrass the Zimbabwean government, it will be cricket that suffers.

Things didn't turn out to be any easier for us on the cricket field. Both the Test matches followed a similar pattern: we lost the first one by an innings and 92 runs at Lord's, and the second one by an innings and 69 runs at Chester-le-Street. I made double figures in all four of my innings, but never reached the fifty mark. It was maybe a sign of where we were as a team. We had just lost four of our most senior and best players, and right away we had to embark on one of the most unforgiving tours in world cricket.

To this day, I say to any batsman that if they wish to finish their cricketing education then they have to go to England. That's where you learn how to deal with the moving ball. I reckon that if you can spend time at the crease in England, then you will be able to spend time at the crease against any fast bowlers in the world. The key when batting in England is to move as late as possible. Because of the extravagant movement on offer, you can only deal with the ball once it gets to you. In these conditions many batsmen become too eager to try and cover the swing, but you can never do anything until the ball actually reaches you. A swing bowler like Jimmy Anderson will tend to do one of two things: he will either move the ball away from you or swing it back in towards your pads. If you remain calm and collected and wait for the ball to reach you before dealing with it, you are giving yourself the best opportunity possible. If you are able to wait for that long, it also means that your balance is right.

There were times on that tour when we collapsed as a team. In the second Test match up at Durham, we made just 94 in reply in England's first innings of score of 416. I made 31 of those 94 runs. It's easy to get frustrated in situations like this, but as a vice-captain I now had more responsibility towards my teammates. I always reminded myself that the best way for me to take responsibility was to perform out on the field. Performing with the bat and the gloves was the first step in me being a good vice-captain. If my own game was in order, then I could start to help others as well, but while I was out there I had to deal with what was in front of me; the ball I was facing. I couldn't waste time worrying about the bigger picture. While I was out there, I believed I could do my bit to change the situation, but I couldn't worry about the same situation, about wickets tumbling around me. I almost had to close myself off to what was going on at the other end. The situation certainly wasn't going to improve if I got distracted and lost my wicket too. My mantra was that I was a wicketkeeper before I was a vice-captain, and a batsman before a vice-captain.

I was very aware that I was learning on the job. I was no longer just thinking about my own game; I had to learn how to look after a team. I had to study fielding positions, learn when to make the right changes and I also had to become adept at reading how the wicket would play. I was constantly observing Heath as he made these decisions. I had to learn how to inspire players; a trait that others said came very naturally to me later in my career. You start to open your mind up a lot more to other people.

I never felt overawed by the job, and I think that's because things were moving at such pace. Even at that stage, when a problem arose – and there were plenty of them – I didn't tend to dwell on it. I instead like to focus on the solution to that problem, no matter how tough it might have been. Given what was going on in

Zimbabwean cricket at the time, I think that was an important mindset to have.

It helped that I had a good relationship with Heath. By no means was I as close to him as I was to Andy, but our relationship was very professional and still is today. I understood Heath quite easily, and I think he read me quite easily as well. I studied his captaincy style up to the stage where I knew what he was trying to do and the gameplan that he was implementing. Off the field, Heath's character was different to mine. He was very much the joker of the pack: he would make fun of everyone, and he was particularly good at imitating everyone else's batting style. He used to win people over and get them on side with his sense of humour, whereas I am naturally a more serious person.

On the field, I felt he was a cautious captain. He never instigated the team to play defensive cricket as such – he was actually a pretty attacking player himself – but he always wanted to have a Plan B up his sleeve to turn to if Plan A wasn't working. He never wanted to end up in a situation where he was left scratching his head. When I became captain, I was the opposite – I believed so much in my original tactics that I wouldn't have another plan to fall back on during a game. I went all out, convinced that my original plan would work. As vice-captain at the time I felt he could have a little bit more belief in his original plan, but I wouldn't come out and tell everyone that. I respected him greatly, and at the end of the day it was his decision. I was only in the role by default anyway at this stage. I'd offer to advice, but 100 percent back him with what he went with in the end.

As a bowler, he knew his own game very well. He knew when he wanted to strike, and he knew exactly what to do to make that happen. He was particularly strong at setting right-handed batsmen up. He had a very good off-cutter, a very good away swinger, and he could also bring the ball into batsmen with the new ball. He could probe at the batsman with away swingers before delivering the perfect off-cutter. When there was no movement on the ball he could play the containing role. If I had captained him, I wouldn't have bowled him to contain the opposition, which is what he did himself and a lot of other captains used him for. I would have used him purely as an attacking bowler and let the others do the containing. He was our best bowler and our best chance of bowling the opposition out.

The one game we won on that tour was the first match of our tri-series against England and South Africa. In the five games we completed in that tournament we only passed 200 on one occasion, but in the first game against at Trent Bridge we produced a gritty performance to lift our spirits. We had reduced a strong England side to just 191-8 in their first innings, a good effort on our part, but then stumbled to 15-4 in reply. I was the fourth wicket to fall. As I sat in the changing room watching my good friend Stuart, who had just joined Grant Flower at the wicket, a thought came to my mind: 'If we win this game from this position, the team will finally get to see me drink.' At this stage in my life I had never touched a beer. I was determined to become the world's best cricketer, and therefore I tried to stay away from anything that would hinder my chances. Alcohol was high up on that list. Still, I went ahead and made my pledge to a very worried-looking balcony. Stuey soon took the attack to English bowlers, playing an array of shots that somewhat eased the pressure. That freed up Grant to just play a measured innings, and he ended up making a match-winning 96*. Stuey eventually perished for 44, but by that stage we were right back in the game. We ended up winning by four wickets; our first and last win of the tour. Being a man of my word, fuelled by excitement after my best friend had just played a brilliant innings to help take our team to victory, I decided to join the others in drinking to enjoy the moment.

A couple of hours later I could be found sat on the physio bed holding a bottle of champagne that Grant had won for his man of the match performance. That was followed by a series of different beers – in around 45 minutes I think I drank six to eight bottles. I also managed to find time to pack up everyone else's kit and put it on the bus. My mind is blank to most of what transpired, but I do remember singing along to a song I had never heard of previously several times on the bus back. Walking from the bus back to the hotel was almost impossible, and I ended up getting down on all fours when I went up the escalator. I couldn't trust myself to stand up by this point.

I had promised the team I would join them on a night out, since I never usually went out to the pubs or clubs, but I was in no fit state to be walking outside. I was vomiting in the room and got so sick the whole night that I made a promise to myself that I would never hold a beer again. Stuey took good care of me that night, but still managed to make it out. The next morning, the roles were reversed. As we made our way to Kent for our next fixture against South Africa, he was the one struggling. He barely made it through the morning swim session. I had to nurse him throughout the trip, while the other, more experienced revellers chipped in to help as well.

Upon our return home I was anxious to see the house that Loveness had bought for the pair of us. When we got there from the airport, I was stunned. It was beyond my imagination, and I was absolutely thrilled. The house was gated and had a garden big enough for a cricket pitch. Though it was a bungalow it had three bedrooms, one with an ensuite, a lounge, and a separate bathroom. There was a long driveway and a garage attached as well. It was beautiful; the sort of house you only usually find in the wealthier parts of the country. I asked Stuey to come and join me at the house, so we could continue to practise together. Stuey was in a relationship by this stage as well, dating a woman named Oslie Muringai, a beauty queen who would later become Miss Zimbabwe. We continued to work very hard on our games, but in time, with our extra workloads and our relationships, we started to grow apart somewhat.

Shortly after I moved in with Loveness, her mother became seriously ill and had to be hospitalised in Chinhoyi, a town a couple of hours' northwest of Harare. The news had reached all the family, and so she had many visitors. I decided not to go at the same time as them, and instead asked Stuey, Oslie and Loveness to accompany me a little later on. It was really sad to see her in such a frail condition. We barely spoke a word for the hour we were there, and we weren't really in the mood to talk much on the way back in the car either.

Loveness received a call in the early hours of the next morning from the hospital informing her that her mother had passed away. I felt empathy with her; I had lost both of my parents, so I knew exactly what she was going through. Loveness was incredibly brave throughout this period, and I offered as much support as I could. Most of my teammates came to her mother's funeral, which was a lovely gesture. The most touching moment at the funeral was the beautiful speech she gave. Watching the girl I loved standing in front of hundreds of mourners, delivering a heartbreaking speech, was incredibly sad and yet incredibly moving. I couldn't help but leave the church with tears in my eyes. One lady came to me demanding an explanation for my tears. 'How dare she ask me that,' I thought. I couldn't answer, though, for my heart had swollen.

After the funeral, I was introduced to one of Loveness's sisters, whom I had not heard much about during the two years of our relationship. It was soon explained to me that she was a staunch Christian and had beliefs that the rest of her family could barely understand. She had therefore become a bit of a black sheep. Loveness had spent four years with her during her high school years in Bulawayo and had been baptised in the church she went to.

At this stage Loveness was still staying with her sister-in-law Esther in Highfield. They were fending for themselves at the house, as Esther's brother had gone to live in England. I would assist them both financially for the time being, but the thought of having two young girls living alone unsettled me. I had to find a way of getting Loveness out of that house, but in Zimbabwean culture it is taboo to live with your girlfriend before marriage. I had already spent money on the house, so I did not have enough money for a dowry for a wedding. What was considered taboo was therefore very much on my mind.

In the meantime, cricket tours waited for no one. We soon had to set off for another series, this time away to Australia, who were quite comfortably the best team in the world. Granted, in the two Test matches we would not be facing Shane Warne and Glenn McGrath, but the fact remained that they had won seven Test series in a row and had not lost a series since they went down 2-1 to India away from home in 2001. They hadn't lost a home series since 1993 against the last great West Indies side. That series had started just a month after we played our first-ever series.

Wives and girlfriends were allowed to join the tour a little later on, so I invited Loveness. If her mother had still been around, I would have asked her for permission. However, I did not have the same relationship with any of her siblings, so I asked Loveness if she would do the honours and ask. Her brother Alec would not hear any of it – he was of the view that it would bring shame on the family – but luckily for me it was her uncle who had the last say, and he saw no issue with it. Alec asked her not to come back to the family home if she went with me to Australia. Truthfully, that was just what I was looking for. It was not the best way to get her away from that house, but it was what I thought was best at the time.

The tour was a gruelling one, and I knew I had to work harder than ever before. Grant Flower and I started to have extra practice sessions together after the others had gone back to the hotel. Given the gulf between the teams, it is perhaps no surprise that we were comfortably beaten in the Test series. In the first Test on the famously bouncy Perth surface we went down by an innings and 175 runs. In the first innings Matthew Hayden scored an astonishing 380, which at the time was the highest score ever made in a Test match, overtaking Brian Lara's 375 against England. Lara would once again take over Hayden months later, in April 2004, with 400* against England, but it didn't take anything away from the Australian's feat. By contrast I only made eighteen runs across my two innings. Still, in the second Test in Sydney I managed a battling 27 off 70 balls in the first innings and 35 off 150 deliveries in the second dig. We lost heavily again, but at this stage for me it was about learning to craft a Test innings against the very best. I was still just twenty years old.

For me, it didn't feel as tough as it might have looked to those on the outside. Traipsing around the outfield in the baking Australian sun for two days while Hayden makes his way to a record Test score does not look fun to the casual viewer, and it doesn't exactly seem good for confidence either. However, I looked upon it all differently. One of my goals as a child had been to go to Australia and play a Test series for my country. I was barely out of my teenage years and here I was doing exactly that. Throughout this period of my career I felt I was constantly learning, and getting a head start on all other players my age. This Australian team was packed to the rafters with brilliant players in their prime – far too good for us – but players who were much older than me and would have to retire sooner than me. In five years' time, I would have bags of experience, and it would be me playing against the new crop of Australian youngsters. Hopefully by then it would be my turn to dominate.

The triangular series that followed against Australia and India saw more of the same outcomes, as we failed to register a win. Still, we often competed well, and could have won any of our last four games after taking a hammering in our first three. We got within three runs of beating India in one of our matches, with Stuart Carlisle and Sean Irvine both scoring brilliant centuries.

In the months leading up to that series a boy named Mark Vermeulen, who had been educated at the Prince Edward boarding school in Harare, had started to play to his full potential. He was a brilliant player to watch, one that could make you leap out your seat with excitement, but on the field he was one of the quietest members of the team. Towards the end of this tour he was playing some glorious backfoot shots, and his game was becoming more and more organised.

In our fourth game of the tour against India on the rapid WACA track in Perth, I was asked to open the batting. We were bowled out for another low score, and during our innings Mark was struck down by a well-directed bouncer by Irfan Pathan. There was silence in the dressing room as he fell to the ground, blood dripping from his forehead. Mark was taken to hospital, and it was later confirmed that he had to stay in hospital for a few weeks to undergo an operation.

By the end of that tour, there were lots of tired bodies and minds. There were many injuries in the camp; some physical, some not. It was easier for those who had physical injuries to be attended to, because they could prove it to our coaches and medical staff. Seeing is believing, as they say. But we had many injuries to the mind as well. There are many that struggle to come to terms with the mental effect cricket can have, and struggle to carry on in the game. These problems are just as normal as physical injuries. This was the sort of difficult tour that could cause these problems.

Loveness joined me later on during the tour. For her 21st birthday I had surprised her over the phone, telling her to take her passport down to the ZCU offices where they would provide her with a visa for Australia. It was the first time we had been together outside of Zimbabwe. However, when it was time to leave I sensed her mood change. She was feeling the pressure of returning home – she did not know how to face her family after rebelling against them, so she came straight to my house upon returning without contacting them. Even though I was serious about settling down with her, we had never once discussed marriage, and I guess that was a concern for her. Sure, she could move in with me, but she didn't want me to feel obliged to marry her just because it was the norm to do so in our culture.

I automatically took over paying her college fees. Being just 21 and living together was an experience for both of us. Stuart and Oslie would come over for weekends and we'd go on double dates, which was nice, but being the black sheep of our respective families was not pleasant. The unsettling circumstances we found ourselves in made us even closer. We did everything together; she became my pillar and I was her pillar. During that period, a bond developed that has not been broken to date. We were effectively staying together without permission from either family, but it didn't matter to us much.

On one of these many afternoons we spent together we received a surprise visit from Loveness's sister Mercy. The guards had not informed us of anyone coming. My mood took a turn for the worst; it was too soon to be discussing what had transpired. We expected Mercy to storm in angrily, but to our surprise it was a short and peaceful visit. Loveness had expected her to demand she pack her bags and return home.

'What was that all about?' I asked when she had left. Loveness remained silent. All the laughter and joy that was there before Mercy's arrival had disappeared into thin air. Were we closing ourselves off from people had no bad intentions?

Only time would tell.

Soon after Mercy called us and asked if we would meet her again. We agreed a date and when we saw her she simply carried on from where she had left off before. She put across her concerns in a respectable manner; I think she just wanted to find out why Loveness had done what she had done. To her, moving in with a partner before marriage was an unpardonable sin. Eventually she asked me if we had plans of getting married, to which I replied that it wasn't something we had discussed. I also told her that I didn't like discussing my plans with other people, which made her upset. She soon packed her bags and left.

I also feeling the pressure from my side of the family too – my siblings wondered how I could entrust Loveness to buy a house for us both when we weren't even married. The fact that we were both in the bad books helped us to understand each other. We decided to take a trip to Victoria Falls, just so we could take a break from the drama and clear our heads. We spent a weekend there among the evergreen trees, embellished by the misty, glassy colour created by the water from the falls.

On our way, back home we decided to take the shorter route. We had split the journey in two on the way, stopping over in Bulawayo, but we were eager to return home directly and thought it possible to travel the 600 kilometres back in around six and a half hours. Twenty kilometres in, we hit a dust road we thought we'd be out of in no time. Two hours later and the thought of doing a U-turn had completely vanished. With no tarred road in sight I grew a little impatient and started to travel faster than the recommended fifty kilometres an hour. The dirt and sand that came from the road made it difficult for me to see clearly through the windscreen, and Loveness was unable to put her seatbelt on in the passenger seat. Still, I didn't want to stop – it was getting dark and we knew nothing about the area.

After a few minutes of travelling at a greater speed, I started to lose control at the wheel. The car started to slide side-on, and in a flash we were heading for a grouping of trees. I managed to steer us away from them and back onto the road, but I overcompensated and completely lost control. I kept my hands on the steering wheel and waited for the car to overturn. Loveness had one hand on her seat and the other gripping me very tightly. All I saw was dust and all I heard was her scream as the car tumbled off course. Thankfully, the car did not overturn completely – we had plunged into a bush. No one was hurt and miraculously there was no damage to the car. I simply carried on driving, but in complete silence. We were both shaken but decided not to stop. We were in the middle of nowhere.

After another couple of hours of travelling we finally hit the tarred road, a huge relief to both of us. We had lost a hubcap and one of our tyres was losing air slowly. I managed to change it with little help from Loveness, who was still badly shaken. We knew we were not going to make it back to Harare the same day, so we called Walter Chawaguta, who was now living in Redcliff near Kwekwe.

We continued with our journey the following day, well rested after a night at Walter's house, but I could not stop playing the incident over and over in my mind. 'What if Loveness had been badly injured or even died? How would her family, who were already upset, have reacted to that?'

It was at this point that I decided I needed to marry her. It might have been earlier than I would have liked, but I didn't see any way around it. I saw no reason for me to continue being stubborn. Besides, many people spoke of how I was mature beyond my years in other aspects of my life. I was not setting a good example to young children and the general public here on this matter.

In November, the West Indies became the first team to tour our country since the commotion of the World Cup, and the political problems had certainly not gone away in the meantime.

On this occasion it was my best friend Stuey who found himself in the firing line. As if losing a number of our most experienced players to enforced retirement was not enough, we now had injuries to Grant Flower, Sean Ervine and Douglas Hondo to deal with as well. It meant that Stuey, who had already played nine ODIs but was yet to score a first-class century, was in line to make his Test debut in the first game of the series in Harare. Much like Dion Ebrahim before him during the World Cup, there was nothing Stuey could do about being picked to represent his country, and he was hardly going to turn down the opportunity. However, he had now become the latest name cited in the debate surrounding the quota system, which was now reaching breaking point.

I was staying with Stuey at the time and shortly before the series started, we received a surprise visit from Givemore Makoni, one of the figures at the centre of this storm. Givemore had created Takashinga with Stephen Mangongo in 1990, so we both knew him well enough, but it was 1am in the morning when he turned up to the house and asked the guards to let him in. Confused, I asked him why he had come to see to me at such a ridiculous hour, but it soon became clear that I wasn't the reason for his visit – he wanted to speak to Stuey.

Mr Makoni had come to tell us that if Stuey was not selected to play for the first Test, then the tour might not go ahead altogether – there were enough people prepared to make sure that this would be the case if he was left out. That's how serious the situation had become. Stuey and I were awake for hours after our surprise guest had left. There was no way we could get back to sleep after what we had just heard. It really wasn't fair on Stuey that he wasn't being selected on whether he was good enough or not, but instead to satisfy an unofficial quota.

The hierarchy's job should have been to ease as much of the burden on their players as possible. This was cricket at the highest level, so any negative thoughts could have had a huge effect on a player and their ability to perform. The board should have been doing all they could to eliminate any doubts in Stuart's mind about his suitability for the international game, but instead they were piling the doubts on. Sure, if he was good enough his ability would have eventually told, but you have to create the best environment for him to showcase that ability. Telling him he was only in the side because the series might be cancelled if he wasn't was a terrible move and highlighted the additional pressures many young Zimbabwean cricketers faced during this period of strife in our sport. During this time there would also be many players wondering if they were going to lose their spot in the side despite doing nothing wrong. It was an unhealthy environment to perform in.

The next morning, we had to head our separate ways. I was joining up with the national team for practice, while Stuey was off to play a warm-up game against the West Indies for our A side. Amid the chaos, there was still a series to prepare for. The warm-up game was to be played at a new ground among the streets of Highfield where we had both grown up. Brian Lara, by now in the last throes of an amazing international career, had been asked to perform the honours of cutting the ribbon. It was a nice moment, but I'm sure it was the last thing on Stuey's mind. Thankfully, with the eyes of the Zimbabwean cricketing world on him, he managed to score a brilliant, unbeaten 84. It would be virtually impossible to question his selection now, and it certainly gave Givemore and co the ammo they were looking for.

Vusi Sibanda, another of the golden generation of cricketers to emerge from Highfield, was also set to make his Test bow against the West Indies. Vusi had toured England earlier that year but not actually played a match, meaning he was the only one of the Highfield musketeers yet to play an international game. That was soon to change.

About a year before this I had bumped into Vusi in town when I was on my way to an interview with Patricia Mabviko on her *Breaking New Grounds* television show. I asked Vusi why he was no longer playing cricket, and his response was that he had fallen out with the administrators at Takashinga. I knew what a talent he was, and I didn't want to see that go to waste, so I asked him to try and not dwell on what had already happened. I still believed he wanted to play the game, so I advised him to go and see the administration at Takashinga and drop off a letter, which I would help him write. Together we wrote a letter of apology for him and he was back playing in no time. Not long later that he found himself in the national side.

Despite the aforementioned problems, we performed superbly in the first Test. We batted first, and I was lucky enough to join my best mate at the crease when we were reduced to 154-5. It took me back to 1995 at the same ground, when Stuey and I were supposed to be selling programmes to raise funds for our trip to South Africa. Instead, we had spent most of the afternoon daydreaming as Inzamam-ul-Haq compiled a masterful hundred. When the time eventually came, we more than took our opportunity, sharing a partnership of 77 before Stuey fell for 57. We were so used to batting together that we hardly needed to call each other through when we ran. I was absolutely thrilled when he reached his half-century, especially given all the pressure he was under. I was so happy that it felt I had reached the milestone myself. After Stuey's dismissal I continued to bat with Heath. I ended up with 83, while he made a stunning 127*. In the end, the West Indies held on for an agonising draw. We had needed just one solitary wicket to win the game.

In the second Test match they turned the tables on us after Brian Lara's 191 in the first innings. Though we bowled them out for 128 the second time around, we never really got close to the 233-run target they had set us. Both Stuey and I were dismissed for single figures in our second innings, unable to replicate our first Test performance. For Zimbabwean cricket as a whole, more trouble was just around the corner.

In May 2004 I had started captaining Mashonaland in order to gain more exposure to the job; after all, it seemed that I'd be in charge of my country sooner rather than later. Grant Flower was in the same team and was far more experienced than me, but he understood that it was a step I needed to make. The spotlight was on me, but I felt little extra pressure due to the team's dominance – the 2004/05 season saw us win our sixth Logan Cup title in a row.

The ODI series with the West Indies at the end of 2003 was as close-fought as the Test series, but unfortunately ended up with the same winner. We actually took a 2-1 lead in the series after excellent work with the bat from Mark Vermeulen and Heath Streak, but they clawed their way back in the final two games to take it 3-2. In our second victory I joined Heath at the crease and made a run-a-ball 37*, and in the fourth game I scored a valiant 66 in a big loss.

By now I was becoming more consistent with the bat, leading to Heath promoting me to number five when Bangladesh visited in the new year. I repaid his faith by scoring a pair of half-centuries in our crushing win in the first Test, before our series decider ended in a draw after persistent bad weather. We went on to win the ODI series as well, showing that although we were still some way behind the established Test-playing nations, we still had the edge over Bangladesh, who had only become a full member nation in 2000. We had played twenty Test series since our 1-0 win over Pakistan in 1998 and won three of them. Each had been against Bangladesh. In the one-day arena, we had only achieved series wins against Bangladesh and Kenya since winning away to New Zealand at the start of 2001.

Soon enough we had a fresh crisis upon us, one which had been threatening to boil over for some time. On 2 April 2004, with Sri Lanka's visit to Zimbabwe a month away, it was announced that Heath had resigned from his role as captain of our side. 'Instead of accepting his demands, the ZC board unanimously accepted his resignation from all forms of cricket with immediate effect,' read a statement from our board. 'Tatenda Taibu becomes the new captain with immediate effect.' Just like that, I was the new captain of the Zimbabwe national team at the age of twenty. It made me the youngest international Test skipper in the history of the game, and also Zimbabwe's first-ever black cricket captain.

It was a momentous occasion, but in far from ideal circumstances, Of course, that was not the whole matter done and dusted. This was another seismic moment in our recent cricketing history. The day after the ZCU had announced Heath's resignation, more news filtered out that the Union chief executive Vince Hogg and Heath were meeting to try and settle the differences that had led to his exit. The news was that Heath had resigned after the board rejected an ultimatum from him over the composition of the selection panel.

'He wanted us to reduce the number of selectors to four,' said chairman Peter Chingoka. 'We currently have five. He wanted us to have selectors who had played

Where it all started for Dad: his barbershop in Highfield, Harare, which helped support the family. [NICK GORDON]

113th Street, Highfield: the road we grew up on in the same neighbourhood: Mum, Dad, me and my seven siblings. [NICK GORDON]

My dear mother, Margaret, who guided us all through our childhoods.
[AUTHOR'S PERSONAL COLLECTION]

Waiting outside primary school with Mum, my two sisters Julie and Jackie, and Dad. We were all there to pick up an end of year award. [AUTHOR'S PERSONAL COLLECTION]

The Zimbabwe Grounds: the venue of Robert Mugabe's first post-independence speech, and later the home of Takashinga, the club that gave me my cricketing education. [NICK GORDON]

The four musketeers: Vusi Sibanda, me, Stuart Matsikenyeri and Hamilton Masakadza outside Bill Flower's truck. [AUTHOR'S PERSONAL COLLECTION]

Front and centre: me with the boys before the Under-19 World Cup, where I won player of the tournament.
[AUTHOR'S PERSONAL COLLECTION]

A grainy newspaper cut out of me and Hamilton with the country's president, Robert Mugabe.
[AUTHOR'S PERSONAL COLLECTION]

On my second tour with the national team at the age of sixteen in England, 2000. [GETTY]

In England again in 2000. I did not make my international debut on this tour, but I did get my first taste of the prodigious seam movement in English conditions. [GETTY]

Keeping my eyes on the prize as the great Sachin Tendulkar gets down on one knee. [GETTY]

On my way to a fifty against New Zealand at the 2003 World Cup, the highlight of my tournament. [GETTY]

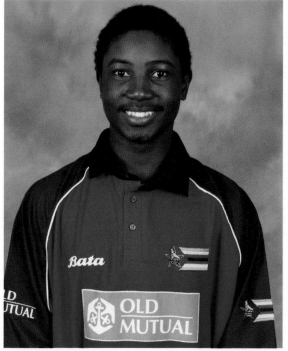

England, 2003. Slightly more experienced, but still very young to be a vice-captain. [GETTY]

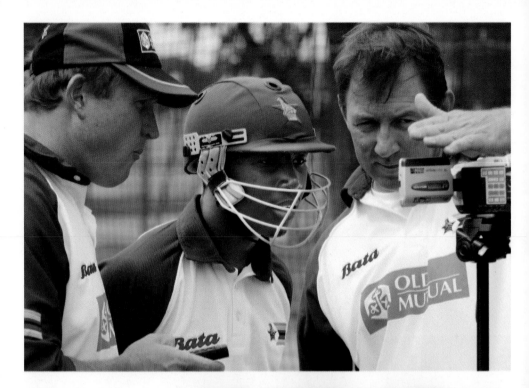

Watching my own batting with coach Geoff Marsh *(right)* and assistant coach Shane Cloete *(left)* in Perth.
[GETTY]

Me and Heath pose with a pair of signed bats in Australia, which were to be auctioned to raise money for the Black Rhino.
[GETTY]

With the other captains ahead of the
2004 ICC Champions trophy.
I was by far the youngest among them.
[GETTY]

Leadership material?
Arriving for a press conference in
Lahore, 2004. By now I was just
getting used to life as captain. [GETTY]

Me and my best friend Stuart Matsikenyeri celebrate victory in Bangladesh, January 2005. [GETTY]

The look of love: me and my soulmate Loveness on our wedding day. [AUTHOR'S PERSONAL COLLECTION]

Me and fellow captain Sourav Ganguly in 2005. I had just gone 27th in the ICC batting rankings, but it would be my last Test match before 2011, and my last game as skipper of my country. [GETTY]

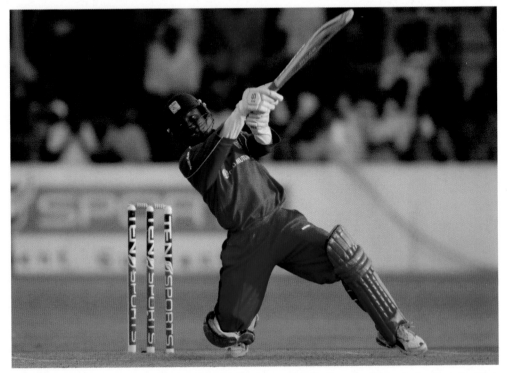

In the zone: on my way to a hundred against South Africa in 2007 after my return to international cricket. [GETTY]

Diving to make my ground during the 2010 Twenty20 World Cup against Sri Lanka. [GETTY]

In the nets with my good friend Brendan Taylor, a man I shared many a partnership with, during the 2011 World Cup. [GETTY]

In conversation with my former teammate and now selector Alistair Campbell in 2011. The two of us would later row about players' pay on our return to Test cricket. [GETTY]

Final bow: despite this tour of New Zealand being my last as an international cricketer, I still had some passion for the game left. [GETTY]

With Nick Gordon, the man who was so influential in getting me to England and helped me so much with my Rising Stars Academy. [AUTHOR'S PERSONAL COLLECTION]

Trying to stand side to side with Blessing Muzarabani, the fast bowler I helped to nurture, in Scotland. [AUTHOR'S PERSONAL COLLECTION]

Me and Loveness, the most important person in my life. [AUTHOR'S PERSONAL COLLECTION]

My two boys, TJ and Gershom, looking resplendent before heading to school in the UK. [AUTHOR'S PERSONAL COLLECTION]

Loveness and Gershom basking in a rare bit of sunlight in the UK and reading about Nelson Mandela. [AUTHOR'S PERSONAL COLLECTION]

Loveness, TJ, Gershom and my nephew Stanford with Reaz Al-Mamoon and his family in England. Reaz was a great help to me when I fled to Bangladesh. [AUTHOR'S PERSONAL COLLECTION]

Taming a lion on one of my more recent visits back to Zimbabwe. [NICK GORDON]

either Test or first-class cricket. That's out of his jurisdiction. It's not for him to say who can be on the selection panel or how many selectors there should be or what other responsibilities a selector can or cannot have.' Amid all this, Heath was insisting that he had not resigned. Yet I had been named as the new skipper to the media. It was the usual chaos.

The main difference between this stand and the one taken by Henry and Andy would end up being the size of it. Henry and Andy had made a deliberate effort not to get too many other players involved; they believed that the stand they were making would carry more weight if it was a stand made by one black player and one white player. Heath would need numbers to back him up if he was going to get anywhere here. Luckily for him, there were many others who agreed with him and were willing to back him, demanding the board meet his demands for reform. Many of the squad shared his concerns.

One unnamed player who was backing Heath had also discussed my appointment with the media: 'There are quite a few guys who don't want to play under Tatenda Taibu, and it's not a racial issue. It's because he's twenty years old and he's still trying to make it in international cricket.

'We've asked them to reverse the captaincy situation back to Streak, and they have said they won't. If that's the case, there are a few of us who are going to leave purely on that basis.' Shortly after, it was announced that thirteen players originally involved in the boycott (it would later be fifteen in total), with Heath the leader of the pack, would refuse to play in the upcoming Test and ODI series with Sri Lanka. It meant that just four of the squad for the upcoming games had played against Bangladesh just three months before.

It would have been normal for those comments to affect me negatively, but I made sure they didn't get to me. Of course, I could understand what they were saying – I was becoming a captain at twenty years old — but I was too busy trying to find solutions to our predicament to pay attention to that. In fact, my mind went blank to everything that people were saying. And there was a lot of talk to ignore.

The players announced their boycott while calling for Heath to be reinstated, while they also called for the removal of Geoff Marsh and Max Ebrahim from the selection panel (the latter because of his lack of playing experience). They wanted them replaced with former cricketers Mpumelelo Mbangwa and Ethan Dube. The thirteen players involved in the boycott were Heath, Stuart Carlisle, Grant Flower, Craig Wishart, Andy Blignaut, Raymond Price, Gary Brent, Sean Irvine, Travis

Friend, Barney Rogers, Trevor Gripper, Richard Sims and Neil Ferreira. In an open letter, the players revealed their problems with the hierarchy in great detail. They started off by making it clear that they shared Heath's concerns, and that as far as they were concerned he hadn't 'threatened' to resign, but that he had said he would 'consider possible retirement' if his concerns were not addressed.

Their main concern in a nine-point document was focused on 'interference of a non-sporting nature'. The players talked of how they supported the ZCU's wider objectives in taking the game to the majority of Zimbabweans, but that they believed there had been 'racial and ethnic discrimination in selection of the National Team'. The 'rebels' noted that they believed players of all races had been excluded solely because of race or the region they came from.

They spoke of how one board member had tried to reselect a team after it had already been ratified by the ZCU, and how another had threatened 'boycotts and pitch invasions' if he did not get his way (something Givemore Makoni had mentioned to me and Stuart when he had visited us in the middle of the night).

These are the reasons why my teammates believed that interference had gone beyond the developmental objectives of the union – who were championing the idea of having five non-white players in each Zimbabwe side – and why they were calling for selectors to have minimum playing qualifications before being given the job. They did not believe that this meant there could not be a predominantly black board, but they did believe it would lead to more accountability, and a better chance of any interfering selector facing punishment.

This was not the only thing concerning the boys. They backed Heath's call for a players' association representative to ease the pressure on the captain, a representative that had to be elected without interference. Further to this, they also detailed how Heath had been pushing the ZCU to introduce a minimum wage for those contracted to the organisation in order to make life easier for the youngsters making their way in the game. These were both issues, in the words of the players, that the union had been typically slow to act upon.

Alongside measures to help other players become more financially secure, the rebels wanted to see the return of National League Cricket in the country and clubs given more financial support, so they could improve the quality of their infrastructure. To help finance this, the board could start by cutting down on their own expenditure on overseas tours – did certain board members really need to be on these tours anyway?

There were many specific accusations against the board present in the text as well: how one member had allegedly intimidated the journalist Mehluli Sibanda and an unnamed black player into not siding with Heath; how they had been 'reliably informed' that a Provincial General Manager and Chairman of a Province both threatened to boycott the fourth ODI vs. Bangladesh, along with making threats of a 'pitch invasion and digging up the wicket'; how one member had suggested at a meeting that Mark Vermeulen be offered double his usual match fee not to play, clearing the way for Stuart Matsikanyeri to play.

Fundamentally they believed there were three board members who held too much power and were bulldozing the other board members into accepting their decisions. Heath had not even been granted a hearing with the board before having his contract terminated, despite him being the country's all-time leading wicket taker. It is also worth remembering, the letter noted, 'that the ZCU have often stated that they are an apolitical organization'.

This left me in a pretty difficult position, and throughout the whole process I was rarely consulted by my teammates. But when the stage was all set and it was time for them to deliver their final blow, they began to realise that their stand might not win over the public – the most important people in all of this. Thirteen players had decided to strike, and all thirteen of them were white. As a group they had been discussing these issues exhaustively over the previous months, and yet they never included any of the black players in these talks. It was only very late in the day that this realisation was made, and they soon realised they could be in trouble.

Heath approached me two days before their statement was to be released, where they would bring all their issues to light. I found it very unfair to be asked to consider joining the other players at such short notice. I was being asked to make a huge decision without any proper understanding of how the process had unfolded so far and what the repercussions would be if I was to join them.

To be fair to Heath, a lot of the issues that he discussed with me were very valid, but I was left wondering why all of the white players knew and were involved, while none of the black players were. It didn't really sit right with me. In particular I remember him saying, 'This is going to turn racial if you don't come on board.' I wasn't comfortable with that. I was thinking, 'Okay, only because it has reached this point you are now asking me to come on board with you and make a stand. If I was supposed to be standing with you, we should have stood together from the beginning.' I felt as if I had been left in dark.

When I became his vice-captain, we had decided that he would go to most of the team meetings alone, because I was still young and was busy enough learning my own game. We decided that if I had anything important to say, the message would go through him. But for him to plan something like this without me – I thought it was wrong. I asked for some more time to think it over, but in the end decided I was not going to join them. A day later, Grant Flower – who was my regular practice partner – came for a heart to heart with me, citing the same issues as Heath had, but by that stage I had already made up my mind.

I watched from afar as the statement was made without involvement from any black player, and ultimately this proved to be a problem for them. In terms of numbers, since the World Cup more of the black population from each of Zimbabwe's major cities had started to show an interest in cricket and had started to come in their numbers to our games. Now the board had a chance to turn the rebels' issue into a racial one, and they took the opportunity gleefully. The way it was put across to the public was that the whites wanted to keep cricket for the white minority – they did not want reform. Inevitably the black spectators were not going to take kindly to that. The issue soon turned racial and that silenced a lot of people.

Ultimately, I can understand the disappointment that Heath felt towards me. He was trying to fight something, and he didn't win. If he had me onside, the board wouldn't have been able to use the tactics they did. If I had joined him a lot of my own questions would have been answered too, of that there's no doubt. But at the end of the day I think principle is principle. If you are doing the right thing with the right motives from the start, things should move in the right direction. My question at the time remains my question now – why wasn't I included in the first place? If we had made the stand together, who knows, we may have ended up solving a lot of the problems.

Although my joining them could have had a positive impact, I try not to dwell on it too much now. Generally, in all aspects of my life, I avoid thinking about what might have been. I always believe that things are meant to happen the way that they are meant to happen, and I can't do much to change it. It goes the way it is supposed to go. If I open up that thought, what can stop me from opening up my other thoughts, the other 'what if' moments in my life?

With all this drama unfolding, Sri Lanka had arrived and were gunning for us.

Life had to carry on. Not only did I have to ready myself to face this excellent Sri Lankan side, I had to start considering how I would lead an incredibly young and inexperienced side. There was a lot of class in the touring party's squad: Muttiah Muralitharan, Kumar Sangakarra, Marvan Atapattu, Chaminda Vaas, Mahela Jayawardene and many others. A mighty task awaited me. Geoff Marsh was still the coach at least, and he had acted in an incredibly professional matter given everything that had gone on. I put all the commotion to one side and tried to concentrate on the job at hand.

The numbers from our squad(s) for the Test and ODIs players spoke for themselves: out of all of us, Mark Vermeulen was the only one to have reached the age of 25. There were other players older than me – Dion Ebrahim was 23, Douglas Hondo was 24, Alester Maregwede was 22, Mluleki Nkala was 23, while both Blessing Mahwire and my good friend Stuey reached the age of 21 just before I did, which was at the end of this Test series. We had four players under the age of twenty in our squad. The fact that me, a twenty-year-old soon to be 21, had been chosen to lead us in both formats, told you everything you needed to know about where we were as a team.

The first ODI was to take place at Bulawayo on 20 April, just days after I had been named as the new captain. Despite the circumstances, I managed to keep the outside noise at bay and not let the hype control me. The main benefit of having such a young team to look after was that they were all incredibly eager, and there was a good vibe at training. That said, it was a weird feeling as well. Though the youngsters worked incredibly hard, barely a word was uttered during the whole of the first training session. You could hear the delivery stride of the bowlers so clearly, because there was no other background noise. I was like, 'Wow.' I had never seen so much nervousness and yet so much concentration on the task at hand.

The presence of Geoff also helped me a great deal as well. Despite all I had to think about, the first major contribution I had to make in the series was with the bat, way before I could implement my ideas on the field. I had put myself at number four in the order but found myself striding to the crease as early as the third over after our two inexperienced openers, Brendan Taylor and Vusi Sibanda, had been dismissed for ducks. Talk about a baptism of fire as captain.

Still, backing all the hard work I had done in the nets and embracing the responsibility that came with being captain, I scored 96*, my best score in international cricket at that point. It wasn't a bad time to come up with the goods. Meaningful contributions down the order from Maregwede and Nkala meant we reached a score of 211-6 in our fifty overs, which was respectable. Rain meant that Sri Lanka were set a target of 133 runs to win from 27 overs, and they reached their goal on the last ball of the innings. We had knocked off Jayawardene and Atapattu early, but the class of Sangakarra eventually shone through. We had lost, but we had made a very good side work very hard for their victory. At the conclusion of my first match as captain I was named man of the match by the panel of commentators. It provided a huge boost of confidence to me. That was as good as it got for a good while.

The series continued, and it was eventful to say the least. I found myself doing a lot more than I had expected. I literally did everything; an all-rounder in the truest form of the term. Not only did I keep wicket, bat and captain the side, but I also chipped in with a few useful spells of medium pace bowling. 'Do you want to be chairman of the ZCU as well?' was Sangakarra's witty take on my workload. He and Jayawardene, experienced and intelligent campaigners, were never short of a wise word or two, which meant there was rarely a dull moment. Throughout the series I continued to perform pretty well, but I wished I had turned up to the party in game number three, when we were on the wrong side of a world record. We were bowled out for just 35 in 18 overs, which was and still is the lowest score in the history of ODIs. Batting at number four I got a golden duck, one of four players on our side not to make a score that day. No one reached double figures. To say it was highly embarrassing would be an understatement. It was a huge blow.

Still, I had no option as captain but to stand up and fight. It was what I had been taught since the day I walked into Churchill Boys High, so I carried on. At the end of the five games I was named man of the series, which was very pleasing, but it hurt me that we had not managed to win a game. Throughout my years in cricket I never grew used to the losing feeling, even though it was something that happened to us incredibly often.

The Test series was next, and this was going to provide us with an even bigger challenge than the ODIs. There were relatively few players in the squad who had played much first-class cricket at all, and in the first game of the two-match series five were making their Test debuts. There was no doubt we were in real trouble. In the midst of all this I was making history again, becoming the youngest-ever Test captain in cricketing history. Needless to say, we were absolutely smashed in both games. In our first innings in the first Test we were bowled out for 199; Sri Lanka had 281 runs on the board before they lost their first wicket in their innings. We were dismissed for 102 the second time around. There was more pain in the second game, as Sri Lanka racked up 713-3 with the bat. Atapattu made 249, Sangakarra 270. Combined we made 228 in the first innings and 231 in the second innings. It was clear there was much work to be done before we could compete in the purest form of the game.

Because I now held so much responsibility, our performances on the field were already weighing me down. I found myself exhausted both mentally and physically. There was so much for me to take on, and I was just trying to keep my chin above water. I wouldn't allow the others to see how I felt as I tried to remain strong; the only one who knew how I was feeling was Loveness. All the complaining I had to do I did to her. Our home was my safe place to let the emotions pour out of me. I felt my body was breaking down. I was keeping wicket for long periods of time, batting at four, occasionally bowling, constantly captaining. At practice, I never had a moment to myself.

It was at this point, only a couple of months into the role of captain, that I wanted to quit. Nothing about the job felt right, and I started to ask myself a lot of questions. When I had taken the job initially, none of it had seemed real. What was happening with Heath and the others did not feel real. I just assumed that they would eventually come back. We played the series, and throughout it all no one from the board uttered a word to me. I had to keep asking all the questions. I was captain, so I called Max Ebrahim. I knew the way to get him to take our conversation seriously was to talk about the captaincy, because frankly no one else was good enough to take over.

'I want to give in,' I said straightaway, and he asked me why. 'Look, if I play well we are losing. If I play badly, we get embarrassed. We can't even talk about winning at the moment. I played out of my skin in the first game, got 96, and we still lost. I got man of the series, but we lost every game. This isn't working; we don't have enough players. What's the story with Streaky? I really need to know what is going on. How have we ended up in this situation?' I told him I hadn't enjoyed the board meeting I had been present at, and Max agreed that I shouldn't have been there in the first place. That decision had been made by Ozias Bvute.

He started talking to me in detail about the main issue, the quota system. 'One side is saying that if there is a quota system, how is that fair on you? Would it have been fair for Henry [Olonga]? Would it have been fair for Pommie Mbangwa? Would it be fair now for Hamilton Masakadza? You all made the side purely because you can play.' There was no doubt that question marks over the selection of Stuey existed. Stuey was my closest friend, but I looked at things objectively. He also made the point that there had been question marks over some of the white members of our squad as well; Stuart Carlisle and Dirk Viljoen, for example. This is why the unofficial quota system cast such a dark cloud over Zimbabwean cricket. No one really knew whether some players were being selected to satisfy quotas or they were genuinely considered to be good enough. As a result, it put people like Stuey under even more pressure.

I didn't take the issue of selection any further. I always had believed that if a player was good enough, then there would be no question marks. Performances eventually speak for themselves. I used to think like that because that's how I saw it at the time. When I had first got into the team, it wasn't as a wicketkeeper, as Andy was number one in that position. I knew I wasn't going to take his place in the near future, because I wouldn't have played enough games to prove I was better than him with the gloves. But I knew I could improve my batting and challenge others in the line-up, which is what I did. Clearly Zimbabwean cricket did not quite operate like this, though.

After Max had answered my questions, I still wanted to leave, but his final words to me made me reconsider. 'Tatenda, I will never ask you to do something you don't want to do. Zimbabwe's current situation is not good, but at the end of the day you have to make a decision you are happy with, and I accept your decision.' Though Max had been involved in all the unsavoury events which had recently taken place, I thought, 'There is someone who is not being selfish. He is not just thinking about his position as a selector. He is actually thinking about me as a human being.' Because of that answer, I decided I would give it another shot.

World number one outfit Australia were the second team I would come up against as captain in a three-match ODI series, and there was no chance they were going to give us an easy ride. They had waltzed to victory in the World Cup final just a year before in South Africa, beating India by 125 runs, and their batting line-up was a scary proposition: Adam Gilchrist, Matthew Hayden, Ricky Ponting, Michael Clarke, Darren Lehmann and Andrew Symonds. Shane Warne was not part of their bowling attack for the tour, but they could still count on Glenn McGrath, Jason Gillespie and Michael Kasprowicz.

Despite being Australian and knowing a lot of these players well, Geoff did not provide us with an awful lot of insight into their line-up, or how we might enjoy success against them. All he had to say was that they were a good side and we would need to bowl well. After the battering we had taken against Sri Lanka, I didn't think that was enough, so I had my own meeting with the team without any of the staff present.

As captain, I was always looking for answers to the situation we had found ourselves in, and I drew strength from learning about the difficulties other sports teams had faced in the past. On 27 April 1993, an aircraft carrying most of the Zambia national soccer team to a World Cup qualifier against Senegal in Dakar crashed into the Atlantic Ocean shortly after taking off from Gabon. All thirty people on board perished in the accident. Many players who had not previously been in the squad had to take on the responsibility of representing the nation. Ours was clearly not the same situation – no Zimbabwean cricketers had lost their lives – but I was able to at least study how these players had continued in such difficult circumstances for their nation.

Walking in to bat at number five in the first game was an interesting experience. As I walked to the end where I would be facing my first delivery, I had a little look at the condition of the pitch. Looking down, I soon spotted where the Australian bowlers were pitching the ball. The majority of the marks were on that good length area that is so difficult to play – you would have only needed a couple of A4 books to cover the area that they were constantly hitting. There was one mark halfway down the pitch where one of them had attempted a bouncer, and one mark close to the crease, where one of them had attempted a yorker, but the rest were gathered together in a little clump. Classic McGrath.

'How are you going to score your runs with groupings like this, Tiba?' I asked myself. 'If you don't find the answer, who do you think will? All the others are so young and inexperienced. This is not the time to be talking yourself like this – it's all about the next ball you are going to face.' So much used to race around my head during these moments out in the middle. The series went as expected, and we lost all three games by heavy margins: seven wickets, 139 runs and eight wickets.

My performance was mixed; I scored 57 in the first game, just one in the second and 27 in the third. They weren't scores that were going to help decide a series. Of the young players starting out their international careers for Zimbabwe, it was Brendan Taylor who was having most of an influence with the bat. He and

I shared a partnership of 61 in the first game as we both passed the fifty-mark, and he went on to score 65 in the second game. He was showing plenty of guts against a high-class bowling attack that simply didn't let up at any moment. Lesser players wouldn't have risen to the challenge.

Meanwhile, our young bowler Tinashe Panyangara was improving all the time. He was learning how to use his crease more, how to bowl a slower ball and how to maintain control when swinging the ball all while bowling at the best batsmen in the world. At the other end, Tawanda Mupariwa was picking up wickets regularly, compensating for his lack of pace by getting the ball to swing into the batsman nicely. When you're in a position where it's virtually impossible for you to go neck and neck with your opponents, you at least try to find positives for the future.

'Maybe one day we will have Streak opening the bowling with Panyangara – what a combination that would be.' It is easy for the mind to dream up such scenarios when you're spending all day out on the field. After the presentations had been completed at the end of the series, I made a point of heading to the opposition dressing room for a chat – I knew after my last tour of Australia that I was welcome there. Adam Gilchrist and I spent some time exchanging notes on wicketkeeping practices and techniques. He would have a beer while I stuck to a soft drink. Adam was always unfailingly positive, and at the end of this series he was his usual self. He spoke highly of Panyangara and Vusi Sibanda and kept mentioning we'd have a really strong outfit once those on strike returned to the fold. That's all I could think about as well.

Still, tours waited for no one, and we had to head to England for the ICC Champions Trophy in England without Heath and co. Most of the youngsters were so excited about travelling to England for the first time, but despite being only a little older than most of them, I had other things on my mind. I had already been to England twice before. I now had to do the majority of press conferences, attend captains' meetings and get involved with team selection.

I was beginning to feel like an old man, so I decided to do what I wouldn't usually do: I allowed myself a night out with the physio and one of the other squad members.

No one was expecting much from us during this tournament, and we didn't deliver much either. We even contrived to lose to the USA – who were about to play in their first official ODI matches – in a warm-up game that I sat out due to injury. I had a grade one tear of my hamstring, but I didn't go home like I might have done in usual circumstances – leaving these boys alone did not feel like an option. I managed to play our two group games on a limping leg – scoring 40 in a 152-run defeat to England and 16 in a six-wicket loss to Sri Lanka. Elton Chigumbura was our shining light on an otherwise disappointing trip: he made 42* against England before scoring 57 against Sri Lanka and taking 3-37 with the ball. Unfortunately, the individual performances of one man were not going to take us through.

There was no time to rest when I returned home as I started to work on improving many aspects of my game: my balance, my sweep shot, my cut shot, the flow of my bat through the ball. I worked at these shots until they became part of me. I needed to trust my sweep shot, as it would be part of my defence on the subcontinent, where we would be travelling next to face Sri Lanka and Pakistan in a tri-series. Loveness, meanwhile, was occupied at home with her college work, and she had also started to learn to drive. She was doing well with her studies, and after just a few weeks of driving she managed to pass her test, so I bought a car for her.

Following the Champions Trophy our next assignment was the Paktel Cup in Pakistan, where we would face the hosts and Sri Lanka. Without Loveness there by my side I had a lot of time to think in between our practice sessions and matches, and it was at this point I decided to buy an engagement ring. I would ask her to marry me upon my return. Loveness and I were going through a rough patch after she had mistakenly found out about how I had behaved in England during the Champions Trophy, sharing numbers with an English woman I had met on my drunken night out, but I wanted to spend the rest of my life with her. I just hoped she felt the same way.

I did at least have a perfect plan in place for our engagement and subsequent engagement plans, should she say yes. In the meantime, I headed to South Africa to buy a bowling machine ahead of our series with Bangladesh. It was a mission getting everything in place just how I wanted it, but I was a perfectionist and I managed it in the end. Up went the net in the back garden, and up went the machine. I had 75 balls to go with it, and I was going to make sure I was practising more than most in the world. Loveness would feed balls into the machine while I tirelessly hit them at different speeds, angles and levels of swing. Blisters on my hands became a regular feature.

*

10
That's a Big Shot Tatenda

OUR NEXT ASSIGNMENT WAS IN BANGLADESH, WHICH MEANT WE were back playing against an opponent who we could realistically compete with. Given how depleted we had become in recent months, they were perhaps the only full member nation we could hope to beat in a series at this stage. Before reaching our final destination, we made a stop-off in India for a training camp and some warm-up games. This would give us an opportunity to get to know our new coach, the former West Indian international Phil Simmons, and also allow us to prepare for the conditions we would be facing in the subcontinent. Given all that had been going on in Zimbabwean cricket, Simmons taking the job was seen as a controversial move in some quarters from his own perspective. Phil had only retired in 2002 after a successful playing career, and now his first major coaching role was Zimbabwe. It was still only just over a year since Andy and Henry had fled the country after their protest, and just two months since Heath had quit as captain and walked out on the national team with fourteen others. Coaching us wasn't exactly the most appealing proposition in world cricket. However, by this stage most of our team was made up of black players, and I think this was one of the reasons the board saw him as an attractive option – they believed he would be able to relate to us.

One of the first things Phil had done was to call on the services of a new fitness trainer named Dean Woodford, who had been working with Bangladesh's national team. There was no doubting that Dean was very passionate about his job, but he and I never saw eye to eye. I was clearly the fittest member of our squad, but there were a lot of instances during his sessions that I felt close to breaking point. If that was the case with me, how much would my teammates be suffering? As captain, I did my best to communicate the fact that we were doing too much. Given how thin on the ground we were already in terms of numbers, we couldn't afford to lose anybody. Dean placed the blame on Phil for the length of our practice sessions.

The training camp in Visakhapatnam was incredibly tough, but if we were going to get better as a team then this is what we needed. The practices went as well as they could have done – the batters got some time in the middle, while the bowlers acclimatised to the conditions. We were to be there preparing over the Christmas period, so the wives and girlfriends were allowed to come over in the lead-up to the Test series. It was really nice for me to have Loveness there, and it helped ease the feeling of a burden I was carrying round with me as captain. Still, with all the walking she made me do around the shops she certainly helped Dean out.

On Boxing Day in India, we woke up to the news that a tsunami had hit the Indian Ocean and lots of people had lost their lives. Indonesia was the country hit the hardest, while Sri Lanka, India and Thailand also suffered badly in a disaster that killed an estimated 227,898 people in fourteen different countries. It was a very sad morning looking at pictures on the news from places that had been affected the most.

The girls left us in Mumbai. The business end of the trip was upon us, and it was time for us to lock in and get to work. It was at this time that I came across a Christian song named 'Show me your mercy' by a South African praise group. That song really did something for me, and I had it on repeat for pretty much the whole trip. It ministered me in an amazing way. All my fears seemed to lift when I listened to it, so that was my song when I was in my hotel room and before I went out to bat.

On a personal level, I performed really well in that series. In the first Test in Chittagong I made 92 in the first innings, though I scored a duck in my second dig as we slipped to another defeat, this time by 226 runs. In the second match in Dhaka I performed even better, scoring 85 unbeaten in the first innings and 153 in the second innings, where I teamed up with Brendan Taylor to put our hosts under pressure. This was the beginning of some meaningful partnerships with Brendan, which soon became known as the 'TT partnerships'. He was strong on the leg side and I was strong on the off side – it was similar to having a left hander and a right hander at the crease. Unfortunately, we could not get the five wickets required to win, handing Bangladesh their first-ever Test series win in eighteen attempts – another unwanted record. It wasn't easy seeing them celebrate at our expense, but they had deserved it.

We quickly took a 2-0 lead in the ODI series, until they realised they could target us with spin in that form of the game as well. We still didn't have any answers to it, and they ended up taking that series 3-2 as well. That hurt even more and outlined more forcefully than ever how difficult a job I had on my hands.

Following the Bangladesh tour, we had a few days back in Zimbabwe before we were due to be on the road again in neighbouring South Africa. It was around this time that I decided if I was going to be a good captain I'd have to start doing things differently from the accepted way. I started learning about my young teammates; I'd invite them to my house for a meal, while I'd also find a way to go and see them in their homes, to find out how they were living themselves. I learnt so much about them. If I am to take a trip down memory lane now, most of the stuff I learnt during this time was quite sobering. Some players were the breadwinners in their extended families despite only being in their teenage years. There was so much pressure on them. I felt as if it was up to me to start teaching them the basics of life and the demands that come with being a professional sportsman. I knew I had a long way to go, but a journey of a thousand miles starts with one step at a time.

At this stage I was young but experienced, whereas they were young but inexperienced. I think they found it difficult to confide me, and they rarely used to approach me for advice. I think it would have been beneficial if they had done this more, but at the same time I understood the culture they were coming from. In Zimbabwean culture, it is very difficult for a young man to go and ask for advice. Given how many young players we had in the team at this point this wasn't ideal, and probably slowed progress down.

Your elders are your elders, and of course they are to be treated with respect, but you lose something if you don't ask questions, because you'll never know the answer. I knew why they were like this, so I used to go and seek the information myself. I would therefore be able to draw any doubts they had from them and tried to help them with any problems they had. It took a bit more work, but I used to look at it this way: Andy Flower had done exactly the same for me – he had been able to draw information from me at a young age. If someone was able to do that for me, why shouldn't I be able to do that for someone else?

The tour in South Africa proved to be a difficult one for me. I struggled to score many runs, and the boys there with me were still just boys. I was still just a boy myself, albeit one who could hold his own at this level. It did not help that we had lost Ed Rainsford, Tinashe Panyangara and Douglas Hondo to injury as well. We lost both the first two ODIs by over 100 runs but were at least boosted by the return of Heath Streak for the final match, despite our series defeat already having been confirmed.

Heath had been absent from the side since his very public falling-out with ZC ten months before, but he wasn't returning as captain – those duties would still be left to me. Still, Heath being back along with the likes of Andy Blignaut and Gavin Ewing would only strengthen our side. 'I am putting my weight fully behind the captain, Tatenda Taibu, and the rest of the lads,' part of his statement read. Heath's and Andy's return unfortunately didn't stop us from crumbling to 54 all out in the first innings of the first Test in Cape Town. Only Stuart at the top of the innings made double figures with his twelve. I made seven, Heath nine. Though we showed some fight in our second dig we slid to an innings defeat, as we did in the Second Test, where I once again could not register a meaningful score. Heath's 85 and Andy's 52 in the first innings at least prevented further ignominy on the batting side of things, but there was no contest between the two sides to be honest.

For me the memories of that series are still very vivid, and it changed the way I played against South Africa for the rest of my career. The South Africans had a gameplan. Normally, they would like to aim for the head of the snake, and so if you were the captain they really came hard at you. I got a good taste of that on this tour. I remember at one stage being out on the field and getting it from all angles, so much so that I started to count how many players were chirping me. It was eight of the eleven. I wasn't going to back down. I had played well in Bangladesh, but I wasn't getting any runs here. I hadn't chirped back all the way throughout the series, but by the final Test I'd had enough. By this point emotions were running high. I was a losing captain and I wasn't performing. I started to chirp back, and it lasted the whole time I was out in the middle.

The South Africans played like that; they didn't let you off. When you do well against South Africa, you know you've played out of your skin. It's not difficult to find some of the exchange from that match on YouTube; in fact, one video in particular has become quite famous in cricketing circles. I'm facing the slow left arm bowler Nicky Boje, and fellow wicketkeeper Mark Boucher is giving me plenty behind the stumps.

'The only time you're looking to score runs is when we've got one seamer on the field.'

The video cuts to me driving a ball straight to cover, and another South African shouts, 'That's a big shot Tatenda.' Boucher, meanwhile, continues on his way: 'Where was your mouth when we were in Cape Town and we had a full seam attack? We've got one seamer and now all of a sudden you've got a big mouth.'

Still he carries on. 'You don't want to get out now because I think you might be averaging single figures this tour. I'll walk you to the changing room as well.'

After another delivery goes by, he delivers his final blow. 'What are you averaging? You must know your average? Nine? Ten? Nine point five so we'll give you ten.'

Mark Boucher was the one to continue once everyone else had stopped. I remember Graeme Smith and AB de Villiers both got involved as well. I specifically recall Hashim Amla being one of the three players out there who did not open his mouth. Pretty much everyone was involved, but it's the Boucher part that I remember most clearly. I remember it was the fast bowler Andre Nel who started it, but with Andre you knew everything was strictly on-field. Everyone knew that when he had a go at you it was just part of the battle. I don't remember exactly how it did start, or one particular thing that was said.

However, I do remember telling Jacques Kallis that he was a big name for nothing and that he must shut up. He did. I strongly believe that something takes you over when you start to say these things out on the field. I wasn't usually the sort of person who would have a go at eight people at once – in such a situation I'd usually run out of things to say. I think a certain spirit inside takes over during these moments.

Most players would keep matters like this on-field only, but as you travelled around the world you started to hear about certain characters who would like to push the boundaries. At the end of this Test match, being captain of our team, I had to go to the presentation ceremony. I was walking alongside Boucher and AB de Villiers, and AB turned and said, 'Tough luck, no hard feelings about what happened on the field.'

'AB, you're being weak,' was Boucher's response.

In general, I believed sledging to be a waste of time because it didn't usually affect me when I batted, though this is maybe the one occasion where it did. Before doing it to someone else I would think, 'What if they take it the way I take it?' If it did anything to me, it got me to concentrate more.

I always thought New Zealand were the best at sledging anyway. They would say things that actually made you think. It wasn't just mindless outrage with them; having a go at someone for the sake of it. When you get someone to really think, you actually begin to play on their mind.

There was one innings in particular I played in the 2003 World Cup against them. We had started badly, but I had built partnerships with Andy Flower and then Andy Blignaut, until I ran the latter out. I was gutted, kneeling down on the floor. One guy running in from the boundary passed by and said, 'We've got an extra man on our side boys.' Heath was next in, and someone else said, 'Don't worry, Tatenda will run him out as well.' It's simple enough, but it was delivered at the right time. I had just run my teammate out in my first World Cup, which was on home soil. They weren't having a go at me, but they were adding to my guilt.

Despite the run of results we were enduring at this time, I was always full of faith whenever we played. I never looked at the other team as being better than us, even though the results almost always suggested that. I always saw each day on the field as different to the last; what has been does not mean it will be. What a person has already done before does not determine how they will play today. This day has never been seen before. I was never one to head into the dressing room feeling sorry for myself and for my team. I always walked onto the field positive that there would be a good outcome.

The one thing my teammates say, the ones that have heard me speak in front of groups of people, is that I inspire with my words. I wasn't necessarily much of a strategist as captain, but I used to speak from the heart. I never used to write anything down or say, 'We're going to do it this way,' I just used to pour out my heart. I think that's part of what defines me, and I stuck to that regardless of what had happened on the field of play.

At the end of this series I met the South African commentator Mike Haysman. He was enjoying a few drinks, while I was holding a Powerade. He called me over, and we chatted about the series just gone. During our conversation he said something that really stuck with me. 'Tatenda, when you speak at press conferences, you speak with so much faith regardless of results. I would like to encourage you to keep going.' That was really comforting to hear. I don't remember ever walking to a press conference with my face or shoulders down, even after we'd been bowled out for 35. The reporters used to say they liked calling me for press conferences because I was always positive. I also used to give them plenty to write about.

If I thought one of my team had messed up, I would not dodge them, I'd go and tell them to their face. For us to improve, we needed to iron things out in the dressing-room environment. I would tell them how it was, and the guys wouldn't take it personally. I think they knew I had them at heart.

Nevertheless, the sledging in South Africa was not really me. Upon returning to Zimbabwe, I was killing time at home when the phone rang. It was my old coach Bruce Makova. He was angry with my performance in South Africa. He always used to say I had more potential than I delivered. We had previously spoken about me bringing back the World Cup for Zimbabwe for the first time. This time we spoke for two hours and he made some very valid points.

He'd picked up on my verbal exchange with the South Africans. 'Tatenda, I've never known you to have a go at the opposition. You usually like speaking with either your bat or your gloves.' He wanted me to change my approach. I tried to defend myself, telling him I had to respond to their chirps when I was not performing well. 'That's not how you do it,' he said. 'Remember that hurt next time you meet them. Lock yourself into that hurt and tell me how you perform after that.' I didn't fully understand what he was telling me, but I was going to try anyway.

One evening while back home I asked Loveness to dress up, because I wanted to take her out to a local restaurant for dinner. After the dinner I told her that I had lost my driver's licence, but I had a good idea where I might have dropped it. I asked if she minded accompanying me while we drove back to this spot. When she said yes, I drove her right to the place where I had first asked her to be my girlfriend. On the very same spot where I had asked that original question, I got down on one knee and asked her to marry me. She was in a state of shock for several seconds, but eventually, in her shy and tender voice, she said, 'Of course, honey.'

We were soon preparing for Roora, an African custom which a prospective husband undertakes to give to the head of a prospective wife's family in consideration of a customary marriage. According to the Shona dictionary, Roora means to acquire a wife, and the word is also interchanged with bride price or dowry. The primary purpose of Roora is to build relations between the respective families, and it is done prior to the wedding taking place.

Because I had stayed with Loveness long before the bride price had been paid, I had to be fined for that first before paying the actual Roora itself. I was accompanied by my mum's brothers and my siblings to do this, and everything went smoothly. Finally, there was peace between the two families, which allowed us to get on with preparing for the wedding.

Mrs Chasinda, a former teacher of mine at Churchill, knew of a wedding planner named Zillah and put us in touch. It was our special day and the wedding had to be to our taste, and there was no doubting that Zillah knew how to provide that for us. We wanted an intimate affair, with only around eighty guests, but we ended up having to compromise and our final number was around 150.

The Wild Geese Lodge lies on the edge of a private wildlife sanctuary a short distance from Harare and it was the venue we decided to use. It was a place that we felt reflected our personality as a couple, and we fell in love with it at first sight. The sanctuary offered around 30 acres of indigenous garden, where majestic antelope, sable, eland and zebras roamed.

As soon as he heard the news of our marriage, Ozias Bvute got in touch and told me not to worry about sorting a wedding video – he would take care of that, and the cars for the bridal team. We didn't always see eye to eye on a number of issues, but that was a nice touch. In 2005 he would become the chief executive of Zimbabwean Cricket, replacing Vince Hogg in the role.

In the end we decided to have two bridesmaids and two grooms. My best man was Farai Mukahiwa. Farai and I were good friends, but we were not as close as me and Stuart. There was no doubt Stuart was my best friend, and he was going to be my best man until a misunderstanding prior to the big day. Our disagreement had resulted in him moving out of my house and so I decided he was not going to have the honour. In truth I overreacted.

Nonetheless we had a really beautiful wedding evening, and our families were delighted that we had finally tied the knot. The highlight of the wedding was our first dance. The song of choice was 'Have You Ever Been in Love' by Celine Dion. Candles were lit as we made our way to the dancefloor, and both Loveness and I had changed into Asian wedding attire. We had purchased these outfits when we were in India and had effectively been exiled from our families for living together before marriage. Because of this, we had virtually planned our own wedding.

Most of our guests spent the night with us at the lodge before we headed to the Sun City resort in South Africa the next morning for the first part of our honeymoon.

We spent three days there before we travelled north to Sanyati Lodge, which had been our first choice as a destination all along. The lodge was on a little island at the foot of the Matusadona mountain range which you could reach by speed boat, and it also overlooked the expansive waters of Lake Kariba. We spent seven nights there with no phone signal or access to technology.

During our time there we did game drives at dawn and boat cruises at sunset. On one our game drives we had the privilege of watching two cheetahs hunt down an impala. It was remarkable and thrilling to watch, and after a rapid chase they caught their prey. I got a little overexcited and stood up to take a picture, which the animals did not seem to enjoy, and I was quickly told to sit down by the driver.

I had taken ten days' leave after the wedding for our honeymoon, which meant I missed the crucial inter-provincial Logan Cup match we had scheduled against Matabeleland. There were rumours that I had forgone my honeymoon to see out the end of the domestic season, but that was not the case and I had actually been granted leave. However, Kevin Curran – the father of the current English internationals Sam and Tom, and my coach at the time – had not been informed and was livid that I had been given so much time off at such a crucial stage in the campaign. The truth is I didn't care. I had been playing cricket almost every day of my life since being introduced to the game. The one time I did something more important than cricket, people questioned it.

Once back, I had to prepare for a match against Midlands in the final round of domestic fixtures. We had secured the Logan Cup for the sixth time in a row. Despite my controversial one-game absence I was named player of the year for Mashonaland that season. I had been outstanding with the bat with two well-made centuries and a top score of 151 against Manicaland. With all the hard work in my newly-built garden nets I was starting to understand my game more and more, and this was reflected in my newfound ability to bat for longer periods.

Soon after the Logan Cup I started preparing for our series with New Zealand. I was practising as hard as I possibly could. Shortly after our honeymoon, we had found out that Loveness was pregnant. I was thrilled to hear the news, but I was also a little concerned for Loveness because I knew how much time I spent away from Zimbabwe each year. We now depended on each other so much. She was suffering severe morning sickness and we knew that soon enough I would be back out on the road, so she decided to head to the UK for a short while. Her brother Alford and her sister Barbra were staying over there, so we thought it best for her to spend some time catching up with them while I really got my head down to practise hard.

I was home alone, and I knew the size of the task we had ahead of us. We had Heath back in the side, and he was a credit to any attack, but we had other injuries to contend with. Perhaps the most impressive thing about Heath's return was how much his batting had improved – he was a very bottom-hand player, but he had worked hard on his game and he was a very-good lower order player in all forms of cricket.

In both Test matches we slid to an innings defeat, once again unable to deal with the challenge of facing one of the stronger nations. In the first Test in Harare we reduced New Zealand to 113-5, but centuries from Brendon McCullum and Daniel Vettori took them to a score of 452. After letting them off the hook with the ball, we were then dismissed for 59 and 99. Only seventeen times in Test match history has a team been dismissed for less than 100 in both their innings in a match. This was one of those occasions. In the second Test match in Bulawayo we put up more of a fight with the bat, helped by my 76 in the first innings, but we were unable to get any closer to a desired result.

After the Test matches, New Zealand stayed for a triangular series with us and India. We were well beaten in our first three matches but ran India very close in our last one. I had walked into bat with the score at 4-2, but a 116-run partnership with Charles Coventry, another player who had returned from exile, saw us post a competitive 250. We were massive favourites when we reduced them to 36-4 and then 91-5, but a masterful century from Yuvraj Singh, one of the best shorter form players in the world at the time, and a half-century from MS Dhoni, then a relative novice, saw them home. That was the difference – Charles and I had batted well but had failed to convert our scores into centuries. Yuvraj hadn't.

He had some words of advice for me at the end of that match: 'Next time you are in that position, don't try those fancy shots, just punch singles all the way to your century. You had done all the hard work to get your team out of trouble and you were supposed to reward yourself with a century.' He had just picked up the man of the match award.

Like New Zealand, India faced us in two Test matches as well. There was no Sachin Tendulkar in their side, but with a batting line-up consisting of Virender Sehwag, Gautham Gambhir, Rahul Dravid, VVS Laxman and Sourav Ganguly it was hardly likely to matter anyway. In the first Test match I made a good fist of competing against them on my own, scoring an unbeaten 71 in the first innings and 52 in the second innings. The second Test did not go so well on a personal level: I made nought and one. As you can probably guess by now, 2-0 to India was the final score.

Most of the attention during that series didn't seem to be focused on the cricket itself, but rather the public falling-out between India's captain Sourav Ganguly, 'The Prince of Kolkata', and their Australian coach Greg Chappell, who had told Ganguly in a meeting that it might be best for him to step down from the role to focus on his batting, a suggestion that was not well received. Ganguly had scored a very timely hundred in the first Test to make the issue even spicier.

What people didn't know at the time was that the second Test would be my last international match until mid-2007, while Zimbabwe would not play in another Test match until 2011.

After arriving back from the UK, the first thing Loveness asked me was why we never prayed together before going to asleep. I had so many questions running around my head already that I didn't know how to answer. We had lived together for all this time, why was she asking this now? What had happened in the UK? I didn't ask her why she was asking, but instead just asked her to pray with me as I knelt with my face towards the wall. I really didn't know how to pray out loud; the only prayers I had made before were silent in my heart. This became the start of us doing it every night before bed, each of us taking it in terms to speak, and it was something that I liked a lot.

Loveness used to talk to me a lot about the time she had lived with her older sister in Bulawayo and her experiences at the church they used to go to. She explained to me how her life had been during that period, and how she longed to return to that routine. She even liked how they dressed back then – modest apparel, long hair and no make-up – though she no longer wore this sort of attire in day-to-day life with me.

We agreed that we would look for a church to go to where we could find fellowship with others. I knew that we would realise instantly the moment we found the right one, but that moment did not arrive straightaway, so we temporarily stopped going altogether. Instead we would spend our weekends visiting children's homes and donating clothing. I had several personal sponsors at the time, one of which was Faith Wear, a local clothing company which had blossomed from a single store to a chain of shops in different Zimbabwean cities. I immediately got on well with the owner Brett because of the love and respect we both shared for God.

I would receive over one hundred items of clothing a year from Faith Wear, so we would give away all the clothes we didn't use any more. What was more important to us was the time we spent with the children, and we nearly adopted a little boy called Ngoni from the Harare Children's Home, but unfortunately our commitments were just too great. We became pretty popular with the kids over time, so much so that we were allowed to take them for a day out one weekend.

When I wasn't with the kids, I often spent time in the company of an old veteran of the game named David Lewis, a man who had captained Rhodesia for ten years straight. I learnt a lot about captaincy when speaking with the late Mr Lewis, and Loveness got on very well with his wife, too. We didn't tell a soul that we were spending time with them but kept everything they said close to our hearts.

However, these conversations did not seem to make things any easier for me as I searched for life's answers. I still a felt a little empty to the point of being dissatisfied with everything that was happening to me. I would go and play, score runs and take catches, but all the joy I got from that seemed to be in vain. As soon as I got home, it would be gone. I often sat down on the floor of the living room enjoying the morning sunshine, but deep thoughts would occupy my head: Where have I come from? What am I doing here on earth? Where am I going? The question I continually used to ask myself was, 'What then?' It seemed to me that life was nothing but vanity.

I started to thirst for something more than just scoring runs, more than just the screams of the crowd. I wanted a meaningful life. My relationship with Loveness felt bittersweet. On the one hand we felt we could discuss absolutely everything together, but on the other was the fact that neither of us had the solutions to the problems we faced in life.

One evening Loveness was telling of how much she missed her sister in Bulawayo, and in particular her sister's children. They were struggling badly with their finances after the death of her husband, while only three of her six children were still alive. Loveness really wanted to help, and so I made a promise to myself that I would pay her a visit the next time I was in Bulawayo for cricket.

After a few months I was finally able to fulfil my promise. I had to call Loveness's other sister Mercy in Harare to get the directions to her house, as Loveness did not know I was making the visit. On my arrival I beeped my horn until a teenage boy came to the gate to ask who I was and what business I had come to discuss. The young boy was named Tinashe and he hadn't met me before, but he let me through.

Tinashe was no ordinary teenage boy, and there was something about him that I loved. I just couldn't tell what it was. We spoke for two hours, a mixture of Bible stories and general life chat. He was incredibly mature for his age. He told me about Moses in the Bible, while his favourite verse was Psalm 103:1-3. There was something about him when he recited that verse to me; it was not just a normal boy reciting any old verse. He meant what he was speaking. During all this his younger brother Peace was sat with my phone, asking if he could play with it. Their mother had already gone to church for prayers, so I did not see her until the next day.

I came back to see Pamela the following day after she had returned home from a church service. She was sick and frail, but we spoke for a long time before she asked if I would return to attend church with her. I failed to make it on the day she had mentioned, but I kept my promise at the forefront of my mind. When I returned to tell the news to Loveness, she could not believe what I had done, and she could not stop herself from shedding a tear – it was obvious how much that family meant to her. We spoke at length about my trip, and she kept asking me questions until I revealed that I had been asked to return for a church service.

On the field I was playing well, and with my performances came lots more money. The new addition to the family was arriving soon, and we wanted a new house to go with it. We soon moved into a new Spanish-style villa, which had two houses in one yard plus the staff quarters.

Things were going well for me in that regard, but I was being tested more than ever before as a captain. Being in charge of such a vulnerable team at such a young age was a tall order. A lot of the boys I was captaining had dropped out of school in order to establish a cricket career. It had worked for me, Hamilton Masakadza and Stuart Matsikanyeri, so why shouldn't it work out for them? That's why I felt it was my duty to help them get them contracts that would secure their future. It soon became clear that the senior figures in our sport were not so bothered about the commitment of these young boys to the game.

The youngsters had no idea what was going on behind closed doors between me and ZC. They had no ideas that I was holding talks with my superiors, and they had no idea that while I was being offered a bumper US dollar contract, they were only being offered Zimbabwean dollar contacts and far less money.

Principle would not let me survey the contract I was being offered, lest I became tempted by it. I wasn't going to captain a less privileged team while I enjoyed the benefits they couldn't enjoy. If they weren't going to dish out these US dollar contracts to the whole squad, then I certainly wasn't going to take mine. I disregarded all the offers put in front of me – my players had to get their fair share. I wasn't going to see them deprived because they were ignorant to the situation and were perceived to be of no value. After all, it was they who were representing their country in such tough circumstances.

11
More Than a Game

NOW I WAS MAKING MY OWN STAND AGAINST THE ZIMBABWEAN Cricket board, it started to dawn on me that the rebels who had had taken the hierarchy on a year before were fighting for a system – a system that works. The racial picture that had been painted at the time had obscured the real issue. Sure, I was protesting against something slightly different to those rebels, but the point remained: the current system was inadequate, and so were those in charge. My players were not being valued properly, and I felt as if I had a decision to make, and so I did: I was going to the quit the national team. With all that was going on, I felt it was the only way to attract to attention, to hopefully make things change for the better.

I called the team together and made them aware that I was retiring from international cricket with immediate effect, though I did not reveal what had been going on behind closed doors. Blessing Mahwire was the first to react, and he threw his weight behind me: 'Skipper, you can't fight this alone.' He then went around the dressing room rallying the other players, asking them to sign a petition to show that they backed me. If my demands were not met – transparency in the union, players getting their fair share of the funds, money being made available for the development of the game at grassroots level – then they would refuse to play as well.

I had been speaking to Clive Field, a good friend of mine and a lawyer, about how to get my message across. Clive, being the level-headed gentleman he was, had advised me to think carefully about what I was about to embark on, especially when I informed him that the young players were backing me as well. Clive knew what ZC were capable of, and he wasn't sure whether the youngsters had it in them to last the distance in a propaganda war. On 11 September, Clive released a statement on behalf of the players, in part a response to an article that had appeared in the *Independent*, titled 'The money Zim's cricketers are refusing.' The article, Clive said, was 'misleading, irresponsible, and inaccurate', which was hardly a first for the Zimbabwean media. We had just finished our triangular series with India and New Zealand and were two days away from the first Test of a two-match series against the former. Our contracts with ZC had ended on 31 August 2005, so we were effectively saving the face of the organisation by agreeing to play in the first place.

As Clive detailed in the statement, what ZC effectively wanted to do was impose a one-month extension to each of our 2004/05 national Contracts by writing individually to the players involved in the 'current tours'. The indication was that the new contracts would be offered from 1 October, after the conclusion of the two-match series with India. As players we rejected this extension:

In law, extensions amount to a material variation of any existing contract, so prior consent is required from both parties because any contract is a binding consensual agreement. It follows that variation/s cannot be imposed by either party without prior agreement. In this case, consent was not sought by ZC, who simply imposed the extension.

ZC subsequently undertook to supply new contracts on 14 September – during the first Test against India – backdated to 1 September. On 1 September they had unveiled their Player Contracts Structure for the upcoming 2005/06 season, indicating in writing their intention to offer 12-month time-specific national contracts to three players: me, Heath Streak and Andy Blignaut. They would also offer around 27 'Level One Contracts', which would be paid as a monthly retainer. In other words, there was no provision made within these Level One contracts for differentiation based on seniority and experience. Meanwhile, the contracts that Heath, Andy and I had been offered would be separately negotiated with us as individuals. ZC also created eight apprentice contracts, which would be paid for by other companies, subject to the stipulation that ZC could call any of them up for national-team duty.

On 2 September ZC had advised our player representative that they had reversed their intent to offer three contracts to three players on the list of 27 – Stuart Carlisle, Barney Rogers and Neil Ferreira – just two days before our next match with India. No reasons were given for their decision, but despite our concerns we went ahead while the Zimbabwe Professional Cricketers' Association sought clarification on the matter. None was provided.

During this dispute, a lot of the attention was unsurprisingly on me and what offers I was supposedly refusing. Apparently, I was unhappy with the new terms I was being offered, the details of which differed in various media outlets. The truth is, though, that individually I was being promised a lot of money in private meetings with the hierarchy. They effectively wanted to buy my silence. At that time, we were being paid our salaries in Zimbabwean dollars, and our match fees in US dollars. They were offering to pay both my salary and my match fees in US dollars, and were also offering to double what I was already making.

What they didn't seem to understand was that I wasn't there to fight for myself. I wanted the best for everyone I was captaining, for the good of Zimbabwean cricket as a whole. I was in charge of a whole dressing room, and I knew when things were not well with the players, whether they came to me directly or not. It was clearly affecting our performance on the pitch. ZC were trying to move to a more incentivised contract model based more upon individuals. They were trying to completely change the nature of our contracts without our consent, and in turn were making the players feel insecure. I wasn't just going to stand by and watch while this happened. As Andy told me, it was better to stand up for something worthwhile than not at all, even if the chances were stacked against me.

Just before Clive's statement had been released, a huge group of us as players had signed a petition, calling for Peter Chingoka to step down as chairman and Ozias Bvute as managing director. I was the first to sign a petition that ended up including 74 signatures from players at all levels of Zimbabwean cricket. Alongside these 74 signatures, six cricket provinces demanded an independent audit of ZC's accounts and accused the administrators of fraud, of breaking foreign exchange regulations and other irregularities.

The India series passed with two more heavy defeats, and as time went on ZC started to act in a way that came very naturally to them. When my decision to resign was announced they decided to go on the offensive, trying to push the issue of race like they had done so successfully against Heath and the rebels before me. At one of the press conferences I had called to outline my concerns, I deliberately made sure that I was joined by two black members of my squad, two white players and two Asian players. I didn't want race to be a factor in the way the media reported the story. An article in one of the next day's newspapers began with the headline, 'Taibu being used'. The picture used was of myself and three others, none of whom were black. The two black players who had joined me at the conference had been cut out of the picture.

I felt that most of the journalists were being paid to do the administration's dirty work. We all used to say they were being given brown envelopes. The trouble was we had no concrete proof. In many ways we were in a no-win situation: none of the journalists in Zimbabwe were prepared to back us or to even report our issues fairly, meaning we'd have to approach the media outside of Zimbabwe to get a fair hearing and to gain legitimacy. The problem was that as soon as we did this the media back home had something else to use against us. We weren't loyal to our country. I often looked around at the scores of Zimbabwean journalists in the room at these press conferences and thought there must be someone with the decency to report the truth. Too often I was let down.

Supporters of the board constantly accused me of being used, but my response was simple: 'I have got my own mind. I make my own decisions. I have managed to lead a young side in international cricket. Why should I allow myself to be tossed up now?' Their race argument didn't stack up quite so nicely when I pointed out that ninety of the country's cricketers were black. Many had signed the petition.

A lot of people could not fathom my retirement from the game. They could put the exodus of Heath and the other white players down to the fact that they were white. With me they simply could not do that, and it certainly raised eyebrows. Soon enough, I was approached by a gentleman who I believed had the game of cricket at heart. He knew that my retirement had everything to do with the system I was playing under. He didn't want me to retire and he didn't want cricket in the country to die because of players leaving the sport. We had a long chat about what had happened and why, and he suggested we meet with one of the two vice-presidents of the country at the time, Joice Mujuru. He thought if I could talk to her and let her know my reasons for retiring, she would be in a position to come in and help clean up the mess, giving hope to the sport. I had at least made a point with my retirement.

The gentleman in question organised the meeting and took me to her house.

Upon arrival at the heavily-guarded property we were escorted to the lounge, where we sat and waited for her arrival. She looked busy when she arrived and told us of the funeral she was preparing for, but she wasn't leaving without hearing my story. That day I spoke straight from the heart, pleading with her to help our dying sport. She was glued to what I was saying, and as soon as I had finished she asked us to arrange a meeting with Dr Gideon Gono, the govenor of the Reserve Bank of Zimbabwe. She called him right away and summoned him to see me.

As I expected, there was an even higher level of security at the bank than there had been at the vice-president's house. I walked in with a gentleman who took us to an elevator. From there we went into a room, before being ushered into another room with doors on virtually on every side. Dr Gono eventually opened one of these doors and asked me to come in. I could tell he was a little worried, because he made a very conscious effort to make me feel comfortable. I could understand how many would have been intimidated by the surroundings, but I was just young Tatenda, a sincere-hearted boy.

Just like Joice Mujuru had been, Dr Gono was glued to my words when I started to speak. After a short while, he stopped me to ask how I spoke so confidently about events and allegations that I had no proof of. He must have laughed inside at my response: 'Sir, you have a team that can investigate what I am telling you and find out more.' That signalled the end of the meeting. At this stage he asked me not to make any further plans on going abroad, because I had told him that three teams from three different countries were waiting on my word before signing me up. I was happy to put on all my plans on hold as I waited for Dr Gono, who by this time had given me his contact details, including his private line. Every time we talk to this day he addresses me as 'My icon', which I dismiss.

As a young boy growing up in the streets of Highfield, I had never once imagined that one day I'd be meeting with such important government figures, even though I dreamed of being one of the country's best cricketers. Now I was virtually having daily meetings with ministers of the state. Most of them spoke to me in an effort to sway my thinking, but I managed to hold strong. All I wanted was cricket in the country to be sorted out, to be administered well and for the game's interests to be taken care of before individuals.

When word got out of my considerations, I was called in for an urgent meeting with Bright Matonga, the Deputy Minister of Information in Robert Mugabe's cabinet. The meeting was hastily arranged because he was supposedly travelling to China with the president that evening, and apparently had to see me beforehand. This seemed like good news, so I rushed to my destination with great expectance. Upon my arrival, once all the greetings were out the way, I wasted no time in explaining my decision not to continue playing for Zimbabwe. To my disappointment, someone had got to him before me, so there was nothing I could say that would be able to change the opinion he had already formed on the matter. I therefore just decided to listen as he spoke. On and on he went, until finally I could hold my peace no longer. I tried again to make him see the light, but he brushed it off without much thought.

Bright needed to get his passport photos done for his trip, so we took a walk. When we reached the downstairs entrance of the building, we bumped into a lady who was in charge of distributing farms for one of Zimbabwe's ten provinces, Mashonaland Central. It didn't feel like a coincidence.

'Comrade, where is Tatenda's farm?' Bright asked her.

I told him that I categorically did not want a farm, that I was happy making my money playing cricket. That's all I wanted sorting.

'Don't be silly young man,' he said, 'you can have your farm and enjoy the money from it.'

He didn't seem to get it. What on earth would I do with a farm? We both stood in silence for a while as it became clear that neither of us was willing to budge on the issue. We headed back upstairs.

When we returned to his office, Bright made his next move: he opened his desk drawer, pulled out a brown envelope and threw it towards me. Never normally a good sign. I had seen this type of thing in the movies, but never before in real life. I picked the envelope up to see what was inside before asking any further questions. What a mistake that turned out to be. What I saw inside was despicable, completely horrific. Inside were dozens photographs of dead people, and not people who had died of natural causes, but people who had died at the hands of violence. I made my way through the first five but could not continue any further than that, and instead pretended to look at the rest. I could not work out what his message was to me at this stage – was it a reminder of the War of Liberation, and how our people had perished at the hands of the white minority?

The meeting had gotten too heavy for me, and I could not tell where it was headed. I had gone in with so much hope, but this had knocked me back a fair bit. I left the meeting and for a while just wandered about town searching for answers from somewhere. Anywhere. I really was a defeated man. I came across a cathedral and decided to go inside. I needed some comfort from somewhere and hoped this would provide me with some. There was no one inside and so I took refuge on a bench. I just lay there and fell asleep. Eventually the janitor woke me and advised me to see a priest if I was so troubled. He was particularly rough in his approach, and so I left with no answers.

This was by no means the only threat I received during this period – the notorious Temba Mliswa was on my case as well. Temba was a well-known ZANU-PF activist, and had just become chairman of the newly-created Mashonaland West Province. He was very much on the side of Chingoka and Bvute, whom I and the other players had openly criticised. In fact, it was during a meeting with the Sports and Recreation Commission at a hotel in Harare – a meeting at which Peter Chingoka was present – that Temba made one of these threatening calls to me. He asked me if I knew who he was and proceeded to say I was a 'black boy being used'. When I interrupted his rant, he told me he knew where I lived and that he would come and beat me up. I was trying to sort out the problems in a dignified manner, and this is what I was getting in return.

The links between ZANU-PF and Zimbabwe Cricket were hidden slightly better than they are now, but I was no longer under any illusions. I was being threatened by the chairman of a new province in our domestic league, a man who was also a well-known ZANU-PF activist. These days they don't seem so fussed about hiding it.

On another occasion Temba got through to Loveness over the phone and got angry with her. Mliswa had been arrested for assault as recently as 2003, so it was no laughing matter that he was acting in this manner to my wife. Loveness was also receiving other anonymous calls threatening her, and she was terrified. Dr Gono had organised for guards to watch over my house, and I was given the numbers of officers of the Central Intelligence Organisation – Zimbabwe's secret police – close by.

One of these threatening phone calls led to Loveness and I moving ourselves and our two-week-old child Tatenda Junior, into a hotel for our own safety, before we eventually went to stay with friends. I wasn't going to be deterred in terms of fighting against injustice, but I had to take these threats seriously. We were thrilled that our first child had entered the world, but it came at a time of such difficulty, meaning it was hard to fully appreciate the moment. When people talk to me about their problems now I sometimes laugh to myself, thinking of what I had to go through. That period of time taught me the importance of just being free as a person. It was something my mum had said to me as a young boy when talking to me about growing up in a Zimbabwe no longer under colonial rule. I had lived my whole life free, but now I felt the opposite of it. There were cars constantly parked outside of where we were staying, and I couldn't walk around outside without looking over my shoulder. Real problems cannot be solved with money.

Perhaps the most frightening moment was not a call, but an encounter that Loveness had just three streets away from our house. She had recently given birth to TJ and was out on a jog, listening to some music to relax, when three cars pulled up beside her. All three cars were the same; it was a government motorcade.

Alarm bells started to ring. A man, most likely a bodyguard, got out and opened one of the backseat doors, and Joseph Msika – one of the two vice-presidents of the country at the time along with Joice Mujuru – emerged. 'Come inside,' he told my wife. Loveness motioned to take the headphones out of her ears so she could hear him properly, but all the while she was looking around for places to escape to. This was clearly not a friendly offer. In the end, she ran in the opposite direction from where the cars were facing, and headed straight for the main road. After a couple of cars ignored her signals for them to stop, a taxi driver eventually pulled over and picked her up.

Soon after, the intercom at our house rang and Loveness rushed in, frantic and unable to speak. I went out to the taxi driver, who had explained where he had picked her up and what she had told him. After she had calmed down Loveness and I drove out to the place of the incident, where a street vendor corroborated everything they had both told me. The cars had long since disappeared, but we couldn't carry on in this fashion.

I was waiting – hanging on – for a second meeting with Dr Gono. He had listened intently when I had outlined my issues to him initially and had promised to meet me again. He had provided me with security and a direct line to him. I was confident that he would come back to me with findings that backed up what I had told him. Unlike Bright Matonga, the last person I had spoken to, I believed he had taken me seriously and at face value.

When I met Dr Gono for the second time two weeks later, I could sense that something had changed. When he arrived at the meeting he had a thick file with him, the results of ZC's findings. We chatted for a while, but the way he spoke seemed to suggest that I should just continue playing for the national team, ignoring everything that had happened. Crazy, considering the threats that had been made to me and my family. He was far more jovial in his tone than he had been previously, far less serious and more diplomatic. In other words, it seemed as if he, like everyone else, was prepared to let the regime off the hook and look the other way.

That was too much to handle for a hot-headed little Highfield boy. I felt there was something he wasn't telling me, and those feelings only got worse when I got home to find the guards were not there. I knew I had to leave the country for my family's safety, because I could smell a rat. I was right about all the allegations.

Chingoka and Bvute were arrested for their actions early in December 2005 after handing themselves into police following a week on the run. The two had been accused of funding their lavish lifestyles on the proceeds of international cricket receipts. It wasn't just me making these accusations, there were a string of players and their colleagues making them. Confirming the news, Chief Superintendent Oliver Mandipaka said, 'They have been charged with contravening sections of the Exchange Control Act, and they will appear in court soon.' The investigations were thought to have been carried out by the Reserve Bank of Zimbabwe.

Bvute had allegedly bought himself a ranch-style house close to where Robert Mugabe was building his own retirement home, while both he and Chingoka were accused of recruiting friends and relatives for ZC staff jobs. Chingoka had been warned by many that Zimbabwean cricket would collapse if he didn't stop manufacturing race rows and cut back on expenditure. Ahmed Ebrahim, the vice-chairman, called a board meeting to discuss the situation and to appoint a temporary managing committee. There was also talk of hiring a forensic auditor to examine local and overseas bank accounts, so that the money spent by both of them could be traced.

I knew for a fact they had spent a couple of nights in prison, because Bvute later told me upon my return that he could never forgive me. 'You caused a great deal of stress to my mother,' he said without irony, as if it had been my fault for his dealings. I did not wait around to see what was going to happen to the pair, in fact I had already left for Bangladesh to play club cricket in Dhaka for a side named City Club. A contact of mine, Reaz Al-Mamoon, had organised everything for me. I would gladly return to play cricket for my country in the future, but changes had to be made before I did that.

Words cannot describe the pain of leaving my wife under such threats with a baby, but she wanted me to leave as soon as possible to minimise the risk. She would stay behind and sort TJ's passport. Loveness went to stay with her sister in Borrowdale. Every day I called her to find out how she was. She constantly cried because of a nervous condition she was suffering from, aggravated by the situation itself. A lot was going on for her. Post-natal depression was hard enough to deal with on its own, let alone everything else that was going on.

Despite the fuss I had caused, I don't think I really knew the power I possessed at the time. It was only in 2007, after I had returned to the fold, that Temba revealed this to me. The hierarchy desperately wanted to suppress my stand. Mike Atherton, England's captain during the 1990s, had his own say in the *Daily Telegraph*, the British newspaper: 'Taibu's departure is a severe blow to them (ZC): he is young, gifted, intelligent and black, and a product of ZC's development programme. It is not going to be easy to cast him as a traitor – although no doubt that the pro-government newspapers will try.'

As for my suspicions about the investigation, they proved to be correct. In January, it was announced that the Sports and Recreation Commission had suspended the twelve cricket board members who were backing the striking players and asked Peter Chingoka to continue to run the organisation. Gibson Mashingaidze, the commission chairman, said Robert Mugabe's government would not bow the demands of the strikers for the removal of Bvute and Chingoka. 'We can start afresh without you,' he said. 'You can all go and play in India or South America if you want.'

Judge Ahmed Ebrahim's attempts to persuade sports minister Aenas Chigwedere to appoint an interim management committee until the crisis had been resolved was turned down, and Ebrahim himself was forced from office.

This was the first time I had ever made my own stand against the powers that be in Zimbabwean cricket, and the way that events transpired was a big shock to me and Loveness, even accounting for what had happened to other players who had made similar protests. Still, I never felt scared or intimidated by these people, and at that time I think that frightened Loveness. I was well aware that what I was doing was dangerous, but I was 100 percent convinced that it was the right move to make, so I did not take a step back. I don't get afraid easily.

When you start getting calls from the vice-president, you know it's dangerous.

When you're scheduling meetings with the governor of the Reserve Bank, you know it's dangerous. When the same governor is giving you the numbers of all the CIO officers' in the area and his own private line, you know it's dangerous. Still I didn't stop. I had to make my point.

In February 2006, towards the end of my time in Bangladesh, I found out that sixteen of my teammates had agreed new contracts with Zimbabwe Cricket, thereby bringing the strike to an end. It contradicted everything they had previously said to me, when they had all given me their word and promised to back me as I made my stand. Betrayal is never easy to handle and there is no right way to accept it. I realised that I had been swimming across an ocean for players who wouldn't jump a puddle for me. I could have easily been selfish and secured the best deal for myself as captain. It's funny how the people you take a bullet for are often the ones behind the trigger.

Thomas Dangarembizi, a boy who I had grown up with and I considered to be my younger brother, kept me updated on all that was happening while I was away. Thomas himself was also doing his best to climb the first-class ladder and had just broken into the Manicaland team. He was in disbelief at everything that was happening in such a short space of time.

I can understand why they agreed to these contracts. The media reported that they had become compelled to sign as most of them were broke and weary, and simply did not have the energy to enter into a prolonged legal battle with the interim board. The board's refusal to even recognise our representative, Clive Field, did not help matters, as it meant they didn't have anyone to fight their corner.

Fear would have been another reason. One of the stories Thomas told me was pretty scary. He spoke of a meeting that had been held with the players at the CFX Academy at the Country Club in Harare while I was away. One of the figures the players were meeting made a point of bringing a gun with him just to let them know that he had access to one. He was never going to use it – he soon put it back in his car – but the point was that he wanted to scare the boys into submission.

At the conclusion of that meeting Thomas ran home as quickly as he could – through a shortcut we knew at the Country Club's golf course – and later decided to move to England. He wanted nothing more to do with the national team.

I understood that fear all too well, but what I didn't take lightly was the fact that I had originally wanted to make the stand on my own, and my fellow teammates had talked me out of that.

'Tatenda, we have to do this together, we stand by you.' The same people who had come to me and said this were now all too happy to sign a new deal and tell the others that they should return to play for their country. It was often because of false promises that were made to them, one of them being the captaincy, which was of course up for grabs in my absence. If they knew they didn't have it in them to continue their stand, then they shouldn't have offered themselves up in the first place.

Cricket is an entertainment industry, and the players are the commodity. They are the final product: they provide the entertainment, and they bring unity and hope to the country and its people. If the players stand together, most of the battle is won. If the stand had continued, the ICC would eventually have had to step in – they wouldn't have been able to ignore it, and neither would our government. We had the chance to change the game for the better in our country. It would have fostered a strong team spirit going forward as well. Anyone who has played international cricket will tell you that you can see the difference in unity from team to team. Clearly it has never been our strong point.

All of this reminded me of a question posed in a movie I had once watched: What is worse than murder? The answer was betrayal. I don't agree with that, but what happened during this period was certainly hard to stomach. Some of the players at the forefront of this betrayal did what was done to Andy a few years back. It made me wish I had never had the conversation with them in the first place.

The new deals were agreed despite the fact that the interim board had announced around a month earlier that Zimbabwe were to suspend themselves from the Test arena for a year while 'putting in place a programme to galvanise the development of the Zimbabwe squads'. The news was accompanied by a statement by Peter Chingoka, very much still involved in the major decisions:

The interim board have decided to suspend Zimbabwe's participation in Test matches until early next year. The decision to suspend participation in Test matches was reached by Zimbabwe Cricket after consideration of the recent performances by the national and A teams. The young team remain full of potential and hopes abound for their development into a strong and competitive performer in the Test arena. ZC are now putting in place a programme to galvanise the development of the Zimbabwe squads. They will work with other Test nations and the ICC itself to realise this objective.

Ahead of the ODI series with Kenya in February and March 2006, it was announced that Terry Duffin would captain the side under the leadership of the new national-team coach Kevin Curran, whom I had encountered at state level. Duffin had never played an ODI before and had only made his Test debut at the back end of 2005. It was reported that the decision to appoint Duffin had angered some of the black players who had signed new contracts, as they felt ZC had used them and subsequently broken promises. It only served to illustrate why I had fought against the board in the first place.

In Bangladesh, players such as Tushar Imran, Mehrab Hossain Jnr, Enamul Haque Jnr, Rajin Saleh and Sirajullah Khadim made the stay pleasant for me. We would have long discussions, not just confined to cricket, but on the differences between Christianity and Islam as well. Mehrab's father invited me around for dinner on numerous occasions, even on Christmas Eve. He was a man full of wisdom who was intent on seeing his son represent his country, and Mehrab Jnr achieved that feat later on that year in an ODI against Zimbabwe.

Gradually, the dust settled back at home. Like any other news, what had happened became history. I had arranged to spend the summer of 2006 in England playing for the Lashings World XI with a host of other former international cricketers, and for club side Pyrford, based in Woking on the outskirts of London. It was all organised by a friend of mine named Geoff Atterbury, and both my wife and TJ were able to join me in the UK. It meant we could all forget about the drama that had made us so miserable for a little while.

I kept totally away from Zimbabwean cricket and everything that was happening. The only teammate I shared my contact details with was Stuey, who was one of a declining group of players who were still holding out for what was right. When I silently re-entered the country, I found the time to pay him a visit, and he updated me on all the goings-on. It was Stuey who told me that some of the players had been promised the captaincy when I left, while others had been offered a higher-grade contract. One player had even found time to stick the knife in on me: 'Tatenda is the only guy who has financial security, why should we stand with him when we don't have anything?' The person in question was the sort of man to spend all his money on clothes and girls all over the world while on tour, while I'd save every penny I got. If you can't look after a penny, how can you end up looking after thousands?

Loveness managed to sort out TJ's passport while I did all the paperwork that was required for me to travel to the UK. I was always lucky to be associated with some of the best characters in the game: from the good hands of Reaz in Bangladesh to Geoff in England. We arrived in England in May, which was a shock to the system. I was to be a player-coach at Pyrford and I started my pre-season preparations straightaway. The team was comprised of nice, talented cricketers, but as sportsmen they were clearly unfit. On the first day back outside a couple of the players had to go behind the clubhouse to vomit following our warm-up. It was going to be hard to get anywhere with such appalling fitness levels.

In a foreign country far away from home with few people to socialise with, Loveness would often get bored during the day, so she started looking for a church where she could find fellowship with others. When she found one she invited me to come along with her. I enjoyed the discussions I had about preaching with the other members of the small congregation on the couple of occasions I did visit. It was working out well until one morning when I went to drop Loveness off on my way to a game. It was a glorious summer's day, but outside the church was a letter informing everyone that there would be no service – England's football team had a World Cup match to play. From that moment on we never attended one more service. We always believed that the word of God came first.

At times it was a difficult balancing act representing both Pyrford and Lashings, though the latter at least gave me a chance to still play alongside international cricketers of past and present. I played with the likes of Sachin Tendulkar, Richie Richardson, Chris Cairns, my ex-coach Phil Simmons, Rashid Latif, Chris Lewis, my ex-teammate Henry Olonga, Greg Blewett, Phil Defreitas, Russel Arnold and the England Women's captain Clare Connor.

The relaxed environment surrounding the Lashings side meant that on the playing side of things I had a very pleasant time. We did not have to do a warm-up and there was little order out on the field – anyone could walk in and do a job. Off the field, I found the environment uncomfortable. It seemed as if I was an easy target for the ladies – every other game I was approached by someone else, and they all made their intentions very clear. The fact that I was wearing a wedding ring didn't seem to make any difference.

One thing I didn't get much of an opportunity to do was to talk to Henry

Olonga in much detail about the goings-on back home, despite the fact that we were now playing on the same team again. I had always felt that our stands had been different, and he seemed reluctant to raise the subject. There was one occasion where we did both get talking to a Zimbabwean woman, who started to tell a story about how she used to have a farm and how she had lost it. Halfway through our conversation Henry got up and said, 'I can't listen to this,' and walked off. That was early on in the season, and I rarely broached the subject again. He was thousands of miles away from Zimbabwe, and I don't think he had been home since fleeing. It seemed it was something that he wanted to leave in the past.

Despite the alarming lack of fitness on show at the start of the campaign, I helped guide Pyrford to promotion. My teammates had been very respectful of the fact that I didn't like to drink and go to nightclubs during the campaign, so to celebrate our triumph I had my hair cut like Mr T – known for his role as B. A. Baracus in the popular 1980s television series *The A-Team* – and went out on the town with them all. It was such a brilliant atmosphere, and when they'd all had a few drinks they started to pour their hearts out to me about my game: 'Tibbly, as nice as it is for you to play here and help us to promotion, you are way too young to be leaving the international scene,' said one of the lads. 'Imagine what you could achieve from here if you go back and play for your country for another fifteen years.' For the time being I turned a deaf ear to such comments.

But players at Lashings were also encouraging me to return to the top of the game, especially when I sat down to tell my story. Nantie Hayward, a fast bowler who had represented South Africa on a number of occasions, was part of the Lashings squad and he suggested that I speak to Gerald Majola, the CEO of Cricket South Africa. He gave me his number so I could speak to him about the possibility of playing in South Africa now that the English season had drawn to a close. In fact, I liked the idea of eventually challenging Mark Boucher for his spot as wicketkeeper in the national side. There would have been a four-year waiting period, but I wanted to play international cricket again.

'I will never return to the Zimbabwe side and I want to play Test Cricket,' were my words at the time. 'South Africa is the best option.' I had provisionally agreed to play for the Cape Cobras at the end of 2005, but instead had to head to Bangladesh, and now both they and the Warriors were interested in signing me again. But just as I was about to sign up, Majola spoke personally to Ozias Bvute. Soon the news in the Zimbabwean press was that I was planning to settle in

South Africa.

I didn't enjoy the spotlight being back on me. It wasn't necessarily that Majola had been open about my plans to play in South Africa – I had revealed my intentions to the media myself – it was the fact that he had spoken to Bvute personally in detail about how I was going to execute my plan. That's what I didn't take kindly to. Me speaking out in the media was one thing; people could choose whether or not they took any notice of my supposed plans. But the CEO of Cricket South Africa talking to the chief executive of Zimbabwe Cricket? That was a far more serious matter.

It is worth noting as well how many journalists Bvute held influence over in Zimbabwe. It allowed him to use something against me following my very public stance against ZC. He could go to reporters and tell them that I was 'abandoning my country', and that's exactly the angle he pursued. It didn't matter that I had had to flee Zimbabwe for my own safety. I was somehow abandoning it. For him it was a perfect opportunity to turn the public against me, and I didn't want to give him the satisfaction. It also showed that I couldn't trust Majola, so I decided not to go through with the plan at all.

In the end I joined the Namibian set-up. I wasn't eligible to play in the occasional international match they had set up – again, I would have to sit out a waiting period if I wanted to do that – but I was able to play for them in the South African domestic competition. On the outset it was a puzzling decision, but Loveness was okay with it: it was close to home and the weather conditions were similar. Halfway through my time there I was named their captain.

Perhaps the best part of playing for Namibia was working with the great South African opening batsman Gary Kirsten, who had just finished his own playing career. He gave us some one-on-one coaching, and he changed my game in a wonderful way. His approach was very simple, but he had a great impact on my game. We tackled my weaknesses head-on, and it was then I realised that the only thing I feared was what I didn't know.

From the moment I started working with Gary my average rocketed to over seventy runs per innings for the second half of the season, a run which included back-to-back centuries. Gary himself joined the list of people who suggested I might consider going back to international cricket, telling how much talent I was wasting by sticking to domestic cricket. He believed that I'd now be able to impose myself at a higher standard of cricket.

What happened to me goes a long way to explaining why so many people in Zimbabwe lived in constant fear throughout Mugabe's regime, frightened of doing simple things such as voting. At the end of 2017, his 37-year reign finally came to an end when he stood down as president following mounting pressure.

One of the reasons Mugabe had faced pressure was because of his decision to sack his right-hand man, Emmerson Mnangagwa. Mnangagwa had fled the country after his sacking in 2017 but would later return to rule after Mugabe himself was ousted. That did not change the fact that the two had shared so much history and mostly shared the same political goals. Mnangagwa's reputation was made during the civil war between Mugabe's ZANU-PF and Joshua Nkomo's rival Zimbabwe African People's Union (ZAPU) party in the 1980s. As security minister Mnangagwa had been in charge of the Central Intelligence Organisation, who worked with the army to suppress ZAPU.

A victim himself of state violence after being arrested by the white-minority government in Rhodesia in 1965, Mnangagwa was influential in the campaigns of violence against the white farmers at the start of the 21st century and was also accused of masterminding attacks on opposition supporters during the 2008 elections. Morgan Tsvangirai, Mugabe's rival during that election, ended up pulling out of the presidential run-off shortly before it was held, saying that he couldn't participate 'in this violent, illegitimate sham of an election process'. This was despite the fact that he had won the first round of elections according to the government's own count. I remember that time well, and everyone seemed to accept that Tsvangirai had won – I don't think Mugabe himself denied that, but he stayed put anyway.

Much violence was used, as was often the case at such times. Tsvangirai had been repeatedly detained in the lead-up to the elections, while his party's chief strategist had been jailed on treason charges. According to estimates by doctors treating the victims of the violence, 85 opposition supporters had been killed.

Emmerson Mnangwa needed a legitimate election victory to distance himself from that regime and to prove to the Zimbabwean people that democracy was returning. At the end of July 2018, he ran against the MDC leader Nelson Chamisa. Shortly before the elections were set to place, I called an old friend.

'Are you registered? Are you going to vote?' I asked him. 'Yeah, I'll see,' was his response.

'You haven't answered the question,' I said. 'Are you registered? Are you going to vote?'

'Yeah, I'm going to vote.'

'Who are you going to vote for?'

'I'm not so sure.'

The first thing that came to my mind was that he was sacred of telling me who he was going to vote for. A lot of people in Zimbabwe like to keep it secret who they have voted for – and he may well have just been conforming to that tradition – but I suspected he might also have been worried about who I knew in government circles. Over the years I have constantly been in communication with a lot of different politicians, and people have therefore always been preoccupied with guessing which side I am on. As soon as they saw me pictured with Grace Mugabe, the former First Lady, they'd interpret it the wrong way. The mundane truth was our paths just happened to have crossed.

I could have picked up the phone and called the late Morgan Tsvangirai. Again, people would have interpreted that in the wrong way. I met the current MDC leader Nelson Chamisa when I was out in Zimbabwe in March of 2018. We started to chat because he knows me from cricket, and I know him as the leader as one of Zimbabwe's two main parties. People therefore wonder: if I talk to Tatenda, will he talk to them? The fear in Zimbabwean society remains.

What happened in the 2008 elections and at other points in our history has coloured the view I have of politics to this day. The definition of politics I have been exposed to is lies and corruption. I think most people in the country knew that Tsvangirai had won that election, but if Mugabe wanted to stay in power, the likelihood was that he was going to find a way to do so, and there was nothing the people could do about that.

Since the start of the 21st century Tsvangirai and the MDC have been the realistic alternative to ZANU-PF. Tsvangirai had formed the MDC – his Movement for Democratic Change – in 1999 and in February 2000 he helped defeat Mugabe's new proposed constitution, which would have given the government more power to seize farms from white farmers without providing compensation. He had campaigned alongside the National Constitutional Assembly (NCA), an organisation he had previously been chairman of. The NCA would gather individual Zimbabwean citizens and civic organisations in order to campaign for a new democratic constitution, realising the problems in the country were in part down to the Lancaster House Constitution in place.

When he first started to become a prominent figure, the street talk was that he wouldn't make a good leader. He was certainly popular because of the changes he was trying to make and the way he used to rally people, but he wasn't automatically thought of as leader of the country. But as things got worse and worse, he became more and more popular. When somebody becomes hungry, any change becomes accepted. He became the hope of the people, in many ways just because he represented change itself.

I did know certain people that wanted to Mugabe to continue, because at the end of the day there were certain things that he stood for, things they felt would have been compromised if Tsvangirai ever got into power. Mugabe stood against gay marriage and some other human rights laws. Certain people stood with Mugabe on these issues. 'We are Zimbabwe, we don't want to be like other countries' was the thought process. That was one group of people that wanted Mugabe to remain. The other group were those who would constantly just hark back to the old days and the war. Every conversation was based on, 'During the war, this is what he went through. During the war, this is what happened to him.' It was all about how we were with Mugabe when he won the war. I heard no other arguments from people as to why he should stay in power.

In the end, Emmerson Mnangagwa won the 2018 presidential elections, but there were once again rumours of fraud. Chamisa and the MDC spoke of 'gross mathematical errors' and sought either a fresh election or a declaration that he was the winner, though these allegations were later dismissed by the constitutional court. Though this election was not marred by nearly as much violence as campaigns gone by, there were still six reported deaths on 1 August after an army crackdown following the election results.

Throughout much of my career as an international cricketer, I felt as if I was virtually living in hiding, wondering whether certain eyes were watching my every move. Eventually, I started to realise that life was passing me by. People are always going to perceive things the way they want to perceive them, but I wasn't going to let that affect me anymore. I couldn't change what people thought, and ultimately, I couldn't change Zimbabwean politics.

*

12

Lone Ranger

THROUGHOUT MY EXILE, IT HAD BEEN EASY ENOUGH TO IGNORE those who told me to rejoin the national team. Whether it be my teammates at Pyrford and Lashings, or Gary Kirsten, who had done so for much my game, I found it easy enough to brush off their advice. There was no doubting they had my best interests at heart and sincerely wanted me to do well, but it was difficult for them to understand just how much water had passed under the bridge. The one person I found it difficult to ignore was Loveness.

Loveness was different. Unlike the others, she knew exactly the bind I was now in and the pain I had been subject to at the hands of Zimbabwean cricket. She had suffered with me throughout it all. I had found leaving Zimbabwe easy enough, but I still had my career. Even if leaving meant no international cricket, I was a man in demand across the world. For Loveness it was different, and she had struggled to settle in foreign lands. When I went out to play, what was there for her in these countries? Despite everything that had gone on, we were at our happiest in Zimbabwe where we could be close to friends and family. I knew that.

The person I first spoke to about a potential comeback was Farai Matsika. Farai was a director at Croco Motors, one of Zimbabwe Cricket's main sponsors. He wanted to have a meeting with me in Namibia and so we set up an appropriate date for both parties. I was impressed by Farai because he did not go round in circles, instead getting straight to the point: he invited me to come back and represent my country. He at least was prepared to put the past to one side.

The first thing we needed to do was to make sure we'd be both be safe – the last time I'd had any dealings with ZC Loveness and I had been receiving threatening phone calls from shady figures linked to the government. Once that was all cleared, I returned to Zimbabwe to finalise my contract. Everything seemed to be moving in the right direction until I saw on paper what was being offered to me. It wasn't about the money for me – I had made enough over my career and I now had other income streams – but I wasn't impressed, so I decided to walk away from the situation. My decision was more to do with principle.

In 2006, while I was still away from the set-up, Prosper Utseya had become the captain. Naturally, he had been given a contract in the highest band offered by the board. Despite the fact I had not played for a couple of years, I was fully expecting to be offered a contract in the same band as him upon my return. Instead, I was being offered one in the band below. I took offence at that. Both Prosper and I, and everyone else who knew anything about Zimbabwean cricket, knew that he wasn't a better player than me. I had a far more impressive record; it was as clear as day. It was as if I was still being punished, kept down, for the stand I had made against them.

Loveness had tried to be strong but packing to leave Zimbabwe again was the last thing she wanted to do. She had to take matters into her own hands. While I was back visiting my old school, she took the opportunity to take my phone and contact Farai herself. Was there no way of amending the contract in order to satisfy me? The problem, however, with negotiating was that Ozias Bvute and I would have to sit around the same table once again. Ozias had arranged all the video footage at my wedding, but since then I had been at the forefront of a campaign to get him to step down from his role as managing director and he had spent time on the run from the authorities alongside Peter Chingoka. There was now so much tension between us that it was difficult for us to be in the same room.

Farai called me and said Ozias wanted to meet me together with my wife. The meeting was to be held at Farai's house in Ballantyne Park. Loveness and Farai believed we needed to meet in person to get things moving in the right direction. I didn't know what to expect and I didn't know how it was going to help. Farai picked us up from town and we went to his house. Ozias was driving behind in his own car – hardly a standard meeting about a cricket contract. I felt very uncomfortable. That feeling did not go away when he started to speak. He was very angry and told me he was bitter towards me because he'd spent a night behind bars while investigations had been carried out. Apparently that was my fault.

I was at least used to the way he was acting. I remain convinced that he was a bully at school. With me, he always tried to play the emotional game. Whenever we had a meeting, the first thing he'd always do was curse me, and this time was no different. When I was starting out my international career, I used to react to these emotional tirades of his by shouting back at him. As soon as I did that he was winning. If we were having a reasoned conversation I'd have the upper hand, because he knew nothing about the game, but a frenzied argument would always favour him. He used to unguard me by playing the emotional game and for that reason we'd never actually finish our meetings – I'd walk out in anger, slamming the door on the way out. I wasn't going to let that happen this time around.

He went on and on about the night he had spent the night in the cells, bitterly fuming about the whole issue. Eventually Loveness could take no more of his accusations. She broke down in tears and left the room. Without her I could not continue in there myself, so after another period of silence I got up and went to shake his hand. I asked for forgiveness for all the pain he had professed to have gone through. I thanked Farai for the meeting and asked politely if he would drive us back home. On the way back he tried to dilute the drama, but in my own mind I had two points to digest: did they really want me back, or did they just want to set me up for a fall?

A few days later he called me and asked if I had forgotten the drama of a few days before. He had spent a lot of money trying to fix the situation and it was not his fault how Ozias had behaved. I told him I would sign the contract. It was official: I was back playing for my country.

It felt strange being back among my teammates, knowing what had transpired while I'd been away. I'd felt uncomfortable being back in a room with Ozias Bvute, and now I felt uncomfortable back in the dressing-room environment. Playing alongside players who had pretended to stand with me and subsequently betrayed me was as painful and awkward as one might imagine.

I made up my mind that I was going to mind my own business. I would have nothing to do with other people's affairs – my only duties now were to score lots of runs, take lots of catches and make a living for my family. I detached myself from everyone. My private life became completely private – I didn't become quite as private as the former England wicketkeeper Jack Russell, a notorious loner in his time, but I was very much there to play cricket and to play cricket only. I'm a very difficult person to approach if I want to be, and that part of me kicked in. I didn't allow for a situation to occur where I was speaking to my teammates about what had gone on. I just didn't.

Kevin Curran was now the national coach, a man who had never previously made life easy for me at state level. Still, with my new mantra of just playing and not paying attention to anything else, our lack of rapport never really bothered me. Ahead of my comeback against India A in a four-day warm-up match I was made to do a fitness test. I later found out that as usual I had outdone everyone else who had completed it. There were many eyes on me when I walked in to bat – I could feel that I had made a lot of enemies within the camp. I had to make a grand entrance, and that I did, being the only person to score a hundred in the game.

My return to the international arena was a three-match ODI series against our neighbours South Africa, a team still consisting of many of the same players who had riled me up so successfully the last time we had faced each other. Rather than let it get to me again, I remembered the conversation I'd had after the end of the series with Bruce Makova, how I should store up all the pain I was feeling and channel it into my batting. I started to focus intensely on that hurt until I made it resurface, and I locked myself into a state of pure concentration in the practice sessions before the first match. I hardly spoke to anyone during these sessions, and I was happy that no one even tried to bother making idle chat. I felt misunderstood and this helped me stay locked in a state of revenge.

I only managed 22 in the first game. In the second, I made 43. I was hardly pulling up any trees. However, something had clicked in that second innings. I'd heard people talk about batting 'in the zone' before, but up until that point I had never experienced it myself. I hadn't even made a half-century in that knock, yet I'd felt completely indestructible out in the middle. The feeling was so good that I felt I could do just about anything I wanted to do. After the game I passed by a local reporter and told him I'd score a hundred in the final game of the series. Against the likes of Makhaya Ntini, Shaun Pollock, Morne Morkel and Vernon Philander, that was quite some statement.

True to my word I made 107* off 103 deliveries in my final innings of the series, almost single-handedly driving my team to an unlikely victory. Nobody else made a score of above fifty. I shared a good partnership with my old friend Brendan Taylor, and he was constantly telling me not to give it away. All I can remember from that knock is the ball itself and the finer details of how it was behaving. While I was out there, all I could concentrate on was the ball; the seam of it, the rotation.

It felt like it was moving in slow motion, while everything else around was a complete blur. The feeling of being in the zone was quite overwhelming, so much so that whenever I finished an innings having been in that state I'd physically feel like I could not interact with any of my teammates. Instead I would have to take myself away while I recovered. I would literally go into the toilet and cry, and it is impossible for me to explain why. I never told my teammates about these episodes, I simply waited until I had calmed down and headed into the dressing room. I could never understand why it was like that, but I wish I could have batted in such a state all throughout my career. It was such an intense feeling.

It was very difficult to be all bubbly on the field, only to wear another character off it. I found it very tough to pretend that I didn't know what some of them had done to me. I knew that most people both in the team and upstairs didn't want me in the setup. It wasn't an impression I got; I knew it. I knew that even when I batted well or helped the team to win, not everyone was happy in the changing room. I could feel it in the changing room. I really didn't care either. I knew that every time I played well it was going to be painful for certain people. I used to say to Loveness, 'Whoever gets frustrated with me may end up in hospital.' My game was as good as it ever had been, and I was consistently scoring runs.

While I was in this rich vein of form Loveness started getting courageous and would choose to watch me from the presidential enclosure, somewhere where she'd never usually go. We wanted to let them know that their disdain wasn't affecting us. When I scored that hundred against South Africa that's where she was. She told me that though they wanted to celebrate, they just couldn't bring themselves to do it. The South African CEO was delighted, because my century had made it an interesting game, but our board members and administration were finding it difficult to celebrate my success.

I think I always felt free when I crossed the ropes, even if the reality was that I wasn't. I never allowed myself to become distracted. Early on in my career, when I was captain, I'd often look up to the changing room and think that the other players were depending on me to do well. That was not the case anymore. Now I looked up and wondered which ones wanted me to fail. I'd think about that every time I'd walk out to bat, and that only served to make me more motivated. I wanted to show them.

I was so detached from my teammates during this period that I even enlisted the help of a young boy named Clemence, a quiet kid who I always used to see roaming the grounds whenever we were playing. I asked him for a favour if I'd return one myself: if he was happy to give me throwdowns in the nets to help me keep my match sharpness, I'd teach him to become a first-class cricketer. It was too good an offer for him to turn down. We practised on a daily basis and even became close friends. I knew what he wanted to achieve and did not take any notice of the complaints people were making.

With so many people wanting me to fail, I knew I had to practise harder than ever before, and so I got contractors to start work on a cricket pitch in my back garden. Loveness once again went out of her way to help me, feeding the balls into the machine minute after minute, hour after hour. Sometimes we'd be there for four hours straight, until the point where blisters were forming on my hands.

As good as it felt to practise in these conditions, I believe it eventually did some damage to my batting. I would start to play around with aspects of my game, just to see how it felt doing things differently. There is working hard, and there is going overboard. Still, I was looking forward to getting back in the zone against the West Indies and Pakistan. But to my surprise, the feeling never returned. I managed a pair of fifties in Pakistan, including 81 in Hyderabad, but a return of 209 runs across nine innings was nothing to write home about. I could not understand where the feeling had gone. I thought it'd would be easy to rediscover it, but instead it disappeared without a trace.

One morning while I was taking a walk with Loveness around the neighbourhood, I received a call from a man who had been particularly aggressive to me before my retirement: Temba Mliswa. Temba, a ZANU-PF activist, had been behind a number of threatening calls we'd received. He'd described me as a 'black boy being used' when I was standing up for what was right, and he'd also threatened to beat me up. Now he wanted to set-up a meeting. The call brought back memories we hoped we could bury in the past. Loveness was not for it and neither was I, but there were certain pieces of the puzzle that still did not make sense. The only way to change that was to meet him.

I assured her of my safe return, and for that reason alone the meeting had to be in a public space or at the house of someone I trusted. We subsequently met at the house of a friend of mine, Mark Manolis, a few evenings after. We talked for a few hours as I tried to get to the bottom of why so many threatening calls had come my way. He seemed to be suggesting that the stand I had taken was the correct one, but he still seemed so blinded to the bigger picture. He was being particularly evasive.

Eventually I had to get to the point: 'Temba, if you're saying I was fighting for the right cause, then why did I get all those threats?'

'Young man, you have many things to learn about,' was his response. 'Your strength is actually your weakness.' I did not understand what he was going on about, and I didn't want to pretend like I knew either, so I asked him to explain further.

'We had to instil a lot of fear into you, because you had no idea how much power you possessed. When you do something, you do it wholeheartedly and that's why people follow you. You have no idea how many people are willing to follow you. Your innocence is what people followed, but your innocence doesn't think from the head. Instead you just act from the heart. One way or another it was going to trouble your heart and you were going to throw the towel in, and that is what eventually happened.' I was very sad to hear that, and had little left to say apart from, 'I'm not a politician, I'm just a player who wants to be world number one someday and make everyone proud.'

I also felt anger towards him. Temba had effectively confirmed that he and Mugabe's Deputy Information Minister, Bright Matonga, had been tasked with instilling fear in me so I would eventually back down. He made it sound like it was all just a game to them, and maybe it was. I was thinking, 'This is someone's life you're talking about.' It was like we were just playing a game of chess, and that was deeply unfair. I respected the fact that he came clean and admitted he had been wrong, but I still didn't like the fact that it all just came across as one big game to him. Loveness was relieved to see me back home. She was not at all interested in what I had just found out. If she had had it her way, I'd have never gone to the meeting in the first place. She reminded me of what we had promised each other on my return: my job was to play cricket and that was it.

13
The IPL

PREPARATIONS FOR OUR TOUR TO PAKISTAN AT THE START OF 2008 for ODIs were greatly disturbed by several team meetings discussing whether we should go at all. Security in Pakistan had long been a concern for touring teams: at the end of 2007 the opposition leader Benazir Bhutto had been murdered in Rawalpindi, highlighting the instability in the country and the threat of terrorism. The threat led to Australia postponing their tour in 2008, before the unthinkable happened in 2009 when the Sri Lankan team bus was attacked by twelve gunmen as they travelled to the Gaddafi Stadium in Lahore. Six of the Sri Lankan team were wounded, while six Pakistani policemen and two civilians were killed in the tragedy.

I did not utter a word in any of these meetings, instead I just listened and marvelled at a mixture of some good and some silly points. I had already done my deal with the boss. While the others were signing for a compensation fee for their families if anything was to happen to them on tour, I was getting Zimbabwe Cricket to pay for my family to travel over with me. If anything were to happen to the players, their families supposedly would have received $50,000 each. But if anything awful did happen, I did not trust them to release this money. That's what it had come to. Instead I agreed a deal with Peter Chingoka that the board would pay for my family to be out there. The tour had the highest level of security I had ever seen: everywhere you looked, there was a soldier with a gun. I did not worry for our safety as a family.

During our stay at our first hotel on tour, our manager gave me his phone to speak to someone on the other end of the line. As usual I thought it'd be a reporter looking for a comment, so I was delighted when I was presented with the news that my name was among those to participate in the opening year of the much-talked about new cricket tournament, the Indian Premier League. Twnety20 cricket had actually first started in English domestic cricket in 2003 and had become popular enough that the first World Cup in the format had been held in South Africa in 2007. Now the world's biggest cricketing country was getting in on the action with a franchise-based competition, and the sums of money being discussed were mind-blowing. I rushed straight up to my room to tell Loveness the news. Needless to say, she was as pleased as I was.

That same night, with my new venture still on my mind, Loveness and I were kept awake by a swarm of insects in our room. In total I slept about an hour throughout the night before our match the next day. Our team manager even suggested I sat out the game when I informed him of what had happened, but I wasn't having any of that. Instead I walked out to bat at number four having not even done a warm-up.

I tried to hit a few boundaries in the powerplay upfront, but I felt as if all my strength had left me. I had to devise a different plan, so informed my batting partner Hamilton Masakadza that he was going to have to run hard with me. I needed to manipulate the field. In the end he made 87 and I made 81, and we shared a partnership of 137. Hamilton wasn't the quickest between the wickets, but he was a good judge of a run.

I got the green light from Zimbabwe Cricket's CEO to head to the IPL in April 2008, even though it meant missing a chunk of our own domestic competition. After the Twenty20 World Cup it had become clear that this format of the game was here to stay, and it was also clear that it would be hugely beneficial to me as a player to spend time with some of the best players in the world. In the 2007 World Cup we had failed to progress beyond the group stages due to net run rate, but we had won one of our two games against Australia of all teams. By some way the best side of this era, Australia had strolled to the ICC Champions Trophy in India in 2006, winning the final by eight wickets, and had been just as comfortable a year later in the 2007 World Cup in the West Indies, winning the final by 53 runs. For the time being though, as teams worked out the best method for the format, Twenty20 had created a sort of level playing field for the international game.

I think every team had the same gameplan, especially when it came to batting: one guy tried to stay there throughout, anchoring the innings, while everyone else around him played with a bit more freedom. I was the one originally tasked with this anchor role, though I failed to make a significant contribution in either of our games against England or Australia. Instead it was my good friend Brendan Taylor who saw us home against the latter, scoring 60* off 45 balls as an opening batsman to guide us to our target of 139 with a ball to spare. Teams were also fairly rigid with their bowling plans at this early stage: the first six overs, the powerplay overs, were when the seamers were used, followed by the spinners in the middle and then the seamers again at the end. Every team played like that, and that helped us in the beginning.

One person I did not see eye to eye with was our new coach Robin Brown, who had taken over from Kevin Curran towards the end of 2007. Robin would lead us to our 2007 triumph over Australia, and like me he had been a wicketkeeper who had captained Zimbabwe, but that is where the similarities ended. Our relationship was so poor that most of the time we didn't even bother to greet each other. As long as I did not stand in his way and he did not stand in my way, it was fine by me. We both somehow found a way to get the best results working like that, and funnily enough I actually played some of my best cricket for Zimbabwe with him at the helm.

Arriving in India, I was ecstatic to be a part of such a big tournament. There was such a hype and a buzz around the competition, with star names from all over the globe travelling to play. Players with different backgrounds and different styles of play were brought together by one trait: success.

I had signed for the Kolkata Knight Riders, who were co-owned by Shah Rukh Khan, one of India's leading film stars. Every team had many media duties to fill, but Khan's fame meant that we had to engage in a particularly high amount. I soon became his ten-year-old son's favourite player, as my diminutive height made him believe that we were the same age. Who knows, maybe it was even the reason I was offered a three-year contract in a squad bulging full of international stars.

Ricky Ponting, Brendon McCullum, Chris Gayle, Umar Gul, Angelo Mathews, Brad Hodge, Shoaib Akhtar, Brad Hodge, David Hussey, Ajantha Mendis, Mohammad Hafeez and Salman Butt were the other international players in our squad that year. It was a collection of some of the finest shorter form cricketers in the world, and there were just four spaces for overseas players in each team. We also had a host of Indian internationals at our disposal: Sourav Ganguly, Ajit Agarkar, Aakash Chopra, Ishant Sharma and Cheteshwar Pujara, to name a few.

Our coach was John Buchanan, who had led Australia through their golden age. I had never played with such a talented group in my career to date, and I had to try my best to get a game.

John Buchanan was a good coach, and he was complemented well by his assistant Matthew Mott. He preferred a hardworking individual to one who simply relied on his talent, and as much as he tried to hide his frustrations with Shoaib Akhtar, it did not take a rocket scientist to realise that he would have swapped the iconic fast bowler for a more average player who actually bought into the team environment in an instant.

You never get a second chance to make a first impression. My chances of playing a single game that year were next to none, but no one has ever lost anything by trying their level best, so I did all that was required of me. There was no chance of me getting in the team as a wicketkeeper with McCullum and a young Wriddhiman Saha in the set-up, so I devoted all my time to my batting and fielding. Most of our squad worked extremely hard, but some of those who were not featuring soon ran out of patience. I did not allow that to happen to me. I had to be ready if I was called upon. I was only in India for a month, so even if I wasn't required, my practice would prove useful further down the line. Matthew Mott in particular was a great help to me. We called him Braveheart for his resemblance to Mel Gibson, and he kept saying to me, 'Keep going, you are building a strong case.' Due to the size of the squad we could play warm-up games against each other, and in these games I was never dismissed while at the crease.

The players that impressed me most during my time in India were Pujara, Gul and Ponting. Pujara was in a similar position to me; he was struggling badly for game time, even though he was a homegrown player. He was also the other player in the squad to match my work ethic, sometimes bettering it. He wasn't in the national team at this stage, but I remember constantly hitting balls to him in fielding practice until even I was tired. He was not wearing gloves, and we were using a normal ball, but he would just carry on catching and catching. He would never drop any either. I never actually asked him, but I'm pretty sure he had a set number of balls he felt he had to catch each day. I remember saying to him, 'You're not dropping anything, what's the problem?' Still he would keep catching and catching. I liked that about him.

I learnt a lot from Ponting; he was a natural leader. He would never wait for a coach's instruction, he was always proactive in training. He immediately noticed the work ethic Pujara and I had and used us to help get fielding drills going. The coaches would then get into place and we'd be up and running. As someone who had been Indian captain, Ganguly was also an imposing, almost bossy character. The guy could clearly play, but technique-wise you would not put him in the same category as McCullum or Gayle. He had so much inner belief though; he convinced himself he could do what they did, and I liked that.

Umar Gul was another who would leave no stone unturned. He had taken the most wickets at the 2007 T20 World Cup, and over the next couple of years he would establish himself as the world's best bowler in the format. It was not hard to see why. He'd practise his bouncers fastidiously, and when it came to bowling at batsmen in the nets he would bowl these bouncers over and over again before reverting to a good length. That was different to what I had witnessed in Zimbabwe, where bowlers would just go with length from the off. In his own time, he would practise bouncers, good length deliveries, slower balls and then his trademark yorker, the most accurate yorker in world cricket. He would go through the same routine religiously. He didn't get much movement in the air with the ball, but it wasn't hard to see why he picked up so many wickets. He'd groove his skills over and over again. A real artist.

We got so many freebies from our sponsors over the month: Tag Heuer watches, home theatre systems, laptops. It was simply impossible to bring everything home. We left loads and loads of cricket equipment behind. It was extremely difficult to do anything outside of our games – it was even a mission to get past the entrance gates of the hotel without the paparazzi spotting you. One day, we decided to go against advice and left the hotel to do some shopping. I disguised myself and used the back entrance, while Loveness braved it and went through the front.

Yet despite my disguise and the density of the crowds, someone quickly noticed me when we got to the shopping mall. He did not approach me, but I could tell by the way he reacted that he was well aware who I was. I told Loveness that we needed to leave right away. We had not yet bought anything, so we went up another level and entered a shoe shop. After a minute so I looked towards the door to see a throng of people gathered at the window. I asked the owner of the shop to lock the doors as security were called. In the end we had to be escorted to the cars surrounded by police.

I had plenty of interesting conversations with other members of the squad throughout the course of the tournament. The players could not understand why I never watched television and wanted to know why I didn't. David Hussey was particularly interested, and after I'd explained to him that I didn't think that most of the shows were suitable for my children, the conversation soon turned to religion. He was an atheist, a believer in the Big Bang theory. On the contrary, I believe in the story of Adam and Eve and that we all come from the same family tree. Since he is white, and I am black, he found this difficult to comprehend. Many players gathered around to listen to us, and it wasn't long before my teammates started calling me 'brother'.

On one of the last days of the tournament, I walked into a room and passed a big mirror. I saw someone, but did not recognise that someone to be me, so I walked back to take another look. I had my chest and arms pushed out; a pompous posture which I despised. 'That's what living the life of a celebrity does to you,' I thought. You start to think you are better than the next person. This was actually happening without me even being aware of it. I lowered my shoulders and started to walk normally again.

The IPL changed how I saw the game in many ways. I remember I even started to cut off part of my bat handle after the tournament, because it was something that I had seen Ricky Ponting do. I had asked Ricky why he did it, and he had told me that if he didn't cut his handle shorter, he'd never feel like he had completed a drive, because the top of the handle would always hit his arm further up as he followed through with the shot. Chopping a little bit from the top of it prevented this from happening. I took his bat and tried his theory, and it worked. From then on, I started cutting my bat handle and felt like I was completing my shot more fully. The IPL was and still is all about the sharing of information as much as anything else: you pick a leaf from this tree, a leaf from that tree, and who knows what you end up coming back with.

I felt in excellent condition when I returned to Zimbabwe and started playing warm-up matches again, and I started to really challenge myself. Once I'd reached a certain score, I'd set myself targets, like hitting three sixes in an over. It gave me an idea of how players pushed themselves to the next level, and I started to wonder what more I could achieve in the game. Unfortunately, we weren't playing a lot of matches at the time, which didn't allow me to capitalise much on any of that.

I may not have played much, but purely being selected as part of a squad in the IPL was a huge achievement for me. I think I am right in saying there were only six

Africans in total in the first year of the competition, and I was the only Zimbabwean. That was a big thing for me. Going through what I had been through, as well as not playing as many international matches as other players by virtue of playing for Zimbabwe, meant being selected was definitely an achievement.

I also enjoyed the professionalism of everything compared to Zimbabwean cricket. From the moment they contacted to tell me I had been auctioned, from the time I got on the plane, everything moved in a straight line. You didn't have to worry about anything but the game itself. Everything was in place. I was coming from a place where all things being equal you had to go out your own way to make sure certain arrangements were in place. To be able to practise the correct amount I had to build my own net at home. In India, the nets are ready for you at any time; bowlers are ready to bowl at you; pitches are ready for use instantly. It wasn't the same back home.

A word from John Buchanan, Kolkata Knight Riders Head Coach:

I was appointed to Kolkata Knight Riders as their coach for the initial season of the IPL by Lalit Modi, the founder and former commissioner of the league. I am not sure how these appointments were made, but it happened only a couple of weeks before the first auction. I was unable to attend the auction as I was engaged in a conference at Sanctuary Cove, on the Gold Coast at the time with my business, Buchanan Success Coaching.

I do recall being asked to provide my opinions on the type of player and some names of players that I thought we should be chasing in the first auction. I remember being called during a presentation I was giving, and so I had to put it on hold. When I was able to call back, there was pandemonium on the other end of the line: my excited contact informed me we had just purchased Shoaib Akhtar. I must say, I did not share the same excitement, as I did not see Shoaib being the type of player we wanted to build the franchise with – certainly an exciting player, but nonetheless one prone to inconsistency in performance as well as inconsistent on-field behaviour. However, I was informed that the owner of the franchise, Shah Rukh Khan, wanted him and so that was that. I did to get to spend some time with Shoaib that first year and found him to be a pleasant young man, but a young man who seemed to be unable to tell right from wrong, and so consequently Shoaib was surrounded by a whirlpool of darkness from which there was no escape.

Sourav Ganguly was Kolkata's icon and captain of the team. Gayle, McCullum, Hodge, Ponting, Mendis, Mathews, Hussey, Ishant, Dinda and Saha all quickly became part of the squad as well. And of course, there was the diminutive Tatenda Taibu.

I had briefly seen 'Mr T', as he became affectionately known, around the group on the couple of occasions Australia had played Zimbabwe while I was coach. I was always impressed by his approach and attitude to the game. He was a person who trained assiduously to improve his game, and he was a leader by the example that he set. So, I must say I was very happy to see him named in our squad.

However, the difficulty for Mr T in the IPL was that the rules only allowed four foreign players on the field in any game, and of course if McCullum wasn't keeping, this job went to 'Pops' Saha. This meant that Tatenda was then competing for a batting spot against all the big-name international players. However, this never seemed to concern him. He would train just as hard, prepare just as much as anyone else, in case there was an opportunity to play. As coaches we knew of his value in the T20 format – not the biggest hitter when compared with Gayle, McCullum, Hodge and Hussey, but he was creative. He was an inventive player. He was a real competitor who could get the most from a good array of skills. Mr T was also energetic in the field and brought a lot to the squad in our training and dressing-room times.

During our time together, I had the opportunity to talk with him a little about his life in Zimbabwe, why he had left the country, and what his future might be. It was in these precious moments that I began to understand the incredible courage in this young man and his wife. In a country that he loved there was always danger. To not acknowledge the Mugabe regime, especially as a young black man, was especially dangerous. But he plied his trade for as long as he could, representing Zimbabwe in Test and one-day international cricket.

However, he was eventually forced to leave and resettle himself and his family, using his cricket skills to live the life of a nomadic professional player. So, Mr T, Tatenda Taibu was a person we all loved to have as part of the Knight Riders. Unfortunately, he was not retained in our second year, and interestingly that coincided with a far less successful year for the franchise.

I look back on my time in cricket, the people I have had the great fortune to meet, and I count Tatenda Taibu as one of those special people who showed me a lot about life and making the best of what you have.

14
Fight After Fight

MY RELATIONSHIP WITH ZIMBABWE'S NEW COACH, ROBIN BROWN, was not the same as my relationship with John Buchanan. Brown, who had played seven ODIs for Zimbabwe between 1983 and 1987, had been our assistant coach at the 2007 World Cup, before taking over from Kevin Curran in August of the same year. I would never look down on any coach of mine, even though I had worked with others of a higher reputation, but I felt that Brown did not allow me to express myself. It was like we all had to be mechanical, which was a huge frustration for me. There seemed to be no room for that extra bit of flair that the top teams often possess. He wanted me to do things as he said; the problem was I didn't agree with him on certain things. I didn't agree with a lot of my coaches over the years, and it is okay to disagree. With Brown, I felt that if I disagreed with him he would say that it was because of the IPL. Money was often talked about, and the impression he was giving was that I was being arrogant, which was not fair.

Coming back to play in the domestic competition in 2008 after the IPL was a pretty unsatisfying experience. It seemed that the bowlers were slow, and I had always been one to struggle to motivate myself in easy games. I could not wait to play international cricket again so that I could apply all the extras which I had learnt during the IPL.

A return to Zimbabwe also meant a return to the bitter cricketing relationships in my life, and it wasn't long before Ozias caught wind of the problems that existed between me and Brown. Naturally, the fact that the most experienced player in the squad and the team manager were not seeing eye to eye was a problem to him, and one that had to be sorted out. He got us to sit around a table with team manager

Givemore Makoni and another selector so that we could sort out our differences. Things did not go to plan.

In truth, by this time I was so frustrated with everything that I was a little bit unstable. I had a new-found faith – I was trying to be a Christian – and it was a confusing period for me. It had got to the stage where I no longer wanted to talk to Brown, and I had told him so. I told Ozias that I was not going to speak to the coach at the meeting either, and that sooner or later he might have to have a think about who he wanted to keep in the set-up – me or him. He insisted we met at the Rainbow Towers hotel anyway. As team manager Makoni tried to say a few words, but I paid absolutely no attention. I was then asked a direct question – I can't remember what it was – and I didn't answer. That gave Brown his opportunity: 'See, this is what I was talking about. Poor upbringing.' Something along those lines. His suggestion was that I had not been raised correctly.

He had said the wrong thing to the wrong person. In my mind I was thinking, 'What have you just said about my parents?' That was the first thing that registered with me, so I thought it best for me to just get up and go. I got up and started walking out, but just as I got close to the door I thought, 'No, I can't allow someone to speak about my parents like that.'

I remember shouting, but I do not remember what I said. Words were simply flying out of my mouth, and the whole restaurant had their eyes fixed on me. I carried on. I was beyond angry, but I still don't know how I ended up in a position where I was holding a knife to him. That, though, is was happened. What I do remember is the waiter grabbing me and taking the knife out of my hands. The whole restaurant had gone completely silent. There were two waiters there holding me back from my own national team's manager. I was standing right by him, holding a knife to him. He had gone completely red, no doubt petrified by my reaction. Everyone was stunned into silence, and I could hardly blame them. I had to get out of there. I just asked Givemore to drop me home. There wasn't another meeting arranged after that. I was incredibly lucky that the story did not make newspaper headlines.

Our next games scheduled were to come in Canada, where we participated in a quadrangular T20 series with the hosts, Sri Lanka and Pakistan. As usual with foreign tours, we had to go through the rigmarole of sorting our visas. When it came to my turn for my interview at the Canadian embassy, a guard came looking for me. He asked me to go to my car outside right away. The architect who was helping us with our house renovations was waiting outside with Loveness; they had both followed us there.

Loveness was in such tremendous pain she was struggling to speak, and we weren't sure why. Her mouth was so dry and all she could do was sit there and hold her stomach. I could not understand how she had got so bad in the thirty minutes I had been inside the embassy. We needed to get her to hospital, so I asked her sister Mercy to drive her while I went to our home to pick up TJ, who was being looked after by our maid.

I rushed to the bank to collect some funds in the event she needed an operation, only to find that none were available to me. In Zimbabwe, if you can afford to get private healthcare, you get it. The government system does not run smoothly, so it's advisable not to take the risk where someone's life is concerned. I had always left a certain amount of money in my account before the 25th of each month – when we got paid by Zimbabwe Cricket – in case of emergency. I had taken out all our funds on the 24th so I could pay for renovations to the house in the knowledge I'd be receiving my monthly wage the next day. It was now the 29th and there were no funds in my account. I had not been paid. I headed straight for the ZC offices to sort it.

When I arrived, I was asked to go into town and raise the issue with Esther Lupepe, who was the head of finance for ZC – she was sorting out our tickets for Canada. I didn't have much time to explain what was going on, so I called her on my way to let her know what the situation was. When I arrived at her offices, she asked me if I would come upstairs with her so that we could speak together in private. I did my best to explain in the shortest time possible what was happening; it was an urgent matter. Zimbabwe is not a first-world country so for anything to move you have to have cash in your hand. I'd lost my place in the hearts of a lot of ZC workers because of my early retirement and the ructions that caused in 2005, but I expected her to have some sympathy towards Loveness's situation. She hadn't done anything wrong. But Mrs Lupepe was not moved by my plea to get the issue resolved.

I had not gone there to borrow money from them, I was after the monthly wage that I was owed. All I wanted was for the bank, myself and a ZC representative – her in this case – to sit down and map a way forward. I told her in no uncertain terms that we were going to the bank. I didn't mind whether we used her car or mine, but we were going to go right away. I could not believe it when she remained seated, so I grabbed her by the arm. As she told me that she was not going anywhere until she finished what she was doing, my phone rang. It was our team manager, Givemore Makoni, asking where I was. I had an interview to do. I told him everything that was happening. 'Tiba,' he said, 'they are looking for you to make one slip up and they will have you, don't give them an excuse to destroy you.' I was holding her arm the whole time I was on the phone; Makoni asked me to leave her alone and promised to sort the matter himself.

I left the scene right away and went back to the hospital to explain the situation. I obviously wasn't able to pay the hospital anything yet, but I hoped they would have started the operation anyway on account of my name. I really hoped she wasn't in the same condition I had left her in. It seemed Loveness was having an ectopic pregnancy, a complication in the process when a fertilised egg implants itself out of the womb, usually in one of the fallopian tubes. An ectopic pregnancy tragically leads to a miscarriage. Dr Matshaba was Loveness's usual doctor, but she was in Botswana at the time and the only other female gynaecologist we knew of was in Zambia.

This was becoming a particularly complicated case because none of the hospital's machines were picking up what was happening to her, but the symptoms were all pointing to an ectopic pregnancy. I was told there were only two doctors who could perform the operation she would need. At first they needed to perform a procedure to check that she was having an ectopic pregnancy, and if she was then she would need keyhole surgery performed under general anaesthetic to remove the fertilised egg, usually along with the affected fallopian tube.

We started trying to locate the two doctors. The first one was out of the country, and the last doctor, our last chance, had retired from his profession a year beforehand. However, upon hearing it was me, being a cricket lover, he came out of retirement just to perform the operation. Throughout all this time when we were having discussions about the operation, TJ was sat in the car. I was not going to be allowed in the hospital room during the operation anyway, so when they saw how worried I was they asked me to go home and get some rest with my son. Before that I sat for a little while in the car and started to replay the whole drama.

The drama of all the threats, moving from country to country and the breaking of records had not hushed the hunger and thirst for peace in my soul. I felt bad for how I had tried to force Mrs Lupepe to go to the bank with me, so I called her and apologised for my actions. I should not have tried to force her to do something against her will, no matter how serious the situation. It was unacceptable behaviour. I told her I was trying to be a Christian and that I had failed to be one in that situation. I asked her to pass on the same message to her husband, which she said she would. But that was not the end of the matter – on the way home I received a call from a policeman. He wanted me to meet him down at Avondale Police Station.

I went there right away with TJ fast asleep in the back of the car. I parked inside the station, opened the windows and walked inside. The first policeman I saw on the door commanded me to take my shoes off with such hostility. I smiled at him, assuming that he was joking. 'You don't see me laughing, do you?' he shouted. As I was still in a state of shock another policeman walked past and said to the other, 'Leave the young man alone.'

I asked if they could be quick as I had my young boy in the car. That seemed to surprise them – did I not have a maid at home? I told them I had asked her to go home. It was just me and my boy and I didn't want to leave him waiting.

Finally, one policeman said, 'Let the boy go, there is no issue here.' Another one walked me to my car. While we walked he told me everything he knew on the promise that I would not reveal what he was saying to me. Firstly, he told me that this issue had been brought all the way from town to Avondale. Secondly, he revealed that the police had received a letter from a private doctor stating that Mrs Lupepe's hand had been broken when I had grabbed it at the offices. His last point was that the police had been informed that I had dragged her against her will. According to his information, Mrs Lupepe had not wished to take the matter any further, but three unnamed gentlemen did. I thanked him for telling me all he knew and started on my way home to make sure I had enough time to prepare some food for Loveness for that evening.

Later that evening I went to visit my lovely wife. Children weren't usually allowed in the hospital ward Loveness was staying in, but they made a special exception for TJ that night. When we saw her she was crying, telling me how lonely it was in there. Also of real concern to me was the fact Loveness had asked them to pray before she had been put to sleep, and one lady had said, 'This has nothing to do with God – this is science, young woman.'

I gave her the soup that I had made and brought some hill songs for her to listen to. She would cry every time I visited until the nurses started allowing me to stay a little longer. Meanwhile, TJ stayed at my sister-in-law's house. When Mercy and I were both at the hospital, Loveness would always make sure to ask her whether I myself was eating well enough. When I subsequently told her about what had occurred with the police, she got very upset. We spoke at length on the subject, and she believed that it was only going to get worse. I was so angry at how the whole situation transpired that I wanted to pull out of the Canada tour, but it was she who talked me into going in the end. She thought it better to be treated wrong for doing the right thing rather than retaliate.

My heart had been so crushed that the way I started acting was unacceptable to say the least. On the one hand I was trying to walk with God, and on the other hand I had all these emotions to fight after what had happened a few days beforehand. I was called again by the police, but this time I left the matter in the hands of my lawyer, Jonathan Samkange.

Loveness was soon discharged from hospital, and I did not feel good leaving her behind while she was unable to walk, but it was her idea for me to go on tour, so I complied. In the end I ended up our top scorer in two of our four games: 40* from 40 balls against Sri Lanka and 37 from 38 against Canada. Unfortunately, we could only draw against the latter, which given the respective cricketing histories of the two nations was pretty humiliating. I was a bubbly character on the field in my role as wicketkeeper, and ultra-silent in the changing room.

I still had not been repaid the funds I had used for Loveness to come to Pakistan. Eventually I decided to stop minding my own business – I needed my money and I was not taking any explanations. I was fed up with being patient. It is often said that two wrongs don't make a right, and that is the truth. It did not make me a better cricketer, nor did it make my journey to find peace in my soul a smooth one.

By this point Zimbabwe had long since stopped playing Test Cricket, so we had to play as many fifty-over games as possible to try and keep pace with the game as it continued to evolve. It almost didn't matter who we were playing, as long as we were getting enough cricket. After a 5-0 defeat to Sri Lanka, we were invited to a tri-series with both them and Bangladesh in Bangladesh. It was nice to return to familiar grounds; Bangladesh had become a second home to me. My old friend Reaz Al-Mamoon had his house open to me throughout the tour, even though he was no longer involved in cricket. I even took a few of my teammates there. On the cricket field it proved to be a somewhat difficult series for batsmen – it was at the back end of winter, so a score of around 200 was often enough to win you the game.

Our next stop following on Bangladesh was Kenya. Upon arrival, my cricket equipment could not be located. There were efforts made to locate my bag, but I had already decided by then to pull out of the series, which did not go down well with my seniors. I was called in for a meeting with my old friend Ozias Bvute. When I got there, he was keen to discuss the issue at hand but surprisingly also wanted to learn more about my faith. After much discussion he said, 'There is a lot of maturity in your talk, let's pray,' and so he and I – foes in the past and soon to be foes again – knelt down beside one another. When I got up to walk out, he asked me what it would take for me to play. I said I needed a thigh pad and a pair of shoes. I could borrow the rest of the kit from my teammates – I'd explain what happened to my sponsors in my own time – but I needed a specific size in both these items.

Ozias flew back the next day, and I never received either my thigh pad or my trainers. Cricket is not particularly popular in Kenya, which probably made my request a little more difficult than it might have been elsewhere. I was sat on the sidelines for the whole tour and was only reunited with my kit upon return home. When I did get back home, I found out that I had received a ten-game suspension from ZC after they had conducted their own investigation into the incident with Mrs Lupepe.

At the end of April 2009, I was acquitted of assaulting Mrs Lupepe by the Harare magistrates court after they found 'glaring inconsistencies' in the prosecution's evidence, describing it as discredited and unreliable. I had been facing a charge of assault, but the magistrate Tapiwa Godzi had now cleared me.

'It's either this case was fabricated or the testimony of the witnesses is grossly exaggerated to the extent of making it unbelievable. In the premises, the application for discharge at the close of the state's case is hereby granted. The accused is accordingly found not guilty and acquitted. It would be futile to put the accused person to his defence.'

ZC had kept relatively quiet over the course of the court case, but at the end of July they released the findings of their own investigation into the case: '... Tatenda Taibu was found guilty by this Committee of misconduct. The position is worsened by the fact that the Respondent's defence is based on spurious allegations which are not worthy of belief at all. Assault, however minor, by an employee on another senior employee is a serious case of misconduct which ordinarily would attract dismissal from employment. This shows a lack of respect for authority and a negative attitude towards one's employer... he has however not shown any contrition for his behaviour. If anything, he has shown contempt for his superiors by making unsubstantial allegations.

'In view of the above and the fact we have alluded to that he is a young man with a bright future ahead of him, we find ourselves inclined to tamper justice with mercy and not recommend the ultimate penalty of dismissal which penalty is at our disposal. We therefore recommend to the Management of Zimbabwe Cricket Union that the Respondent be suspended from participating in 10 ODI matches with immediate effect.'

Ozias Bvute himself had given a statement to the media saying that I had admitted to assaulting Esther to him shortly after the incident and that she and her husband were not prepared to meet me in person, so I could give my apology. Ozias also told the media that he had held a meeting with me after the outcome of the internal hearing, asking me why my lawyer had made those allegations against ZC and why I had retracted my earlier statement indicating I had assaulted Esther. He claimed I had told him in this meeting that I wasn't comfortable with having lied to the courts via my lawyer.

What he was saying was simply not true. First of all, I had called Esther and she had accepted my apology. Of that I have no doubt. Secondly, I told Ozias exactly what I had told my lawyer. Yes, I had taken hold of Esther's hand in an attempt to get her to come to the bank with me. It was not behaviour that I was proud of, and I had apologised, but it had not gone any further than that. I had not retracted my statement and I had not lied. I told my lawyer what had happened and then left it him to defend me in court in the way he saw fit. It was the people on the witness stand in court who were creating fictional stories. There was one tale that I had lifted Mrs Lupepe with one hand and punched her with another. Someone else said I had picked her up and thrown her against the wall. I could only marvel at this. After a while I stopped listening to what was being said in court. I simply could not fathom the lies that were being created.

When I had returned to play for Zimbabwe after my exile, I very much got the feeling that Ozias Bvute was not done with me. Peter Chingoka was more than happy to move on, but Bvute felt that he had to get me back somehow. He had told me how upset his mother had been when he was forced to spend a couple of nights in prison, and he held me responsible. This was his chance. I was therefore very grateful to my lawyer Mr Samkange, who allowed me to pay him a one-off fee for the legal proceedings upfront rather than an hourly rate, which I would not have been able to afford.

The allegations against ZC that my lawyer had made in court, ones that Ozias had referenced in his statement, were put to the ZC chairman of legal and disciplinary affairs, Wilson Manatse, by my lawyer under cross-examination. Jonathan had suggested the assault charge was part of a long-running campaign to discredit me, referring to a quote made by him about the national team not wanting arrogant and undisciplined players, and asked him to explain what had happened to large sums of money that ZC had accrued in recent years from various different revenue sources. Monatse's reply had been to state that ZC were struggling financially and had very little money. The ban stood, and I missed the ODI series against Bangladesh and Kenya before I returned against the former in October 2009.

I was relieved when the trial came to end – for one it allowed me to carry on my spiritual journey – but it inevitably led to more tension between me and the board from then on, and following my ban I started to struggle to derive any real pleasure from the game.

15

The Awakening

I HAD BEEN LISTENING TO SERMONS PREACHED BY A GENTLEMAN called William Marrion Branham, an American Christian minister. The sermons made me sorry for the life I had lived so far but motivated me for the life to come. One morning, as I was getting ready to head to a team meeting, I started to read a sermon of his titled 'Pride'. I started crying, as I felt I was not worthy of living after the way I had treated my coaches and some of my fellow players. With tears in my eyes I paused the tape and went to knock on Robin Brown's door. Robin and I had not seen eye to eye in the past, but I asked him kindly for his forgiveness. Robin hugged me and told me it took a real man to admit when he is wrong. Walter Chawaguta, another member of the coaching staff, was the next one I apologised to for my past actions.

I then called a meeting with all my teammates and asked everyone to forgive me if I had wronged them in the past. Most of them said it was no big issue, that I had often acted in the right manner, while others admitted fault on some issues. I asked them not to silence my conscience: if I was right in my heart, I was not supposed to act in a certain way, even if I had been wronged myself. I also asked them not to expect perfection of me, as I was still trying to get to where I wanted to be. Until I reached that place, I would continue to apologise if I felt condemned.

It was Walter Chawaguta that became the head coach of the national team after Robin Brown was dismissed in August 2008. There were whispers that I had been one of the main reasons why Brown had suffered that fate, but I didn't pay attention to them. I was now on good terms with him and so what anyone else said didn't bother me. Walter's first tasks were a quadrangular T20 series against Canada,

Pakistan and Sri Lanka – which I had nearly pulled out of due to Loveness's operation – before a tri-series against Kenya and Ireland virtually straight after. A slightly more daunting series against Sri Lanka followed a little later on.

By this point I was spending most of my spare time reading the Bible, and often felt at peace. I would pray on a daily basis, and the sermons I was listening to alongside my reading helped me to understand things that otherwise would have been beyond me. There was a white dog and a black dog fighting inside of me. I did not know how to handle myself in many instances and I did not know how to react in a lot of situations. The dog I fed the most won my inner battles.

Around this stage, many of our games were coming against the same cricketing nations – Kenya and Bangladesh – and that had a lot to do with the way we were viewed as a country by others around the world. A year ahead of our proposed visit to England in 2009, the ECB announced that they had cancelled the tour: 'All bilateral agreements are suspended with Zimbabwe Cricket with immediate effect,' read a statement. The decision had come from the top: the UK culture secretary, Andy Burnham, had written to the board to clarify the views of the Prime Minister, Gordon Brown.

Their decision came after our neighbours Cricket South Africa had announced they were to sever their bilateral links as well due to the ongoing political turmoil – Morgan Tsvangirai had pulled out of the second round of the 2008 elections. The president of the ICC at the time, Ray Mali, and the chief executive, Haroon Lorgat, were both South African and there was talk that we were to be suspended from international cricket altogether.

In the end that did not happen thanks to the support of some of the bigger nations – ten member countries needed to be in agreement if we were to lose our full member status – but we did pull of the 2009 Twenty20 World Cup in England. Peter Chingoka talked about the decision being in the 'larger interests of the game' having been informed that the British government may not have granted our players visas.

The ICC had subsequently set up a team to investigate the situation on the ground in Zimbabwe at the end of 2008. Lorgat was one of those involved in the investigation into our country's cricketing affairs, and he set about speaking to the key figures in the game, both administrators and players. Eventually I was informed that they wanted to speak to me, but it was only due to the intervention of my former teammate Douglas Hondo. Douglas had been interviewed by them and enquired as to whether they had spoken to me yet. After all, I wasn't afraid of speaking my mind. Lorgat had responded that I was on holiday in South Africa. Douglas knew that wasn't the case, though, and he told them so.

Hastily they arranged to see me that evening, two hours after their investigations were meant to have concluded. I was someone who was probably more comfortable than any of my teammates in speaking out against authority, and now I had a chance to do so in front of three members of the ICC board. They were tasked with sorting the game out in our country, and so I spoke from the heart, just like I had done to various politicians in 2005. I quickly realised that Lorgat was not particularly interested in what I was saying. He had spoken to a lot of people already, and it became clear to me that he made up his mind about what was going on. He was not buying my side of events. One of his colleagues, Jon Long, who was the head of Executive International Programmes at the ICC, seemed intrigued by the information I was giving them at least, but the third ICC member was virtually falling asleep.

I felt really sorry for myself after the meeting's conclusion. It seemed to me as if the system above us all was too big – anything that me and any other player said wasn't going to make a difference now, even if it was to the ICC. The only thing I had to worry about now was what Haroon told Peter Chingoka and Ozias Bvute. Had he told them what I had told him?

Midway through 2010, Lorgat came out and revealed how happy he was with the progress being made in Zimbabwean cricket following his visit, declaring that a gradual return to Test cricket would happen soon enough. He said that the most encouraging thing for him since his visit was how most of his recommendations had been 'enthusiastically adopted' by our board. It hardly came as a surprise to me.

In Walter's first fifty-over game in charge, against Ireland, I was awarded man of the match after making 74. I had also devised a plan with our new coach regarding the use of our two spinners, Ray Price and Prosper Utseya, in tandem due to the dry nature of the wicket we were playing on in Nairobi. Both of them were two of the best in the world when it came to the control they could exert – I had seen them both hit bottle tops laid out on the wicket for them in practice on numerous occasions. Both of them had the same weakness as well, their inability to turn the ball a great deal, but they were able to get plenty of spin on this dry surface.

I always wondered how much better both of them would have done if they were just left to play. Instead, they always felt as if they were competing against each other for one place in the side. They were both good enough to be in the team, so why make them compete for one spot so we could mimic other teams' strategies of playing just one spinner? In the golden age of West Indian cricket, they relied on four rapid bowlers and little else and it worked beautifully for them. Sure, Price and Utseya weren't going to catapult us to that level of success, not even close, but our strategy should have been to play them both, to focus on our strengths.

In between our win over Ireland and our next game against Kenya we had plenty of time to kill. I had injured my hamstring, so I personally had even more time to chase up on those missing funds I still had not received following the tour of Pakistan. By now I had started taping every meeting I had on the matter with a personal recorder. All trust had evaporated, so I wanted to make sure everything was available for referral.

I once again reiterated to the team manager, Givemore Makoni, that I wanted my funds. Like everyone in else in the hierarchy I no longer trusted what he was saying, so when he paid a visit to the toilet during my meeting with him I decided to take matters into my own hands. While he was out of sight, I quickly opened his emails and found the thread where he had been communicating with Ozias about me. I forwarded them on to my own address. By the time he came out the damage had been done. 'The truth is always better than lies,' I said to him as I left the room.

I made my way back to my room on the crutches I was on and delved into the emails I had forwarded to myself. Needless to say, I was shocked by my findings. They seemed to be suggesting I was not due the money I was claiming I was due. I quickly headed back to Makoni's room, asking him if he had a few minutes to talk about something very important. I did not make him aware that I had accessed his emails, but I pulled out my own computer and made him listen to the files I had recorded. I informed him of the files I had saved, and also showed him the conversation Loveness had had with Peter Chingoka about her being allowed to travel to Pakistan. I walked out and left him with some homework. I had learnt the hard way and wasn't taking anything for granted.

There was no way I should have been fit to play our second game of the tri-series against Kenya, but on the morning of the game I found myself listening to a sermon titled 'Faith' while I watched the boys prepare. I got so excited when the preacher got onto the subject of healing that I went straight to our physio and asked him to tie a bandage on my thigh as tightly as possible – I wanted to play. He could not believe what he was hearing.

'Tatenda, you are sitting here with a crutch in your hand and you want me to put my job on the line?'

I knew I was asking something of him that seemed pretty unreasonable, but I pleaded with him to do it before the team was announced. I was asking him as a Christian; I couldn't explain any further than that. I just knew deep in my heart that I was capable of playing the game. He asked me to walk around the field with him as a test. I was in such pain, but I gritted my teeth and made sure he could not see. He then asked me to jog, something I miraculously managed to complete as well. He eventually passed me fit, though did not let me keep wicket.

We lost the game by a large margin, and in the changing rooms after Walter was not impressed. He asked us to give two reasons each as to why we had lost the game. I did not want to bring up my issues with our gameplan, so my first point was to mention the fact that we had attempted to chase down a big score with Timycen Maruma opening the batting, a young boy at the start of his international career. I meant no disrespect to Timycen, but he was yet to score a first-class hundred. How could we expect him to go out there and score an international hundred?

My second point was slightly more controversial: 'We pray every morning asking from protection from injuries and to make the correct judgement, but how many people in this room have slept with Kenyan girls on this tour?' The silence in the room surpassed the silence you find in a graveyard. I felt like it was a point I had to make, though. Off-field events had been atrocious. I was always the last to know what was going on outside of cricket on tour because I hardly ever left my room, so if I was aware of how bad things had got then it meant things had spiralled way out of control. The off-field culture of staying out late had seemingly not changed since I was first exposed to Zimbabwean national-team cricket at the age of fifteen.

Quite predictably, Walter was disappointed with the point I had raised, telling me it was it not relevant. I felt myself getting angry again so started to walk out. Stuey got up to try to explain what I meant, but before he had a chance to finish Walter said, 'You can walk out with him too if you want.' Being a rather timid character, Stuart remained sat down while I left.

The rain began to pour for the rest of the tour, and while I was cooped in my room one evening Loveness rang to say she had taken TJ to hospital – he had been crying for over two hours, but doctors could not seem to find what was wrong with him. I felt so useless being in another country. At one stage I tried to convince the manager to let me fly back, though he tried to talk me out of it. Eventually Loveness called back to say that TJ was okay. On top of this our funds from the Pakistan tour had finally been paid into our accounts. Still, we did not see any more action in the tri-series, with every game called off due to the weather.

The board wanted answers for our loss against Kenya. I was always one for speaking my mind, but on this occasion I decided to keep my mouth shut and listen to others. This was before the official travelling party had a go at me for wanting to return home to care for my child. The rest of the players were well aware by now that I wasn't one to back down in a fight, so their faces all turned to me in unison when we were asked to provide these answers. I was absolutely boiling inside, but somehow managed to keep my cool. I didn't utter a word.

Still, I found a way to get my message across. There is an unwritten rule that what happens on tour stays on tour, but that was about to change in a big way. I wrote a letter to all of the ZC staff detailing all the stories that had reached my ears about behaviour on the tour.

I was in court on a charge of assault in October 2008, and I did not get any time off while the trial was ongoing. I did not ask either, since temperatures were running very high. It meant I carried on playing for the national team. I appeared in the ODI series in Sri Lanka in November 2008, the tri-series with Sri Lanka and Bangladesh in January 2009 and the subsequent ODI series with the latter.

During one of our provincial matches during this period, our coach Kevin Curran came to sit beside me and said, 'Tiba, there are lots of things happening in your life and yet it doesn't seem to bother you one bit? Would you like to share with me how you do it?' With the way he asked I could discern that there was something going on in his personal life. He was a tough character who hardly ever showed any signs of weakness. It was a rare moment.

'You seem a little bit down coach, what's going on?'

'Tiba, I'm going through a divorce.'

At first, I didn't know what to say because I hated divorce. However, I soon remembered a sermon I had recently listened to. 'Coach, there is always a Man who can turn on the light. You should try telling God about it. If you really pay attention and keep still, He will answer you too. You ask me why I don't look bothered about things. I'm human like everyone else, so I am bothered just like everyone else from time to time. But after telling Him I know He will make a way, and He has never disappointed.' After I had finished, there was such a hush; a really welcoming atmosphere. He asked me for a copy of the particular sermon, and from that day on our working relationship improved immeasurably.

Once my ban did arrive it covered the two home series against Bangladesh and Kenya in 2009, both of which were five matches in length. After that, it was time to return to my second home, Bangladesh, for another ODI tour. Once there, our tall fast bowler Christopher Mpofu paid a surprise visit to my room. He had come to the point in his career where he thought he was no longer progressing, and he needed help to climb the next ladder. 'Why come to me of all people?' I asked him.

His reply was very humbling. '*Mkoma* (older brother), at least you will tell me the truth. Even if it hurts, I know it will help me.'

I started by referring to a game on our last tour against Kenya. Chris had taken 6-52, which remain his best figures in an international game to this date. Still, as we were leaving the field I had not clapped him off like the rest of my teammates. Yes, he had taken six wickets, but five of them came after Kenya had already ensured they were going to get a total that would be difficult for us to chase down. He had only taken one at the top of the order. 'They call you a strike bowler, which means you must strike. If you don't strike upfront, then you have not done your job.' He understood. We got talking about how neither of us should ever feel content just doing well by Zimbabwean standards. I think we both left the conversation feeling refreshed.

We won the first game of the series and lost the second. I featured in both of them, making nought in the first and 38 in the second, but injury would rule me out of the final three games of the tour. The third game was the first international match I had missed due to injury since I made my debut in 2001. The only player to surpass that was Makhaya Ntini, the great South African fast bowler. I had actually done a few fitness sessions in the gym with Makhaya during the 2002 Champions Trophy in Sri Lanka. Neither of us was playing and therefore we had a lot of time to kill. We had the same method of training; lots of running and working quietly. When people walked in he would often start chatting, and it would seem like we were just wasting time. But when all the people had left we hardly spoke a word. We would run for twenty or thirty minutes at a time on the beach under the unforgiving glare of the sun.

Dean du Plessis, the world's first visually impaired commentator on international matches, whom I had encountered with Gary Brent before my ODI debut years before, was travelling with our first team on this tour of Bangladesh. It was his first time travelling with us, though he had commentated on our matches before. Dean was blind, but he had a sharp memory and his strong sense of hearing helped him to make up for his lack of sight. If he stopped to concentrate, he was able to hear the footsteps of a person walking twenty yards away. The mics placed on the stumps helped him to tell who the bowler was.

Once you had introduced yourself to him once, he would be able to tell it was you straightaway the next time you had a conversation. Dean and I became quite close, so much so that I started to help him on walks from the airport toour hotels. I shared the duty with my teammates Ray Price and Chamu Chibhabha. The first time I ever took him to his hotel room he shocked me. It's one thing being told a person does this and that, but it's another thing actually being able to witness it for yourself.

I went about describing the room's lay-out to him; where the television remote was, where the toilet was. Things like that. Being a man of wit, his reply was, 'Tiba, don't worry about showing me the switches, I can do that from my eyes.' We had a good laugh, and he asked me to turn on the sports channel. There was a provincial match in South Africa on the television, and almost right away Thami Tsolekile clipped a delivery for six. Before the commentators said anything, Dean said, 'That was a good whip off his legs for six.' At first, I thought it must have been highlights of a match he had already watched, but alas, it was live. I looked at him out of the corner of my eye. Funny as it may sound, I really was double-checking whether he was actually blind. I knew for sure later when he pulled out both his glass eyes.

I stayed in the room for a little while longer, and soon enough the other batsman played a nice cover drive between the fielders. 'That was well struck and will run all the way to the offside boundary,' remarked Dean. That was too much for me. I had to ask a few questions. 'Dean, how did you know that the batsman had whipped that off his legs for six? How did you know that last shot was going all the way to the boundary?' I knew about his high level of hearing, about his sharp memory, but this was beyond any senses.

'Tiba, I won't lie to you, I can't explain it. All I know is that I just know.' If he had said anything else I would have thought it a lie. Being a Bible reader and knowing that God works in mysterious ways to perform his wonders, Dean's answer had satisfied me more than he could have imagined.

South Africa were next up. Given the fact that I had missed the last three games of the Bangladesh series in the previous couple of weeks, there was little chance of me making the first match of this series, no matter how much I pestered our physio. I was kept in the squad in the hope that I would be fit to play in the second and final game of the series. We only had two practice games before the first match, but while I sat and watched the boys practise the same feeling that I had experienced the last time we played South Africa engulfed me once again. There was no need to explain my state of mind to anyone else; no one would have been able to understand anyway. I got up, put my pads on and asked one of the junior players to throw some balls at me. I was not disrupting anyone, so I was left to my own devices.

When it was time for treatment I made my move, asking our physio Amato Machikicho to pass me fit to play. 'Tiba, you are starting your games again,' he said.

'Doc, I respect you a lot, I don't play games with you. When I talk to you it's serious business.' Amato and I had shared many conversations on life values and we had great respect for one another. I felt very free talking to him whenever I had any problems. His ability to just listen without offering his own view was appreciated greatly, not just by me but by others in our squad as well. We had a deal that he would put my name forward to play as long as I did not pull out before the game ended.

The coach allowed me to practise under the watchful eye of Amato. I did well to show no discomfort whatsoever, which led to my selection for the series opener. I managed to keep without much trouble: the ball spent more time flying towards the boundary than it did my gloves as they racked up 295. Our strength was spin bowling, and South African pitches were rarely suited to taking it, making our tours there particularly difficult.

Given my fitness, or lack of it, Walter moved me down from my usual position at four to number five. I'd only had one training session and I was about to face a particularly strong South African attack. Stuart had been moved down to seven, but for a different reason to me; he had not performed well on the tour of Bangladesh. I didn't have long to wait before walking to the crease anyway – my time came after 13.5 overs when Brendan Taylor's dismissal left us 40-3. Soon after it was 44-4 and soon after that it was 48-5. It meant that Stuey and I were back at the crease together again. The storm clouds were gathering both literally and metaphorically, and when we were forced off for rain I sat on just seven.

When we returned we needed something like 225 to win off 25 overs with just five wickets remaining. The total was out of reach, but we could save some face. We took the batting powerplay right away and it started raining boundaries. We ended up sharing a record sixth-wicket stand of 188 to take us to the respectable total of 250. I made an unbeaten century and received another man of the match award against our neighbours. I remained in serious pain ahead of the second game. I didn't want to pressurise Amato into passing me fit to play, but I soon realised this time around that the pressure was coming from the coaching staff. The game was not really a contest: they made 331, we made 119 in reply. I made 52 of those runs. It was enough to earn me the man of the series award.

Domestically, there was talk of adopting a new franchise system like they had in South Africa if we were to keep getting assistance from the South African sports channel SuperSport. Cricket was reorganised in time for the 2009/10 season, with five new franchises created not just for T20 cricket, but for the first-class and List A competitions as well. The five teams were Mountaineers, Mashonaland Eagles, Mid West Rhinos, Matabeleland Tuskers and Southern Rocks. The T20 league would attract some household names in the following years: Brian Lara, Ian Harvey and Steve Tikolo at Southern Rocks; Dirk Nannes at Mountaineers; Shaun Tait at Mid West Rhinos and Chris Gayle at Matabeleland Tuskers. The tournament looked very organised on the surface, but what the world didn't know was that local players, if not contracted, were getting US$20 a day for a match.

I was paying more attention to events at home. Loveness and I were expecting a new member of our family. Gershom was to be his name, the name of Moses's first-born child in the Bible. Moses named him Gershom because he himself had been, 'a stranger in a strange land'. I had felt like a stranger in a strange land for much of my cricket career. I had experienced events in my short life that others my age would give their right arm for, but the extras that came with playing international cricket – the offers of alcohol and partying – never really bothered me. If I had performed well, I just wanted to stay indoors. Drinking and parties made little sense to me. If I wanted to have a conversation, why would I go to a noisy place? All this made me realise that I was a stranger.

Local players were no longer transferred by ZC to the respective provinces: the franchises were given the power to choose who they wanted to sign and if one didn't get a franchise then he was not allowed to be selected to represent his country. There was a lot of commotion at the venue on the day that the franchises picked their players. It was each man for himself. At one stage, one of the ZC workers asked me to follow him to a private area. Once there, he informed me that all of the franchises had been told not to select me. In the end, it didn't work out that way: my old coach Steve Mangongo had a chat with Mr Senzani, the new CEO for the Mountaineers, and I was signed by them.

Steve was our coach, and I think it was a little hard for him to adjust from seeing us as the boys we once were to the men we now were. He had coached so many of us as youths, and back then blanket punishment had been his chief strategy. I think a lot of those who hadn't worked with him for a long time now found him and his methods strange. I understood his ways so just got on with my work in a professional manner. The best way to get in the good books of any coach is to play well. If I had my game sorted, I could get away with any other petty issues.

Mangongo got me to bat at number three in all forms of the game, while I was keeping as well. All that action weighed heavily on my body, so I made sure to rest up off the field as much as possible. We played our home games in Mutare in the province of Manicaland. During home games I'd often rest up in the beautiful mountains of Vumba, which were very close by. Instead of staying in the hotel with the others, I would book myself into a place in the mountains, where I would pray and enjoy the surrounding nature.

In the meantime, I had started to grow spiritually. I felt I understood a lot more, especially what caused people to act in certain ways. Mangongo noticed this and gave me a role to play within the team set-up. There were some boys who had great potential to play well but were considered to be somewhat arrogant. One was Tendai Chatara and another was Natsai M'shangwe. However, I was not the captain, nor was I the vice-captain: ZC were not going to consent to me holding one of those posts, not after all that had happened of late.

I managed to break through to Chatara first. I used to invite him back for lunch, just so we could converse with each other. I soon managed to pick up on the boy's general lack of etiquette, which could be mistaken for arrogance. He had been brought up by his mother alone, and she had to work for the family to eat. M'shangwe had a very defensive heart. He had grown up almost all alone; his mother constantly had to work, while his father had a mental illness.

Music had become his sanctuary, and he responded to any little act of aggression towards him in an ultra-defensive manner. It took me a few weeks of spending time with him to get to the bottom of the issue. This arrangement worked well for a little while until I started taking a more hands-off approach. I felt like my role was starting to cause a little confusion. I wasn't the captain, I had a bad reputation within the organisation in general, and I was the one nurturing these two young cricketers?

There were other players who knew what they wanted and were always there to learn, one of them being Njabulo Ncube. In my humble view, I felt at the time that if they handled him correctly, he could become one of the best bowlers to come out of Zimbabwe. He reminded me so much of the South African fast bowlers, especially Makhaya Ntini, always running in hard and bowling his heart out regardless of the condition of the wicket. In the end, he'd play just one Test match and one ODI in his career.

In February 2010, it was finally confirmed that we had a new coach to replace Walter Chawaguta: Alan Butcher, the father of Mark Butcher and the former coach of English county side Surrey. His first assignment was our five-match ODI tour of the West Indies, which came pretty much as soon as he had been appointed. In the short amount of time he did have before that tour started he took the opportunity to speak to a few of the players. Alan and I sat on the side of the clubhouse in Mutare during a provincial practice session, but after the first few minutes I could tell I would not be able to tell him a lot. I could discern that he had already been told a lot of negative things about me. I just had to promise to him that after a few tours he would begin to understand the person I was through first-hand experience. 'Butch, if you forget many things it's okay, but please don't forget this: play it your own way, for that's the only way you will succeed.'

We played well in the warm-up matches out there and carried that into our first match, winning by two runs while Alan watched on from the sidelines. He looked a calm and timid character, a bit on the nervous side, I guess. The West Indies had prepared a spin-friendly wicket, which suited us down to the ground: we had four in our team. We should have won the second game as well, but I missed two crucial stumpings, both off Chris Gayle, comfortably their best player. He went on to make a match-winning 88. In truth, my wicketkeeping was atrocious on that tour. I was lucky that the former West Indies keeper Jeff Dujon was on commentary duty throughout that series, and he was helpful enough to provide me with some tips. However, he was quick to remind me that he hadn't kept to an awful lot of spin as a keeper: he had played Test cricket between 1981 and 1991, the golden age of West Indian fast bowling. Sometimes it's not so much about what you are told, but who's telling you.

In the final three games of the series the West Indian groundsmen had clearly learned from their mistake. All three games were to be played in Kingstown, St Vincent, and plenty of grass was left on the wicket on each occasion. They were very low-scoring encounters, but we only got close to winning one of the three. I could tell that Alan was getting frustrated when it came to us discussing where we had gone wrong. The English believe in discussion; in Zimbabwean culture the youngsters expect to be told by their elders what they need to do. Having spent time in both countries, I could tell how that culture often filtered into sport. We did at least win our one-off T20 match. The odds looked stacked against us when four of our top five, including me, made ducks (six out of eleven in total), and we only mustered a score of 105. However, on a turning wicket we turned to an attack almost exclusively comprised of spin bowlers and somehow managed to restrict them to 79-7.

We were only back home in Zimbabwe for a few weeks before we had to fly back out to the West Indies for our second appearance at a Twenty20 World Cup. In terms of our position on the world stage, things were at least starting to look up: we were readying for our return to the Test arena against Bangladesh and we were back competing in an international tournament. We had pulled out of the last T20 World Cup in England and had not played Test cricket since 2005. We also seemed to be making our cricketing structures more professional. We weren't relying on Alan Butcher to do all the work as head coach: Stephen Mangongo had become assistant, Grant Flower our batting coach and Heath Streak our bowling coach.

Our problem was that we had not actually played enough T20 cricket to be able to be expected to compete with the best sides. Since our first T20 game against Bangladesh in 2006, we had played a total of just eight T20 internationals, four of which had come in one quadrangular series in Canada and two of which had come in the first World Cup back in South Africa in 2007.

Still, we were on fire in the warm-up matches we played, beating both Australia and Pakistan. When it came to the tournament itself, we couldn't raise our game. The weather caused a little confusion during our meeting with Sri Lanka. We were chasing a big score of 174 for victory with rain threatening, bringing the Duckworth-Lewis method into the equation. I was meant to be batting at number three and was sitting in the changing room waiting to come in if a wicket fell. Rain had delayed the start, but we were now ready to go. The Sri Lankans were out on the field, Hamilton was halfway to the crease, but fellow opener Brendan Taylor was nowhere to be seen. He had gone for a smoke and misjudged the time. I just had to go in and open the batting. Once I was out there we got so much abuse. With rain around, the Sri Lankans thought we were holding out for a draw. We reached 29-1 off five overs but were not where we needed to be when the rain did fall. Against New Zealand, I top-scored with 21 from fourteen balls, but we were dismissed for 84.

After the World Cup, we faced India and Sri Lanka in a tri-series and then Ireland. ODIs were coming thick and fast. I was playing really well on the field, and we actually managed to beat India twice and Sri Lanka once in our five games over the course of that tournament, and then easily defeated Ireland 3-0. My individual scores were 13*, 42*, 71, 62, 41 and 22. Off the field, I was doing little to convince our coach Alan Butcher about my value to the team – if he had been selecting purely on performance in the nets, I wouldn't have got near the side. However, I tended to deliver for him when it really mattered out on the field of play. My bat was now doing my talking for me.

Our next assignment was against South Africa in their backyard. Grant Flower had returned as our batting coach but believed that he was good enough to make a playing return to the international arena as well. That meant for the first ODI of the series I was demoted to number six, with my job to support the top order rather than anchor the innings. I didn't complain, but as I looked out from the changing rooms with Alistair Campbell, my former teammate and now a selector, some of our batting out on the field was embarrassing. A few players were backing away and seemed scared of the ball. Especially after my recent form, I could not understand why I was sitting listening to Alistair when I could be out there with Brendan, who went on to make a brilliant unbeaten 145.

With the record I had against South Africa, some of their players even enquired as to why I was batting so far down the order. I didn't have the answer, so I passed it on to our selectors. The pressure eventually mounted on them ahead of the next game and Butchy came to tell me that I was being reinstated at number four. He apologised for the previous game, and I accepted that. I did not let him down:

I scored 78 and was the only man on our team to past fifty. I got out at a stupid time, though – I had been in a great position to kick on and get a hundred. In the end they chased our score down easily, with Hashim Amla and AB de Villiers both cruising to hundreds. I had come across many natural strikers of the ball in my career, but for me AB was the only player who could play any cricket shot effortlessly.

This was the last time I came up against South Africa and some of my favourite players in the world. It wasn't so much their abilities on the field, but the way they carried themselves off it. Hashim Amla was definitely one of those players. I always had massive respect for a person who would achieve good results on the field but carried himself like he had not achieved anything. Another such player was Pakistan's Younis Khan.

My subsequent preparations for the 2011 World Cup in India were not the best. I had been struck on the index finger, which caused me to miss most practices in the lead-up the tournament. It was a shame, because it was eight years since I had played in cricket's showpiece event, which had ended in our team being ripped apart by internal divisions. Brian Lara was also acting as our batting advisor at the time, but because of my injury I didn't get much of an opportunity to work with him. We spent some time in Dubai, where I did not bat at all, but I still believed I'd be ready for the start of the tournament.

When it did begin, the truth is I didn't feel ready, but I was glad we were in a group where we would face more tough than easy opposition – I was always confident of doing well against more esteemed opponents. However, this tournament proved to be somewhat different for me. I did well against our weaker opposition, scoring 98 and 53 against Canada and Kenya respectively in two victories, but disastrously against the better sides: 7 against Australia, 8 against New Zealand, 4 against Sri Lanka and 19 against Pakistan. It wasn't good enough.

David Coltart, who was one of the founders of the MDC party and had just been appointed the country's new sports minister, had come into our dressing room before one of our games and given us a pep talk. I had spoken to him once before when I had been banned from the national side after events in the courtroom, and he had asked me to be a guest speaker at a beautiful school he was chairman of called Petra, based in Bulawayo. I had the privilege of speaking to him alone, and I was allowed to air views I otherwise would not have got across. I was always welcome at his house. He had a warm home which had an old Christian feel to it, and I liked how humble he was. I was glad to have someone who could carry my voice for me, because by this stage I pretty much had no voice. I did not speak to any newspapers at home, and nor was I ever on television or radio.

My 98 against Canada meant I became the fifth Zimbabwean to score 3,000 runs in ODI cricket, but we had not really left a mark on the tournament. We had beaten the teams we were expected to beat, lost to the teams we were expected to lose against. We returned home to an unhappy group of fans, who hardly turned out at the airport to welcome us back. And why would they? We hadn't needed to qualify for the tournament and had made no real impact once we were there.

My time in provincial cricket was coming to an end, and my last game for Manicaland was not a rosy affair. Most of the players were not receiving their funds on time. I had managed to secure mine, but my heart would break when I'd give my teammates lifts to the shop before taking them home. I gave them lifts simply so they wouldn't have to spend their own money on transport; that's how desperate the situation had become in Zimbabwe. I would see them buying bread, and I knew that was to be their dinner before the next game. These were players that were expected to work really hard day in, day out at training, but I knew for a fact that they simply weren't getting enough food down them to be able to do that. These were professional cricketers, but their energies were devoted to finding what they were going to have to eat the next day.

I went to speak to the CEO of the team and asked if there was anything he could do about the players. I was well aware of what had happened the last time I had stood up for my teammates as captain of the national side, but to me this situation was different. These players were really struggling to make ends meet, to provide for themselves and their families. I couldn't just ignore that.

Instead of trying to help, he reported me to Mangongo, who knew that some of the lads would follow everything I'd say. I could tell that what I had said had been reported to him, because before our next game he asked for anyone who didn't want to play to either leave or forever hold their peace. There was silence in the changing room for a while before eventually I said, 'Let's go out and win tomorrow.' We went out and won, but it was then that I decided I would not stay on for another season.

Hyperinflation in Zimbabwe was at its height between 2008 and 2009, but it was often difficult to measure because the government stopped filing official statistics. Still, during November 2008 inflation was estimated at 79.6 billion, its highest mark. In 2009 Zimbabwe stopped printing its own currency. What I was witnessing with my teammates was the human result of this crisis. There are so many distressing stories from the time. Simply having access to a loaf of bread was like holding gold.

A friend of ours always used to walk miles to his home from town so he could save his money during this period. On one day he was making one of these walks when he noticed a queue building on the side of the road. Usually, a queue forming at a time like this meant that something of value was available, so naturally he joined the back of it. It was only after spending several hours in this queue that he realised that it was for transport. He carried on his walk.

Another friend of mine told me a story of how he walked 15km to the bank to pick up his wages and 15km home, again to save money. He arrived home that night with his money, but when he woke up the next day inflation had risen so much that his monthly wage was enough to buy him three oranges. He was a teacher. You almost laugh about stories like that now, but the impact this crisis had on people's lives was astonishing.

Of course, during parts of the crisis I spent a lot of my time travelling the world, but I wasn't blind to what was going on. When we were back in the country I witnessed things I had never seen before. I remember driving from Harare to Bulawayo one time and we passed a woman with a child on her back. She had taken some weeds from the side of the road and she had made them into a broom. She was literally sweeping up maize – a type of corn that is a dietary staple in Zimbabwe – from the side of the road, maize that had been spilt by lorries carrying it from Harare to Bulawayo. She was literally sweeping up the spillages so she could feed her family.

That's what prompted me and Loveness to act. Because I was playing cricket in Namibia at this point, we had easy access to cash. We were getting our money on the foreign exchange market and bringing it back into Zimbabwe. We'd visit the factories such as National Foods Limited and purchase flour, and because we were paying in cash we'd go to the front of the line. Loveness would sell half of what we had bought to companies and make a profit but would give away the other half to people who were in need. What people didn't have access to was food, so that's what we did. A lot of people had resorted to making their own bread.

Givemore Makoni was now the CEO of Southern Rocks, a team that played in the Masvingo province, and he took advantage of my situation to offer me a contract with them. They were the weakest of the five provinces, and he offered me the role of captain, helping out players such as Sikandar Raza, Brian Vitori, Richmond Mutumbani and Tafadzwa Kamungozi. Mutumbani and Kamungozi were quite difficult to get through to because they were not as flexible to change as Raza and Vitori were. Vitori just did everything I asked of him, while Raza pestered me with lots of questions. After everything that had gone on, I had ended up back in a captaincy role at provincial level, nurturing youngsters, just as I had done in the national team at the age of 21.

Part of my contract with Southern Rocks stipulated that I did not have to stay in town with the rest of the team. Instead I could stay away from the noise and be with Mother Nature. I always felt refreshed staying out in the country, where I would hear the animals at night. Stuart would often join me there and we would enjoy good conversation about the days gone by. We lost many games, but I was content knowing that I was helping in my own little way by living an exemplary Christian life. I didn't get into arguments about religion, I simply let people make their own mind up about my actions, which I let the Bible guide. I did less talking and more acting.

16
A Rock in a Weary Land

AHEAD OF OUR RETURN TO THE TEST ARENA AGAINST BANGLADESH in 2011, there was plenty of talk about who was going to be our captain. It had been Elton Chigumbura at the World Cup, but the burden of being in charge of a whole team seemed to weigh on his shoulders and his performances would often dip. He was often batting down at seven and was not one of our strike bowlers. The new favourite for the role was Brendan Taylor, now our most consistent batsman. I really did not mind who got the job. I had finally developed some kind of relationship with all of the players, though I did not invite any of them to my home anymore. I was still something of a lone ranger.

Our one-off Test was to be played in Harare. There was a customary press conference two days before the game, and I was surprised to be one of the players chosen to speak. I found myself sitting alongside fellow wicketkeeper Mushfiqur Rahim, fielding general cricket questions, when I was asked what I thought about Zimbabwe Cricket's recent efforts to reintegrate the nation into Test cricket and the world game. I did not believe in lying and therefore there was no way I could avoid saying what I really thought. I had to speak from the heart, and so I did:

'I don't think much has changed really, the administration is still struggling to run cricket in the country well. For example, the guys haven't been paid their match fees from August last year up to now. At the moment I am sitting here without a contract, no one has got a contract. Those are all things that the administration is struggling to deal with.

'When you walk around and see a house that's painted well you will think that house is really standing strong but if it does not have a strong foundation, it will fall down one day or another. Zimbabwe Cricket has just painted a house that's about to fall.

'I can't fault the coaching staff, they've worked really hard and I can't fault the guys. They come in, day in day out but they are not getting much support from the administration, unfortunately.'

I was only speaking the truth about payments. Even though our chairman of selectors, Alistair Campbell, described my comments as a 'slap in the face', he could not deny the fact that the players did not yet have permanent contracts (these new contracts were due to start in September, a month after the Bangladesh Test) and they hadn't yet received their match fees. There was mention of a global economic crisis as a factor, and Alistair claimed things would be easier once we were playing more regularly again, but we were back to playing international cricket without being paid properly.

The main issue was that ZC seemed to be spending a lot of money elsewhere. In the same year, 2011, floodlights had been installed at the Harare Sports Club so day-night cricket could be held at the venue. There was no doubting that was a positive move, but it shouldn't have come at the expense of players being paid. Perhaps more worrying was the fact that plenty of money had been spent on big-name players to play in our T20 league, as we tried to copy what was going on in other tournaments around the world. Brian Lara, who hadn't played international cricket since 2007, was reportedly paid US$30,000 to make a few appearances in the competition. Hearing what some of these players were getting and then seeing what our national-team players were getting was alarming and didn't make the slightest bit of sense to me. Once again, their priorities were not in order.

All the reporters present were no longer interested in asking any more questions; they were off to write. I, meanwhile, did not know where my future lay. I told Loveness what I had said, and she was in total disbelief. I told her that I had no choice, that it was the first thing that had come into my heart. She did not agree with what I had done. What good was it going to do? Still, it was too late now. There was no way of taking back my comments. I had to face what was coming.

Though there were some who clearly did not want me to play, I did at least now have a coach willing to fight my corner. He was the first person I saw the next day.

'Tiba! You really threw the cat among the pigeons,' said Butchy when I greeted him. 'People are running around like headless chickens after the press conference you gave yesterday. I don't know if you will play tomorrow, it's really out of my hands.' Though my words would not carry the same repercussions as Andy's had on the eve of the 2003 World Cup, especially internationally, I had caused a similar sort of panic among the ZC hierarchy simply for speaking my mind to the media and refusing to sugarcoat what I really thought.

I didn't expect the players to support me, or even to mention the whole affair at all. It had been a long time since I had expectations like that. Brendan Taylor, who had been named captain and was a good friend of mine, did offer words of support. 'Tiba, that was a strong statement and I back you. It will be tough for you on the field if you play.' Apart from that, all I caught were a few negative murmurs in disagreement. That was until our spinner Ray Price addressed our dressing room.

'Don't be negative on Tiba, us not having the courage to stand up and speak like he has done does not mean he is wrong. Tiba, you are brave, my friend. That is why you can go out there and fight until the last punch. Honestly, I do not have the guts to do the same.' That was a nice thing to hear, especially from someone I regarded to be a fighter as well. There were more meetings throughout the day before the game, and every player seemed anxious about the outcome. It was taking an age for the team to be announced, and in the meantime, we were all just sat around in the changing room.

I had my bags packed, ready to be told that I was no longer required. I was a doubt already after sustaining an injury to my index finger, which meant the threat of being dropped worried me even less. Eventually I was called to speak to Alistair and a tense conversation with a lot of finger-pointing ensued. There wasn't a lot of shouting between the pair of us, but a lot of hard facts were presented in a short space of time. The encounter ended with Alistair asking me to take back what I had said, which I refused to do. He then asked if I would pay a visit to the bosses with him, so I could repeat the same words to them. It was an opportunity I welcomed with a smile. What I had said was what I truly felt and believed, so I would have no difficulty in repeating it over and over again.

He asked me if I thought the players agreed, and I told him it would be easy for us both to find out. All we had to do was pay a visit to the dressing room together. He changed his mind about taking me to the bosses, and instead asked me to make sure that my teammates did not leave until this was all resolved. All the players had been peeping over the balcony to find out what was going on, as we had conducted our heated exchange out on the field for all to see. Heath was our bowling coach, and I told him the time for speculation was over: we would soon find out what side everyone was on. There was dead silence in the room.

Butchy appeared and told us all to go home and rest. There was to be no team announcement. Instead, we would all arrive at the ground the next day prepared to play. It was not easy to go through this all without the support of Loveness, who for once was not in agreement with what I had done. I did not have anyone to talk about the incident with, so I just had to digest it on my own. It probably would have been easier for her if I was dropped. She struggled to watch me at the best of times and would only be able to relax once I got into the 20s. With the issue now hanging over my head, how would it affect her?

Still, I had mentally prepared myself to play. I knew the chances were that if I had been asked to come to the ground that I was going to be included. We could not afford to send a weakened team out upon our Test return, and I was still the man in the squad with the most Test appearances. There was going to be a lot of pressure on me, especially when Butchy later informed me that I was going to bat down at number seven, lower than my usual position at four. It meant there was a good chance I would have to bat with our bowlers, and so I had to think of how I would adapt my game to that. Bangladesh had developed a way of wiping out our tail quickly, so I knew there was no room for failure.

We made 370 in our first innings, but I only contributed 23, which only served to heap the pressure on me in the second dig. We had a lead of 83 from the first innings, but I walked in to bat in our second with the team in a spot of bother at 92-4. Luckily, my favourite batting partner Brendan Taylor was still at the crease and we quickly got down to work. I scored 59 in a partnership of 113 to take us clear of our visitors, swinging the match firmly in our favour. Those who witnessed our partnership before and after lunch said it was among the best two hours of play ever produced in the format by Zimbabwe. Brendan went on to make a superb hundred before making a fearless and positive declaration. We ended up winning the game by 130 runs, with the wickets shared out among the bowlers.

My finger was getting worse and worse, but I still had plenty left to prove to those who resented me, so I pressed on to the ODI series. There were plenty still willing me to fail, and so things did not get any easier when I was dismissed for a second-ball duck in the first game. Luckily, we were well on our way to victory anyway after Brian Vitori's 5-30. In the second game Brian repeated his trick, taking 5-20 in Bangladesh's innings and leaving us to chase a score of under 200. It was a realistic target, and Vusi Sibanda and I made light work of it. I finished not out on 61.

It gave us an opportunity to take an unassailable lead in the third match of the five-game series. When we lost the toss on a fairly moist surface, the message from our coaches was to not go too gung-ho. Still, I reckoned we needed a score of 250 to remain competitive, so when I joined Hamilton Masakadza at the crease early in our innings I signaled my intentions to attack. I rode my luck in my innings of 83, but we ended up on a score of exactly 250 and won the game in the last over of their innings. We lost the final two games of the series on a spinning track but had already just done enough. Fine margins.

Pakistan were next in Zimbabwe for a Test and three ODIs. We played well for a good chunk of the Test but, as in any other sport, winning is a habit in cricket, and it was a habit we had not mastered against the stronger sides. Tino Mawoyo scored a brilliant 163* in the first innings to take us to a competitive score of 414, but we crumbled to 141 all out in our second. The worst we should have managed from the position we found ourselves in was a draw, but that is what a lack of belief can do to a side. I was the only one to post a score above 25 in that second innings with 58, sharing a ninth-wicket stand of 66 with Kyle Jarvis, but Pakistan chased down their target with ease.

My finger was not getting any rest and was just getting worse and worse. I could not keep pushing, so I had a meeting with Butchy requesting a little period of recovery. He and I were on really good terms now and he had seen me play in pain without complaining too much. I knew I was placing him between a rock and a hard place, but I felt that I needed the break. In the end I was in the side for the first ODI at home to New Zealand, but it was Brendan Taylor who was grabbing the headlines with some absolutely brilliant knocks. With Grant Flower he had worked very hard at his game and it was showing.

I played my part in us chasing down 329 in the last match of the ODI series with 53 off 39 deliveries, with Malcolm Waller scoring a stunning 99* as we won with one wicket and one ball remaining. We nearly pulled off a miracle in the only Test as well, but in the end fell 34 runs short of our target of 365. Brendan made 117 while I made 63, but we could not quite pull off a famous victory.

Ahead of our return trip to New Zealand at the start of 2012, I gave some advice to Brian Vitori. Brian had been particularly impressive in the ODIs against Bangladesh, and plenty of teams over there were interested in signing him. It would mean him missing part of the New Zealand tour, but I encouraged him anyway. 'Vits, I think you must make a tough choice of letting us go to New Zealand without you. You can join us later, but you need to go to Bangladesh and maximise your earnings. I promise you that you will become a better player after. This will further force you out of your comfort zone.'

I was not surprised to see him at the airport for our flight not long later. I didn't think he had it in him to make such a bold decision. There was a lot of confusion before that flight; it seemed some people had tried to remove me from the touring team without the knowledge of the coaches. It was the same old nonsense, the board trying to take matters in their own hands because they disapproved of someone's character. All this was getting me tired inside, and all the fight I had left for the team and for myself on the international stage was beginning to fade. I was standing there at the airport in my travelling uniform but with no boarding card. I had given my all in every international match I have ever played; I had played a part in spreading the game across Zimbabwe. I didn't feel I deserved to be treated like this.

I had to comfort myself: 'Tatenda, if they don't want you, Christ won't forsake you.' I had found a resting place in Christ, a rock in a weary land. The board had shown in many different ways since my return in 2007 that they didn't like having me in the team set-up, and frankly I didn't care anymore: I had now found something far more important to me than cricket. I was prepared to go back home there and then, to call time on my playing days for good, but Butchy was not having that. He told the manager that if I was not going to the board the flight then neither was he. That was the end of it.

When you are playing for a team and an organisation full of people who do not want you to succeed, it has a negative effect on you; you are fighting thoughts in your head all the time. When I had first returned to the international scene in 2007 I was not yet committed fully to being a man of faith, and therefore I invested more time in being the best cricketer I could possibly be. I was leaving no stone unturned in terms of my preparation, and so it didn't matter to me that were people were willing me to fail. I felt I could prove them wrong. But by now I was spending less time working on my game and more time travelling to and from church. It meant

I didn't feel as ready to perform consistently at the highest level.

The mental battles playing out in my head were getting the better of me, and I didn't want to give the board members the satisfaction of seeing me lose my way. Even if I played well on this tour, I was only going to return and fight the same battles, only with less vigour than I previously had done. The fact that I agreed to go at all was out of respect for Butch, and because Loveness was willing me to. Longer term, it was better if they carried on without me. That's clearly how some people wanted it to be.

I appreciated my coach stepping in, but I was now beginning to feel numb about the game, no matter whether we won or lost. It just did not mean much to me anymore. I spent my spare time on tour in my room reading sermons and the Bible, as well as praying. Most conversations with fellow players about the game did not feel like before. I was not interested in gameplans and batting techniques, but in talking about what Christ had done to my heart.

As usual, at the start of the tour we had a team dinner, initiating the new members of the squad into the group. We went to a restaurant which was not big enough to have one long table like we'd usually sit at, so we had two side by side instead. I knew we were going to be a while, and I had no interest in talking to my teammates about the matches ahead, so I took out one of my sermons to read. Just as we finished eating there happened to be a conversation about marriage and Grant Flower asked me for my views. When I began speaking, all the players gathered around to listen. Clearly, they were interested in what I had to say.

I knew that word was going around that I had lost my mind, but I was at peace. I understood that I was now an outcast and considered odd to most of the squad. I now loved the thing that most people weren't acquainted with and didn't like the things I loved before. Society has acceptable norms, and if one lives outside the brackets of what is deemed acceptable he is considered abnormal. I felt if I had a one on one with someone they would come away feeling refreshed by our conversation, but I didn't often get the opportunity to do that, especially not on tour.

I started talking about how marriage was of the Lord, and thus it is said, 'What God has joined together let no man put asunder.' I asked to give a little testimony of how Loveness and I started having oneness. I went back to how I had received Christ as a personal saviour and how I told Loveness my life story without omitting anything. I said to the boys, 'Everyone has a choice whether to open the book of your deeds while you're here on Earth or on the day of judgement.'

As I was lost in speaking, one said, 'Tiba, some books are better kept closed.'

Another said, 'Moses, what you say is hard, but I like it.'

The tour was over soon enough, and we had lost badly in all formats, despite Brendan Taylor and Kyle Jarvis performing well. That wasn't really of any concern to me. I had made up my mind that this was going to be the last tour I was to go on and I had to start telling people.

'I just feel that my true calling now lies in doing the Lord's work, and although I am fortunate and proud to have played for my country, the time has come for me to put my entire focus on that part of my life.' It was 10 July 2012: the end had arrived. I had played 28 Test matches and 150 ODIs. I had been named captain of my country at the age of twenty and been Zimbabwe's first black captain. I had walked out of the very same job soon after and been forced to leave my own country. I would return, but things would never quite be the same again. I had been a martyr for the cause, and I had suffered for it, living a lonely existence in my last five years on the international stage. Christ had saved me, and now I was repaying the favour.

There's a quote from the Bible that has always stuck with me: 'For you were made from dust, and to dust you will return.' One of the things that anyone finds difficult to deal with in life is a death in the family. My understanding of the Bible and my understanding of God's plan for me did not make an event like this any easier for me, but I now felt the difference between me and others was that I was now able to draw comfort from what I had read in those pages.

It also helped me to understand and come to terms with how people in the game had treated me. When I was younger, I would often wonder if I was in the wrong following my latest disagreement with those in power in Zimbabwean cricket. As I found my faith, that began to change. I knew I was right. I would compare my story to characters from the Bible such as Joseph, sold into slavery by his brothers after receiving preferential treatment from his father. Joseph would eventually find wealth in high appointment in Egypt and had the perfect opportunity to exact revenge on his brothers, but instead he chose to forgive them. I tried to take a leaf from the way he had acted in my own dealings with those who had wronged me.

I was still the same person that I had been before finding God, but the fact that my life was now in his hands meant I was at peace. I still am today.

The away tour of New Zealand had concluded in the February, so my announcement was far from instant, but a finger injury had kept me out of domestic action in the meantime. I had been named in our provisional squad for the Twenty20 World Cup in Sri Lanka in the September, but I had no intention of taking part. I had played in two of the three T20 World Cups, but the game was moving on and I was moving on from the game.

ZC released their own statement: 'Zimbabwe Cricket considers the wicketkeeper to be one of the success stories of its development programme and is saddened to be losing his services, although Taibu was appreciative of ZC's open door policy should he wish to be involved in the future.' It was all very amicable and tension-free. I had been spent all these years in a permanent state of conflict with the board; maybe now we all just wanted to put it behind us.

In truth, cricket had started to feel less important to me since 2008 – just after I had finished my one and only stint in the IPL – because of how I was starting to view the world. Still, between 2007 and 2009 I had found myself in some of the best form of my life, and in this period Loveness had made a habit of collecting newspaper articles focusing on me, especially when I had performed well. It wouldn't just be one particular newspaper – if I'd scored a hundred or contributed significantly, she would buy a few different titles. She would sit by the patio doors in our lounge, where the sun used to shine through, and bask in the glow. Loveness would never read out loud directly to me, because she knew I wasn't interested in hearing what the article in question had to say. Instead she'd read it, comment on how it was a nice article, cut it out and stick it in our scrapbook.

One morning after a game we were going through this same routine when I turned to her and said, 'Loveness, what then?'

'What do you mean?' she replied.

I started explaining that no matter how good or badly I performed, the cycle would continue to repeat itself. We would continue to sit there and analyse performance after performance: if I'd had a good game I would have to continue to practise harder than ever, to not let arrogance get the better of me; if I'd had a bad game I'd have to ignore the critics and keep my spirits up.

But what then? This monotonous cycle would continue until retirement and then manifest itself in different ways in whatever I chose to do after my professional career. I didn't like that thought.

The truth was, a good performance wasn't giving me much joy; a bad performance wasn't getting me too down. I was struggling to experience any real emotion from the game either way. I was worn down. I was struggling to sleep at night and I felt like I needed answers.

At home I had a torn Bible that had been bought for me years before. I'd patched it up nicely, but I still never used to read it. I truly believed I would find the answer I needed in those pages. For another year or so I didn't touch that Bible, but over time it slowly started to dawn on me more and more what I needed to do. The problem was, I didn't understand a lot of what I was reading early on. That is when I decided I needed to start visiting churches. Someone or something had to quench my thirst for answers.

'The Lord knows what's in my heart,' I told myself. 'As long as He knows what is in my heart, He is going to lead me down the right path.'

I didn't get answers straightaway, but nor did the desire to find them disappear. I had to keep trying. Eventually I went to a church in Bulawayo. I had to make sure it was the right one for me: I have visited a lot of churches over the years and heard a lot of things that I was not at all convinced about.

My character is such that if I start looking for something I go all out in full pursuit of it. Because I was beginning to find many answers to my life at this church, cricket was starting to get in the way. I was living in Harare, but I would drive to Bulawayo, listen to a sermon and then drive home, all in a day. Five hour drive there, six-hour sermon, five-hour drive home. I soon found that I didn't have much energy left to give in training the next day. I was starting to put less effort into my cricketing life and more effort into life's answers. That's when the end really started.

17
The Calling

I HAD ANNOUNCED THAT I NOW FELT MY TRUE CALLING LAY IN doing 'the Lord's work', which I think caused some confusion. People seemed to think I had become a pastor, but that wasn't the case. I became a trustee of the church I attended but didn't have any other role apart from that. I had simply decided to devote my life to the Lord. I didn't need any other distractions. Without cricket I was free.

Not only had the Bible helped me to start rationalising what had happened to me in life and in cricket, it also helped me to understand that everyone was different. All I could do was live the best life that I could. I realised that I could not really control anything else.

Loveness and I wanted the spirit of God to be so great in our house that people who visited with a burdened soul would find themselves healed. We wanted a house so governed by love that a person would not walk in and remain the same. Loveness, the boys and I would pray every morning and evening, reading a chapter each time. One of those very occasions, while reading from scripture to my family, I started to feel completely taken over. As I was speaking, Loveness started blabbering; rapidly talking without control. I had no idea what to do, so I just started praying. Both my boys and my nephew Stanford, who was also present, were crying. I had no idea what was happening. I had known Loveness for all my adult life and she had never acted in this way. She was speaking fluently in another language. I finished my prayer, and no one said a word. I left the room, as did she. She was weeping.. Later, it happened again in church only this time lots of people were present. That allowed us to understand: Loveness was speaking in tongues,

THE AUTOBIOGRAPHY OF TATENDA TAIBU

a phenomenon where people use a language unknown to them. We came to realise it was a spiritual gift.

Although I didn't act for the church in any official capacity, I often found myself discussing and expanding on my faith to others. Every time I was required to go to Harare for business I would end up somewhere giving testimony of how I had been changed. It was particularly easy for me to have these conversations because people were interested as to why I had stopped playing cricket, giving me the opportunity to expand on my faith. On many occasions I would be invited to people's homes for a little talk, which would often end up taking up the whole of my day.

One gentleman whom I became acquainted with was a man named Gora, and one day he called me, asking me to take a prayer request to my church in Bulawayo. I had a spent a few days in the company of him and several other Harare friends; they would come to my house, listen to my sermons and then pray. His son had been given up by the hospital and sent home, not because they could not help him but because his family could not afford the medication that he needed.

Gora's little boy had not passed urine for two days and was in great pain. He got his wife and children and we met at the college where he worked. His brother-in-law, named Sakavapo, came over and offered prayer, and after he left we got into a room and started singing until there was a very welcoming spirit. We talked and talked about God's power to heal, and how He had done His healing already when Jesus was crucified on Calvary.

When I felt his wife was really starting to believe, I then asked for the baby and we all started to pray. As we were praying I started to feel my shirt get wet because of the boy's temperature, but as we continued to pray I could feel it drop. I felt him put his head on my left shoulder, and when we had finished I looked down to find he was sleeping. To share the story of how the boy had been granted healing around the table at dinner with Loveness and the boys was such a fulfilling feeling. I was travelling a lot at this point, but I always tried to suffocate my family with as much love as I could in these moments.

There was also Noah, an acquaintance I made on my travels. Not long after we had first met, I received a call from him. He asked me to pray for his mum, whose doctors had given up on her due to the rare condition she had. Her only chance was a possible operation, but owing to the low sugar levels in her boy that option was fraught with danger. Noah had been told to spend his mother's last days with her, as there was nothing that could be done. Loveness and I started praying for her every day, but we did not get word of any improvement. As usual I was listening to a sermon, and I heard something about sincerity that struck my heart. The preacher said that when you are praying for someone you must be sincere, whether it was your mother, brother, father or sister. Right away I went to Loveness and told her that I was going to the rural areas of Shurugwi to pray for Mrs Gabi, the lady in question.

When I arrived in Gweru, the capital of Midlands province, to ask Noah for directions he was surprised to see me, but though he tried to stop me at first, he eventually made the journey as well. When we arrived I realised what a bad state she was in. She could hardly walk and was holding onto the walls for help, and her condition was worsening all the time.

I immediately got my Bible and started reading from the passage that had inspired me to visit her. I could tell she was failing to pick up the meaning of the words – and because I was in a hurry I failed to understand why that was. I continued speaking, until I realised I was reading from an English Bible. I quickly got Noah to read from the Shona language Bible. As soon as I saw that she was beginning to understand, I asked to pray. I believed so much that the Lord heard us during these moments.

Another man I came across during this period was Sam, who was the song leader at our church. Sam had shown me a lot of warmth when I first started attending the church, and I had a lot of time for him. Sam often visited Harare for business, and on one occasion he asked to borrow my car for the arduous journey. On his way home from Harare he was involved in an awful car accident, a head-on collision which put him in a life-threatening condition in the hospital.

Sam had sustained multiple fractures and Kenias, the church usher who was in the passenger seat at the time, had a broken femur. The third person in the car was Nyasha, the treasurer of the church. He had been seated in the back and thankfully hadn't suffered any major injuries.

They had both been rushed to Chitungwiza Central Hospital, a short distance outside of Harare, and I headed straight there to pray for them. Neither Sam nor Kenias were on medical aid and so we had to look for US$16,000 to cover the costs of the operations they needed. A lot of people – church members, relatives and friends – chipped in with whatever they could to help.

We arrived at the hospital shortly before Sam was to be operated on. Sam's wife and two kids had joined me, as had Kenias's two teenagers. We had left in the early hours of the morning and had passed through the place where the accident had taken place. After seeing the condition of the vehicle, we all just thanked God that they had come out alive. After they were both operated on they looked so frail. Sam especially did not look good at all. He had been placed into the Intensive Care Unit and there were a lot of machines, drips and pipes by his bed the first time I saw him. However, when he saw me he smiled, and that gave me a lot of confidence that he would eventually pull through.

I had taken shelter at the house of one of Kenias's boys, Wadilove, around 45 minutes away from the hospital. We lived like soldiers for six weeks, on the go at all times. We woke at 4am each day to wash, eat and pray, before leaving at 5.15am to pick up the wives, who were staying slightly closer to the hospital. We would arrive in time for the morning visit at 6am. It would have been exhausting, time-consuming and a waste of money to drive back to Wadilove's house before the afternoon visit, so instead we would sit in the car under a tree, listening to sermons and reading the Bible. That was how we spent the time between the morning and afternoon visits; in between the afternoon and evening visits we would catch up on sleep.

One day during this time I had a feeling in my heart that if I went in and started to hold Sam's hand for a while then he would eventually regain movement in it. While others visited to pray, I was praying in my heart for his recovery. On the way back, I told his son Tino that when we visited the following day we would see him moving his hand. Naturally, Tino wanted to be the first to witness that, and he did first thing the next morning. Sam was waving his hand and singing when he walked in for the morning visit, and upon seeing this Tino ran out of the room, shouting and praising the Lord. Everyone else in the waiting room had no idea what was going on. There were only two people allowed in a room with a patient at any given time, so no one else had witnessed it. I had to tell the nurses that if Sam felt he could get up and walk at any time then they had to stop him. Sam did start to believe that he would eventually be able to walk, though, and so adamant was he that I began to think the same thing. I was in a state of believing the impossible. It had been done before in the time of old and it could happen again.

Soon after Sam had responded, I received another welcome boost to sustain me in these exhausting circumstances. Noah's mother, Mrs Gabi, was now making a full recovery despite the diagnosis of the doctors, and she was giving thanks to me. I quickly corrected her: I hadn't done anything, it was the Lord that had healed her. Her daughter, whom I had never met before, also called to give thanks.

Despite all of this, I did not consider myself to be a faith healer, and I do not think there is anyone on this earth that can claim to be one. However, I do believe that God will try and carry out all that He has promised. In the Bible, the Lord is said to be the one 'who healeth all thy diseases', and I truly believe that to be the case. I believe it completely.

That is why I spend time trying to carry God's message and did so during this period of time in the hospital. It's also why I took time to speak to people who had already been given up on by the doctors. If someone was still being treated and was likely to recover, I would pray with them, but that was it. However, it was those who had been told that they had no chance of recovery that I really tried to connect with in these moments.

I really tried to get them to understand the Lord in the way I did at this time. Once they started to catch on, to feel His spirit, I truly believed with all of my heart that nothing would stop them healing.

It's hard for me to explain what it is like to visit a state hospital in Zimbabwe if you have not been in one – you will witness things that you have never seen before. There is simply not enough medication to go around in these state hospitals, and you literally walk around seeing people die in front of your eyes. It can be a harrowing experience.

On the opposite side of the bed to Sam was a man named Elijah, who had been struck by one of his drinking partners. He was unconscious, and when his relatives came to visit they would just sit there and cry. I started speaking to them about the Lord, telling them of how Jesus had calmed the storm by saying, 'Peace! Be still!' and the wind and waves had obeyed. I was trying to encourage them to believe and not to doubt. They were not church-going people and they did not know how to pray. I asked them just to say what was in their hearts to God, encouraging them that the Lord knows the heart of a man. Crying had no virtue at all, but faith changes things.

Sam left the ICU soon after that, but Elijah had hardly recovered at all. He had gained consciousness and was now opening his eyes, but he was making noises without saying anything any of us could understand. The doctors had decided that nothing else could be done for him: he would never be able to walk, talk, sit or eat properly again. Upon hearing this news his sister was particularly distressed.

She was on her own, waiting for the elders to arrive and decide who was going to look after Elijah. I tried to get her to calm down like I had done before, using the inspiration of Jesus, but on this occasion, I failed. In the end I just gave her a dollar, so she could call the others to complete arrangements. They had spent so much money only to be told that nothing could be done for Elijah.

As I was leaving I bumped into her husband and started to tell him what I had been trying to explain to them about the power of God. He was very responsive and so I took the opportunity to ask for permission to pray for Elijah before the following morning, when he was to be discharged. The nurses respected me and so allowed me to see him after hours. The doctors informed me that half of his brain was never going to function properly again.

I opened the Bible ready to speak, but first I had to get his attention, so I called for his name. Sure, enough he turned his head, and I asked him to keep quiet for the reading. We read, and I asked him to close his eyes while we prayed. The nurses just stared at me; to them it was not normal that I was sitting there talking to a person they had declared insane. When we finished praying, I told him that I wanted to see him sitting the next time I visited. All the people in the room looked at me as he tried to hold my hand but missed. I sat with the nurse for a while, enquiring about the decision to discharge him. While we spoke, Elijah took hold of the side rails on his bed and tried to help himself up into a sitting position. All the nurses on duty rushed to him and I just walked out.

I returned to the hospital to find that plans to discharge Elijah had been abandoned. The nurse I saw told me that he was now able to sit and say two words, *kumba*, meaning home, and *mvura*, meaning water. He was also able to eat properly again. Months later, word came to that he was now able to do everything he had been capable of doing before the accident. If I compare the feeling when I heard that news with that of scoring a century, there is only one winner. Playing a part in changing someone's life provided me with such satisfaction, a feeling that stays with me to this day.

Though this path I had taken soon became very fulfilling, at first it was very frightening. Imagine if someone you had lived with all your life, who only speaks English as well as some Ndbele and Shona, suddenly starts talking fluently in another language. Loveness spoke in tongues on several occasions, and that was both confusing and frightening for us at the time, because it was something that we had not known.

Meanwhile, I regularly had this feeling that would take over me, a kind of spirit inside of me. It is almost impossible to explain this feeling to someone who has never experienced it, but I know it's real. It happened to me on one occasion when I was speaking to a group of teenagers about my experiences in the hospital. As I was speaking I was completely aware that I was not thinking at all, but words would come spilling out of my mouth nonetheless. While I was speaking to these teenagers one girl in the front row got up and started speaking in tongues. Another one got up, then another one did. I was confused; it was like people speaking different languages but all in harmony. The atmosphere makes you feel very sane. It's very humbling. I just bowed my head and said a short prayer before walking out to my car. I just lay down on my seat. I had no idea what was happening. 'What is my destiny?' I wondered.

I didn't quit international cricket to pursue my faith to prove a point to anyone, nor did I make all of those hospital visits to prove a point. I simply felt as if I was following the path of the Lord. If I felt I could help someone in trouble by speaking and praying to them, that's what I did, no matter the inconvenience. The intense, time-consuming nature of it did not bother me at all, and I felt at peace. It was why I had to quit the game I had loved in the first place.

The feelings I experienced in these moments, whether it be at the hospital or just speaking to others at church, and the emotions I have felt at times since, are far more powerful than anything I ever experienced on a cricket field. Because of that, I don't think I will ever experience the void that other professional cricketers do after retirement. I don't think it will even cross my mind.

18
Trying to Keep the Faith

IT WAS 2016 AND I HAD NOT PICKED UP A BAT FOR FIVE YEARS. My life had become completely detached from the game that had consumed my early adult years. Loveness and I had just bought another property in Bulawayo and were about to go through our usual procedure of renovating and then selling on. After finishing this particular renovation, it was time to decide on what we were going to do for the next three years, which is about as far as we liked to plan ahead. Politically and economically, things were not moving well in Zimbabwe.

TJ had come to the decision that he wanted to be a neurosurgeon. The standards of the schools in our home country seemed to be slipping, and we felt as if it was only fair if we gave him the best opportunity to achieve this dream of his. Once upon a time when we were young our parents did what they could to help us. If the boy wanted to be a neurosurgeon, then we wanted to give him the best opportunity to be one. Part of how we could help him was to get him into a good school, and so we decided to do something completely different for a change. We were going to move to the UK.

From my long years spent playing cricket at the top level, most of the people I knew abroad were connected with the game. That's how I had made my name. The easiest way to come over to the UK was to take advantage of that name. I went on to a site called Pitch Vision, an online cricket training platform where you can also find jobs. I posted an advert, explaining who I was and how I was looking to get back into the game. I got three responses quite quickly, but it was a man named Nick Gordon with whom I instantly clicked. Nick represented a club named

Hightown St Mary's, based in Crosby, a coastal town just north of Liverpool, in the northwest of England. I didn't even do a website check on the club itself: my conversation with Nick alone was enough to convince me that this is where we were going.

We immediately started looking for schools when we arrived, while we also had to work out how we were going to move our money over from Zimbabwe. I wasn't working, I was only playing club cricket, so we needed to sort that first. We came across St Mary's College, an independent Catholic school, and after looking at the prospectus we decided it was the right one for our boys. It also worked nicely for me as well, because thanks to Nick's relationship with the headmaster I was able to use my cricketing knowledge to do some coaching there.

I hadn't picked up a bat in an awful long time, but I told my new teammates that I would be fine; time had moved on, but I didn't feel like my ability and feel for the game had just evaporated into thin air. If I had been returning to the international scene then I might have encountered a few problems, but instead I was going to be playing in the Second Division of the Liverpool and District Cricket Competition. I got into the nets, hit a few balls, borrowed some gloves, borrowed a bat. I scored 66* in my first game. But we lost our first four matches of the season.

I soon realised that I was going to have to adapt my game to this level. I was the prize catch for our opposition; dismissing me would give them a good chance of winning the game. Whenever I got to around 25 they would start to spread the field in an attempt to stem my flow of runs. I needed to be smart tactically. Once I worked out how to pace my innings, I was fine. As a club we also became more diligent in our preparation for the weekend's games, making net sessions available to players on both a Tuesday and a Thursday. In the end we couldn't stop winning, and our first team ended the season in second place, earning promotion.

Of course, it wasn't long before my playing at this level attracted the attention of a few news outlets; Zimbabwe's former Test captain, who had quit the game at the age of 29, was now playing cricket in the second division of the Liverpool and District Competition after not picking up a bat for five years. It was not your averaging cricketing story.

The news quickly reached Zimbabwe. The man who had quit the international scene at such a young age in 2011, seemingly no longer interested in the game and deriving no joy from it, was back playing for no money. It wasn't long before the new chairman, Tavengwa Mukuhlani, a man who I had never dealt with before, was in touch. But before he could even ask the question, I set my stall out: I told him that I did not want to play international cricket again. I was simply helping out an amateur club, who had lost many of their players and had recently had their clubhouse burnt down, achieve promotion. It was as simple as that.

'Yeah, but you are doing that for someone else abroad, whereas Zimbabwe Cricket is struggling and could do with your expertise,' he said. Zimbabwe had hardly been serial winners when I was playing, but things had certainly not got any better since I had left.

'Thank you very much,' I told Mukuhlani, 'but it doesn't fit in with my long-term plan for now. However, we can continue to speak about it.' We continued our discussion, on and off, while my family and I got adapted to our new life in the UK. When Loveness and the kids decided they were comfortable, I was able to go back to Zimbabwe for longer stints to conduct business I had there. On one of my returns Mukuhlani arranged a meeting with me and we ended up speaking for four or five hours, right up until midnight. His main goal was to try and get me to ditch my other work commitments aside from Hightown, so I could return to the fold.

I was as honest as I could be with him. 'Look, my life has gone on without Zimbabwean cricket. I'm really not sure I want to be getting involved, given how much I have suffered in the past.' He gave me his word and was adamant that those problems all existed in the past as part of the previous era. I told him that I would have go away and speak to Loveness about it, but I knew well enough by now that she would give me her backing, whatever I decided on. In the end, I thought I could see if I could help out. But not as a player.

Despite agreeing to return to the fold, I did not believe that Zimbabwe Cricket had sorted out the problems that blighted them in the past. In fact, I thought the opposite. If things were better, there would have been no need for them to call on me. I had spoken to a few people I knew well on the inside as well, and they had assured me that there were still plenty of issues. The reason I returned was because I trusted the new chairman's word. I thought he had the right intentions and that with time his intentions would help Zimbabwean cricket move in the right direction, with the help of people like me. I knew the organisation was still a shambles, but I had some faith in Mukuhlani as an individual.

Primarily they wanted me to be the convener of selectors. One of the things that was agreed on was that I would not move back to Zimbabwe. As selector, I would be able to understand what was going on from afar, and I was still young, so I was happy to travel a fair amount too. I only wanted to sign a one-year contract as well. That way I wasn't committing for too long if I didn't like what I saw. After my first meeting with the chairman we agreed on another soon after, which would also include the director of the organisation and the head of the cricket committee. 'Look,' I said, 'before I make a decision I have several questions to ask.'

It's fair to say that there weren't many answers forthcoming. I started by asking about the development of young Zimbabwean talent, centring on the high-performance pathway. How were players going to make it through our current system? I then moved onto logistical issues such as floodlights. By now all the best T20 competitions in the world – the IPL, the Big Bash – were played under the glare of floodlights. When I quit the Test arena in 2011, one of my gripes was that they were happy to spend money on floodlights but they were still not paying their players properly. Five years on and the pylons at Harare Sports Club were still up, but the problem was, there were no lights on these pylons.

As I was going through this, I could see Wilfred Mukondiwa taking these notes – were these issues not already being addressed? It soon turned out that it would be me addressing them. Not only was I to be convener of selectors, but I was to be a consultant on special projects and development. I wasn't given any help on the selection front – I had to find my own allies to assist me – and I was already taking on more roles before I had even started my new job. Usual service resumed.

I got straight down to work, surveying and interviewing around fifty people as we put our high-performance pathway together. As I was the chief selector for the A side and the development team as well, it quickly became clear to me that the same names were cropping up again and again for selection. That's when I knew we needed immediate change.

I had met with a man called John Armstrong, who was the head of Physical Education at my boys' school in the UK, St Mary's. He loved his cricket and so we met on several occasions, bouncing ideas around. It was after a discussion with him that I had the thought of bringing young Zimbabwean players over to the UK to help further their cricketing experience. I modified what we had talked about and came up with a programme to present to my seniors at ZC. It was to be called the Rising Stars Academy. In my presentation, I noted how many players there were around the national set-up, often playing in the A side, who had been floating around the Zimbabwean first-class system for years. Many of these players were firmly in their comfort zone, and people involved in the game knew that they would not make the jump successfully to the next step, the international stage.

Although a green light was given for the academy to go ahead in the UK, we had a very tight budget and the support from the organisation was almost non-existent. Many people did not see the reason behind taking the players to the UK, and the issue of them being granted a visa was also raised. Our national team national team had not toured England since the ICC Champions Trophy in 2004. In 2008, the British government had intervened to suspend cricketing ties between the two nations, and the two teams had not played each other since in a full international.

I personally got in touch with the ECB to explain the situation in order to try to avoid any problems between the two boards, and I was delighted when our player applications for visas were accepted. The Rising Stars Academy was born.

The UK was the destination of choice because of the standard of facilities there and because of the standard of cricket. We did not need to play against the first XIs of county sides to find competitive cricket. Touring the UK would give the players an opportunity to forget about their worries in day-to-day life in Zimbabwe and allow them to concentrate more on the game of cricket and what they could achieve in it. I studied 'Maslow's Hierarchy of Needs', a motivational theory in psychology comprising a five-tier model of human needs. The final tier is self-actualisation – 'achieving one's full potential' – and that was the level we hoped the players would reach. We wanted them to make the most of their obvious talents. Perhaps more importantly, we also wanted the project to take them out of their comfort zone, so they could grow as human beings.

My small working team consisted of Stuart Matsikenyeri, who was coach; Nick Gordon, the team manager; and Alec Gezi, the life coach. Alec had been my personal manager during my playing days and had often been a great help to me. However, we were really up against it.

At first, the programme was despised in all corners of Zimbabwean cricket, and I had to fight tooth and nail to get it off the ground. Something like this had never been done before and people just could not seem to understand how it could possibly work. Many of these people did not understand the game itself and had not seen it being implemented elsewhere. It meant they couldn't paint a picture in their heads. In the end, I told them to just let me get on with it.

They could come back to me in six months and if it wasn't working I would accept any criticism.

In our first year we did not achieve our goals but enjoyed some success on the cricketing front. Our squad of sixteen played in 48 matches across the English summer – a tour Nick Gordon was very helpful in setting up – with the opposition ranging from club sides to first-class second XIs. We had a training base in the Liverpool suburb of Aigburth where Lancashire sometimes play, which allowed us to closely monitor the players, and highlights included wins over the MCC and a strong Surrey second XI. Of the 48 scheduled games we won 29, drew three and lost just eight (due to the English weather, the other eight were cancelled). It was a good return.

Further to that, we soon became the fifth franchise in Zimbabwean cricket ahead of the 2017/18 season, giving the players a chance to prove themselves at first-class level. The boys struggled in the Logan Cup, losing three of their first four games in an eight-match competition, meaning they finished bottom of the table, but they excelled in the fifty-over format, winning the final against Mountaineers after topping the group stage after the same number of fixtures. It was a real achievement against players who had competed at this level for years. Of the players who competed in that final in June 2018, not one has yet passed the age of 25.

Winning that competition told me two things: firstly, it told me we did achieve some good things on the playing side almost straightaway. It also told me that while these players were at a higher level than we had originally thought, the standards in Zimbabwean cricket remained critically low. Of the four games we played against second XI county sides in England we won one, drew one and lost two. If we were able to then win the fifty-over competition in Zimbabwe against first XIs, then how far behind was our cricket?

Of the sixteen players we took to England on tour in 2017, four had already represented Zimbabwe at full international level – Ryan Burl, Tarisai Musakanda, Richard Ngarava and Carl Mumba. However, three quickly made their international debuts soon after – Tinashe Kamunhukamwe, who featured in two ODIs against Pakistan in 2018, Brandon Matuva, who made his Test and ODI debuts in the same year, and the tall fast bowler Blessing Muzarabani, who has recently signed for Northamptonshire in England.

This was after six months' work. I told the board that if we kept this academy running all year round for the next five years we would be able to achieve so much more. Unfortunately, we would never find out.

At the start of 2018, we also had the small matter of hosting qualification for the 2019 World Cup in England. Because of the ICC's decision to cut the number of teams competing at the main event from fourteen in 2015 to ten in 2019 and 2023, we had to face up against three other full member nations in Ireland, Afghanistan and the West Indies, and four associate nations in Hong Kong, Nepal, Papua New Guinea and Scotland in qualifying. Only two would make it through to the full competition. Zimbabwe had competed in all nine World Cups since our first appearance in 1983, so all our focus was geared towards making sure we would be at the next one.

I strongly disagree with the decision the ICC has made to make the World Cup – the biggest tournament in the sport – smaller. Ultimately, it boils down to money, TV money. It's the way a lot of sport has gone. It's a money industry. If that wasn't the case, there wouldn't be so much noise about the USA becoming a more prominent cricketing nation. They've got an economy that works already. There wouldn't be talk about China either. They've got an economy that works already. If more African countries had economies that were working, then you can guarantee the ICC would be taking a closer look at them.

I think the ICC have to ask themselves if cricket really is that much better off as a sport than it was when money wasn't the dominant factor. When the great West Indies side was the dominant force in cricket during the 80s, it wasn't just because they had the most financial muscle. I think it helps sometimes to take a step away from it all and see what you are actually doing to grow the game, rather than just thinking about money, money, money. Sport is always evolving. If you start to build the game in more countries around the world and commit to helping these smaller nations, then the game will continue to grow, and the money will eventually follow as a result. My view is that the money follows the sport eventually. Sport should not follow the money.

What has happened with the World Cup as a case in point does not bode well for the future. Cricket is a game which is very difficult to get better at if you are not playing better opposition. The game is the same at associate and full member levels, but the difference is the margin of error and speed at which it is played. The quicker the speed, the sharper your reflexes become. It's a simple thing, but you can't emulate that match simulation anywhere else. It has to be on the field.

Think about it: pace has been so crucial to the best teams of so many different eras. The West Indies team of the 80s often played with five quicks; Australia at their best in the early noughties had Glenn McGrath, Brett Lee and Jason Gillespie; South Africa have constantly churned out great pacemen, names such as Allan Donald, Dale Steyn and Kagiso Rabada; the England side that so famously beat Australia in 2005 could call on the services of Steve Harmison and Andrew Flintoff. The advent of the IPL has helped India to produce perhaps their best-ever pace attack, and they have just won a Test series in Australia for the first time in their history. Jasprit Bumrah, the unorthodox star of that attack, mastered his craft in the IPL. As a result of the IPL, Indian batsmen have been exposed to more quality fast bowling on a regular basis, and they therefore learn how to make their game better. How will players not from the big nations keep up with this? I worry deeply about how often the smaller nations will meet the bigger nations in the years to come, now there is no major tournament to bridge the gap. It's up to the powers that be to decide.

In December 2016, Heath Streak returned to coach the national team. Heath and I go back a long way: he was my captain when I was vice-captain; I was his captain when he was vice-captain. We had worked together a lot. Heath got me very involved in the process, even inviting me down to the meetings where gameplans would be discussed. I had a hand in that and I don't think the players felt uneasy with it.

We worked together closely, understanding that once again we were in a bit of a crisis. After a tri-series with West Indies and Sri Lanka our first main opponent was Afghanistan, whom we lost to 3-2 in February of 2017. But after a 1-1 draw with Scotland in June, things really clicked into place on a tour of Sri Lanka in July: we won the ODI series 3-2, and nearly pulled off an equally miraculous victory in our only Test match. It was our first ODI series win against any of the full member nations, barring Ireland, Afghanistan and Bangladesh, since we had beaten New Zealand in 2001. It was some achievement.

That result was followed up by the return of Brendan Taylor, Kyle Jarvis and Solomon Mire to the national-team set-up. Taylor and Jarvis had both been making more money in the English county game than they could hope to make playing for their country, but with a slightly more professional set-up now in place, it was left to me to try and convince them to come back ahead of qualifying. Both players respected me from our playing days, and ZC knew that if they had spoken to the pair themselves there would have been no hope. I was able to talk them round, which was a big boost ahead of the qualifiers.

Heath and me were generally trying to improve the name of Zimbabwean cricket, which had taken a real beating over the years. The perception of us was not good, and it's something we have brought upon ourselves as a cricketing nation. It did not take long for that perception to present itself as reality again. At the start of 2018, in our last series before the World Cup qualifiers, we were playing against Afghanistan in the UAE. I was there, and so too it transpired was one of our board members from Zimbabwe. He soon demanded a meeting with me, Faisal Hasnain – our new managing director – and Heath.

Apparently, the board were not happy with how we were selecting the team. There was, he reported, a feeling that some players were only being picked because they had come through my academy – chiefly Blessing Muzarabani and Ryan Bell. Heath backed me up, telling the board member in question that it had been his decision to select both Blessing and Ryan, while Faisal also questioned the board's approach.

After this meeting, I decided to write to the chairman and Faisal to voice my concerns. I told them that it didn't make sense that they had sent a board member all the way to the UAE for a thirty-minute meeting. It's something that could have been done over the phone or, failing that, when we got back to Zimbabwe. They could have used that money to reimburse me for funds I had used to help get the academy going. I was not amused.

Faisal called me not long after and broke the news to me that Heath now had the final call on all selection matters – the board wanted more accountability. It heaped the pressure on an already overburdened coach and made my role as chief selector pretty redundant.

My academy wasn't the only thing not being paid for properly in the organisation – the first team were not receiving their wages fully either. In November 2017 staff were only paid in part, and in December they were not paid their wages at all. ZC were able to catch up on outstanding payments by mid-January thanks to one of their two annual ICC distributions, but in the very next month staff were not paid properly again, only receiving forty percent of their salaries. Our players were still owed their match fees from the Sri Lankan tour. What was happening felt eerily familiar.

Given how involved in the organisation I was, I was very aware of what was going on. I believed it was my duty to stand with the players. If you were to take a look at my letters to the chairman and the managing director around that time, a lot of them will have been addressing the issue of pay and why the players weren't receiving theirs. When I was a player, the time we were playing our best cricket was when getting paid regularly; the 25th of every month. Very simple. The last thing you want on your mind as a player is nagging doubts about your life on the outside: have I paid my rent? Have I paid my child's school fees? You're hardly going to be concentrating on the ball if those are the issues at the forefront of your mind.

I used to raise these points in meetings, bringing me into direct conflict with board members. I didn't think much of them anyway; I was there because I believed in the chairman. I didn't want to be the sort of person who only raised these issues once I had left the organisation and was speaking to the media. I wanted to tackle the problem head-on.

I tried to bring up the idea of having a players' representative. There is always a fence between players and the administrators, and I found myself as the man in between them, trying to get them to work together. The players needed a union. When I was meant to be discussing selection with them I was discussing ways of making this happen. The players would be stronger and better protected if they could work together and with a representative. Unfortunately, some of the lads just could not see the thinking behind it and so it never got off the ground. It was frustrating.

I believed that throughout my career I always tried to fight for the right cause, and I had huge respect for others that did as well. It's why I stood up for Brendan Taylor more recently when he was not selected for the tri-series against Australia and Pakistan in June 2018. Brendan – along with Graeme Cremer, Craig Ervine, Sikandar Raza and Sean Williams – was demanding a payment plan for outstanding salaries and match fees they were owed. The players were negotiating through their resurrected player association, which Brendan had been the driving force behind.

I know for a fact that all the captains that came after me when I left for Bangladesh in 2005 were offered something by the powers that be to keep quiet about certain issues. I had been offered similar incentives myself. It meant they wouldn't stand up for anything in the future. For Taylor to stand up then made me think that when he was captain, he did not take whatever was offered to him from our hierarchy. If you look at everyone else who has taken the captaincy role, a pattern emerges.

To accept money in these circumstances is pure greed. How can a captain derive joy from knowing he is sorted out as an individual, but his team is not? What kind of captain and leader does that make him? A leader is meant to pull everyone through, not wander off on their own. I cannot understand how a captain would accept something that only benefits them and no one else. What sort of team are you going to end up with? It's a cancer that needs cutting out, otherwise it will continue to be like that. The youngsters will come through the same system, and who will be the one to stop them doing the same thing?

At one point shortly before the qualifiers, the players were planning a boycott, which forced me to step in with the board again. 'The money we get from the ICC, where is that? I heard the players are going to boycott. Why is that?'

'They don't want to believe that we have managed to secure some funds for them,' came the reply.

'Well have you managed to secure funds?"

'We have, here is the letter.'

'Why don't you just go and tell them?'

'They don't want to hear anything from us.'

It ended up being me who took the letter to the players. 'Okay, this is the situation, and you know I wouldn't be coming here if it wasn't. The money has been secured.'

One of the lads responded by saying, 'Tatenda, the reason why we are doing this is we trust you and know you wouldn't lie to us, but these people have lied to us before.'

What was frustrating was that if ZC did not have the necessary funds to pay the players all their wages at once, why weren't they just saying so? If they only receive their money in instalments, why not tell the players that? You get more respect that way, and people trying to help. It saves so much hassle in the long run.

We were fast approaching the qualifiers. I don't care what people say, these issues affect players and their mindset while they're out on the field. If you're dealing with car park issues, carrying things on your shoulders while you are out there, you don't have much chance in international cricket. Their play was being compromised to begin with, and they had to try to put that aside and perform.

It was almost possible. They were really up against it. As well as that, they had the board trying to get involved in selection. Heath was not being given enough time to come up with a specific gameplan. We were behind from the word go.

Our first game in qualifying was against one of these associate nations, Nepal, and the margin of victory was convincing: 116 runs. Both Brendan Taylor and Sikandar Raza scored hundreds as we amassed a score of 380-6, and Nepal could only make 264 in response. I wasn't happy, though. For the game I sat in the presidential enclosure, and so did several of the board members. After the victory, one of those board members made a remark about how well Zimbabwe had played.

'You don't even know what you're talking about,' I told him. Shocked by my tone, he asked me what I meant. 'Right now, you haven't approved my plans for the academy this summer and we are already in March. We are late already. Surely after the results it has given us after just one year, you should be jumping on it. You should be saying that this should go on for the next five years, but you're not. That shows that you don't know what you're doing. Yes, we have played Nepal and won, and it looks clinical on the eye. But I have been in cricket a long time, and it's not there.'

At that point, one of the other board members came up to me and said, 'We're not going to approve kids going to London just to see street lights.'

'The sad thing is you sit here and talk about that when you've got no idea what it takes to produce a youngster who will go out there and perform at the highest level,' I said. 'You sent someone to come to England and assess my academy and what did they do? They spent one day assessing. What can you assess in one day? He had a look at where the boys were staying, where we were practising, the food they were eating, the gym they were using, the facilities, and then he went to London for the rest of the weekend before heading back to Zimbabwe. Surely, he does some assessment? When he came to see me, I said, "If you do not change and start to listen to people who know the game, we are going to go the way of Kenya. Unfortunately, when you realise it will be too late." I'm not going to continue sitting here listening to this rubbish,' I said, finishing my tirade.

I got up to leave, but the board member sat closest took me by the hand and got me to sit down. 'No, let's finish this.' By this point there were vulgar words being exchanged in Shona, words that can't be repeated. There was no good in this conversation continuing, so I messaged Loveness and asked her to call me. When she did, I used it as my excuse to leave.

The boys out on the field continued to perform admirably given the situation. Blessing Muzarabani starred against Afghanistan, picking up 4-47 as we defended a total of 196. An easy win over Hong Kong and a thrilling tie with Scotland saw us comfortably into the Super Sixes, where we would face Ireland, the West Indies and the UAE.

The first game of the Super Sixes brought perhaps our best win yet. After 69* from the inspirational Raza allowed us to reach a score of 211, three wickets each from Tendai Chisoro and Graeme Cremer in a brilliant bowling performance saw us bowl Ireland out for just 104. We had thrashed a fellow full member nation, and now needed just one win from our games against the West Indies and the UAE to progress to the World Cup. The game against the former was a stunner, with Taylor once again coming to the party when we needed it most. His masterful 138 from 124 balls lifted us to 289 from our fifty overs, an eminently defendable score. We nearly did defend it as well, but contributions from Evin Lewis, Shai Hope and Marlon Samuels helped the West Indies reach their tricky total with just an over left to spare.

In our do-or-die match against the UAE, we asked our opponents to bat and Raza, the standout player of the tournament, picked up 3-41 from his ten overs. However, their total of 235-7 in 47.5 overs was a threatening one, especially with rain likely to play a part in the chase. In the end we were set 230 to win in forty overs and looked to be in some trouble when Taylor was bowled for fifteen, leaving us 45-3. Peter Moor and Sean Williams brought us back into contention, the former making 39 and the latter a run-a-ball 80. However, by the time Moor was dismissed we still required 106 runs from 12.2 overs and some serious impetus. That was provided by Raza, who made 34 from 26, and Ervine, who was left unbeaten on 22 from seventeen, but we were left in trouble at 209-7 when our captain Cremer was bowled first ball by the pacy Mohammad Naveed. Ervine and Kyle Jarvis took us to the last over needing fifteen runs for victory, but we could only manage eleven. In the most agonising of circumstances, four runs the margin of defeat, we had failed to qualify for the World Cup, the first time we would not be at cricket's biggest tournament since we had become a member of the ICC. It was heartbreaking for all concerned.

We had been supported in big numbers throughout the tournament, and for our final match the Harare Sports Club had been packed out. Eventually the gates had been closed and people had been turned away from the ground. The pain they were feeling was the worst thing about it all. I got along with several players in that side and would have loved to have seen them perform at the World Cup. I grew up with Hamilton Masakadza and knew this was his last opportunity to play in one, so I was gutted for him. First of all, I am Zimbabwean, and I would have loved to see my country compete. It would also have meant me continuing in my role with Zimbabwe Cricket and I would have tried to keep effecting change. I have always believed, especially in a country like Zimbabwe, that you have to make changes from within. It is impossible to effect any meaningful change from the fringes.

There were some similarities in the problems between co-hosting the 2003 World Cup and hosting the qualifiers for the 2019 edition. However, in 2003 the house was at least painted. Sure, the foundations were messed up, but until the tournament itself things in Zimbabwean cricket were rosier than they ever had been. This time around that wasn't the case: everyone knew the problems with Zimbabwean cricket and had known for a long time.

These problems did not go away once the games began. Ahead of our crunch match with the West Indies, half of our players did not turn up to training because they had not been given their allowances. For the tournament, cash arrived in Zimbabwe from the ICC to pay the players. To all the teams who qualified for the Super Six stage, the ICC released daily allowances of US$100. However, the Zimbabwe side received their allowances by means of RTGS bank transfer into their bank accounts. When our players realised the other teams had been paid in US$100 bills, they protested. ZC responded by paying them $450 each in old tatty US$5 bills. When some players questioned this with the ZC authorities, they said the cash crisis was to blame, without explaining what had happened to the original money provided by the ICC. It seemed like the Zimbabwe Cricket management had kept the US$100 bills to themselves, eroding trust straightaway.

Since 2009 Zimbabwe has not had its own currency and has relied on the US dollar or South African rand. Officially, every kind of dollar has equal value – the US dollar, the Zimbabwean reserve bank-backed 'bond note' or a digital dollar held in a mobile wallet – but in reality, that's not the case. An article that appeared on *The Christian Science Monitor's* website in August 2018 neatly illustrated why being paid in US cash was more preferable for the players. According to the article, to get $100 US dollars on the blackmarket, you would need around $170 in EcoCash (the digital dollar), or $135 in bond notes.

There were many other problems as well. The liaison officers, the changing-room attendants and the drivers found themselves overworked and stretched too thinly, meaning there were times when they had to drive from Bulawayo to Harare and then back again in the same day. Net bowlers were supposed to receive a fee of $30 whenever they were involved in a session, but they were transferred just $12 each time. They were literally stealing money from net bowlers. Groundsmen were not getting their dues – these were things there for everyone to see. There was a list of machinery that was meant to arrive in the country for the qualifiers that never did. If the groundsmen had access to the Super Soppers that they were meant to have access to during the Zimbabwe v UAE match, then we would have lost no overs due to the weather, and things may have been different.

Though it was hugely disappointing not to make it through qualifying, I think that if we had done so, it may have created a false picture that everything was fine. The fans wouldn't have known what was going on behind the scenes and a lot of things would have been brushed aside. Even I would probably still be trusting the chairman like I had done when I first returned. Maybe I wouldn't have considered that he was not the right man for the job and didn't really know anything about the game. There wouldn't have been much accountability, instead it would have been a case of, 'We've qualified, like we have done on every other occasion in the past.' The truth is, there is not one kid in Zimbabwe now with a cricketing scholarship. The school system that used to produce so many cricketers is virtually dead in the water, and the talent stream has dried up.

Twenty-four hours after the defeat that had left us reeling the board members had an urgent meeting. How they managed to get everyone to that meeting within 24 hours, God knows. It normally takes around three weeks for such a meeting to take place, with all the board members present, but they had one right away. Once they were done they called Faisal Hasnain and told him that he had to call eighteen staff members and tell them all to resign. Faisal initially refused their order, but the pressure was applied and three days later he started ringing around.

Soon it was my turn to receive the call. I told Faisal I had no problem in resigning, but I wanted to know why: I was no longer in charge of selection, so the failure to reach the World Cup could not be pinned on me. I also pointed out how many different roles I had within the organisation. They could not replace me with any other members of the coaching staff, because they had sacked them all as well. I was done fighting with these people.

For the record, Heath refused to resign, instead daring ZC to sack him. Days later, they did. It wasn't long before comments accusing Heath of racism were streaming down from the top, from the chairman himself no less.

'Streak was the coach and selector, he was entitled to change the team as he found fit, but the question is: why did he change the team in the manner he did?' said chairman Mukuhlani to *Daily News*. 'The white players knew that PJ Moor was going to play [against UAE] but none of the black players knew about it. Cephas Zhuwao was only informed [he had been omitted] in the warm-up. Why didn't Streak inform the entire team?'

It was silly that Heath was forced to defend himself on these grounds. I spoke to Heath and his lawyer and promised I would speak for him in court if that's what it came down to. Once again it was a case of members of our board not being knowledgeable about the game of cricket. As soon as they were asked proper, simple cricketing questions they tried to make up for their lack of knowledge of the game by turning things racial. It's a technique they have used on countless occasions. By accusing Heath of being racist they were trying to work on people's emotions, trying to get the fans to turn against him. Heath was asking them simple, direct questions about his own dismissal, so that's the road they decided to go down, and it is a road well-trodden by them.

This time, though, the fans were not buying into what the board were saying. Not at all. They had seen me and Heath come in, and they had started to see some positive change. When Heath and I were dismissed, hardly anyone turned up to watch the T20 tri-series against Pakistan and Australia in July. The ones who came cheered whenever Australia's Aaron Finch hit a boundary in his record-breaking 172 from 76 balls, and even jeered some of our players. They were finding it difficult to support their own team, and they were definitely not on the board's side.

In all my years in Zimbabwean cricket, little has changed. Andy Flower and Henry Olonga were the first to make a stand against authority in 2003, protesting against the death of democracy, and in 2004 Heath followed after a row over race and selection policy with the board. As a young boy in the nascent stages of his international career, I often wondered why there was so much conflict between the players and the hierarchy. I did not agree with Andy and Henry's stand at the time because I did not believe sport and politics should mix. To me, they were two separate entities with different rules. As professionals, why couldn't we just get on with playing sport? I soon found out why.

In 2005, I was next to stand up to the board as I campaigned for my players to be paid what they deserved. It was a stand that left me at loggerheads not only with powerful figures in Zimbabwe Cricket, but powerful figures in Zimbabwean government. In Zimbabwe, I soon realised that dissent in the cricket world was crushed in the same way as it was in politics. It means you cannot separate the two, as desirable as it may be.

Fast forward to 2018, and Heath and I were both being sacked after Zimbabwe's failure to qualify for the 2019 World Cup in England. Upon my return to the set-up in 2016, I had found myself imploring the board to pay the current crop of players on time, just as I had done so long ago. Upon our dismissal in early 2018, Heath was accused of a racist selection policy by the ZC chairman, Tavengwa Mukuhlani. The problems were still the same ones that had plagued us during our playing careers.

Elsewhere in Zimbabwe, not a great deal has changed. In January, several people were killed and many more were injured after the Zimbabwean people took to the streets to protest against the government's decision to double the price of fuel overnight. The crackdown on protestors was so brutal that the government was forced to come out and say that it would investigate reports of violence against demonstrators, after the country's human rights commission said they had been 'systematically tortured'. The year? 2019.

Until violence and treat of violence cease to be the chief tactic among those with power in our country, a sense of fear will continue to pervade our society, and things will not get any better.

A Word from Stuart

STRONG-WILLED, HIGHLY FOCUSED, TRULY RESEMBLING A SMALL *package of dynamite. This is how I can describe, in a few words, the man whom I have had the privilege to walk hand in hand with. To fight, to disagree with, to battle alongside, to love. A legend of our time.*

I would have been around nine years old when I first met him, through cricket, of course. Cricket was still in its infancy in the high-density areas of Zimbabwe, and it was an exciting time for those of us that were coming into contact with the game. This pint-sized fellow was among those of us who were keen to swing some willow and throw the ball around, as was I. Whether it was our size, ability or the fact he owned a video game I can't remember, but somehow we ended up spending a fair bit of time together. From then on, a friendship was born and a brotherhood forged.

From the onset I could see I was in the presence of a special guy. We had different minds and yet we found common ground more often than not. One of my earliest memories of his loyalty is an incident not long into our friendship. Tatenda and I decided to open a joint piggy bank, but he'd put more money into it by virtue of getting more pocket money from his parents than I did. Eventually the time came to split our loot, and I suggested that he took the lion's share of the money out, given that he had put more in. That idea was crushed almost instantly. 'We share equally.' It's a quality of Tatenda's that remains to this day, even if we disagree on an awful lot.

Tatenda enjoyed a lot of success in his early cricketing years at school, and that was largely down to his attitude and determination, characterised by constant afternoons practising – rarely did we spend our spare time without bat and ball in hand. Every weekend we'd hop the fences of Chengu School just so that we could play the game we had fallen for. Being Tatenda, there had to be some drama involved at some stage. Being a highly talented athlete, he was also more than decent at soccer, and so at some stage he decided to start turning out for the Zimbabwe Crackers, a team that played in Highfield. It was I who had to deliver a message to him while he was at football from coach Steve, who demanded he returned to cricket, otherwise he would face the consequences. Luckily, he heeded the warning. I was also present when he got involved in a fist fight on the eve of our cricket scholarship trials and turned up to those trials without being able to use his dominant hand.

I was a witness when Tatenda first became infatuated with a girl. He thought he was in love, but how could he have known then? He'd write her name everywhere and save her half-eaten candy bars – it was highly entertaining watching him go crazy at this time. Of course, Tatenda lost his father around this time, and it was a confusing and traumatic thing for a young lad to have to go through. He took it in his stride and did okay in the circumstances. A highly determined, hard-working mum was there to be his shield, and what a wonderful job she did.

The loss of his father made Tatenda become all the more responsible very quickly, and this period shaped the character he was to later become. The long afternoons and the hard work with the bat became more purposeful. Our first taste of an international tour came in 1995. A development side was put together to play games in South Africa, with me and Tatenda both selected. I remember Tatenda's excitement at getting his first passport; his infectious laugh when our mate Arnold Rushambwa could not replicate his signature; the long trip in our hired VW vans. He fully enjoyed all that tour had to offer – friends made, cricket matches won and lost. He had a fairly successful tour on the field runs-wise, and it was here that we discovered what a good runner between the wickets he was. I was batting with him in a game against a team from Soweto, playing good-looking shots without really getting any runs. Coach Steve soon grew frustrated and instructed us to run for everything. It was here where he learned to become one of the best runners between the wickets that Zimbabwe has seen.

His early years in high school were filled with many new experiences for him, and it was the same for the rest of us. To me he seemed to have a little bit more of an edge than most of us, willing to put a little bit more into his cricket. We went on to have a very successful year with the Churchill Under-14 team, which saw us rewarded with national selection at the same age group. That meant another tour to South Africa and another opportunity to be exposed to a different level of cricket and *different cultures. At this stage he was still a batting all-rounder who bowled some off-spinners.*

When he returned from South Africa, his club side Takashinga exerted more pressure on him to keep working on his game, and in my opinion, he continued to put more effort in than most. I feel privileged when I look back at all the special moments we shared on the field for Churchill and Takashinga, and there are many achievements I could list here, but I guess that's down on record anyway. The most special thing was achieving these milestones with my best mate and a man I respect greatly.

Another incident that shaped Tatenda and gave him extra determination to succeed was the unfortunate passing of his mother while he was at school. As if he didn't have enough purpose already, this was when it went to a different level altogether. The shield of his family was now gone, and it had become clearer than ever that there was no option for him other than to win and win well. Still, he pushed hard while retaining his love for the game – he seemed to love it all the way through.

It was during this period that he was picked to represent a Zimbabwean side at men's level at the Africa Cup. It was not the main Zimbabwe side, but to be picked at such a tender age was special nonetheless. His new-found wicketkeeping skills played a big part in his development, and huge credit for that must go to Bill Flower, who used to take us all over the country to play cricket. Tatenda returned with stories of other talented African cricketers, such as Kenya's Martin Suji and Steve Tikolo, and it brought inspiration to us all back home. It seemed that he returned with even more hunger and drive from that trip, and plenty more accolades and disappointments occurred throughout the years. I loved him dearly through it all.

I remember both him and Hamilton Masakadza, another boy we had grown up with, winning their first international caps while still school boys. What a proud friend I was, especially for Tatenda. The school year of 1999/00 was another big turning point in his life for reasons outside of cricket. As sixth formers by now we enjoyed certain privileges at Churchill, and we used to hang around on Nigel Phillip field on both mornings and afternoons. A beautiful girl used to walk by every day, and she turned more than a few heads and had boys break into wishful conversations. Unbeknown to me, my mate had more than just an eye on her. Her name was Loveness, and her codename to us was 'bling bling.' Boy did she have his young heart and mind all wrapped up. Being the man Tatenda was, he had to win. There were a few suitors, but my boy Tiba captured her heart, and it remains captured to this day. From the moment they started dating, she became a huge part of his life. They were really happy in each other's company, and I could sense a genuineness in their relationship very early on.

I went to Australia in 2000 for a year of cricket, but I never fell out of touch with my good mate. The funny thing was I never really spoke to him directly during this time. Because he was touring most of the time I would call Loveness to find out how he was doing, and he would do the same thing. She was perfect to say the least. Our respective cricketing careers continued to push forward; successful periods and not so successful ones came and went, but his love life shaped him from there on.

Tatenda had been a person searching for a spiritual understanding for a good while, but never seemed satisfied with the answers that he found. Loveness had spent a lot of her upbringing living with sister in Bulawayo and had attended church from a young age. It was through her that Tatenda eventually came into contact with the church, and it was in that environment that he finally felt at home and found the truth as it were. This would eventually lead to a lot of change within the man. When he believes or gives his heart to something, he gives absolutely everything.

Noticeably, for a guy who for all his life had been brought up in a sporting environment, he was happy to turn his back on it once he had found his calling. My last cricket trip with my best mate was in New Zealand and by then he was not the same man off the field. He would still try hard during games, but results would not shake him left or right. Through his conviction of faith, he ended his playing career to lean on God, and He follows His instruction as He understands it. Nothing else matters, nothing else is true.

A Final Word

I HAVE NEVER REALLY SAID A LOT ABOUT THIS HIDDEN LIFE WHICH I have lived, but one speech has always kept me going:

Others May, You cannot:

If God has called you to be really like Jesus, He will draw you into a life of crucifixion and humility, and put upon you such demands of obedience, that you will not be able to follow other people, or measure yourself by other Christians, and in many ways He will seem to let other good people do things which He will not let you do.

Other Christians and ministers who seem very religious and useful, may push themselves, pull wires, and work schemes to carry out their plans, but you cannot do it; and if you attempt it, you will meet with such failure and rebuke from the Lord as to make you sorely penitent.

Others may boast of themselves, of their work, of their success, of their writings, but the Holy Spirit will not allow you to do any such thing, and if you begin it, He will lead you into some deep mortification that will make you despise yourself and all your good works.

Others may be allowed to succeed in making money, or may have a legacy left to them, but it is likely God will keep you poor, because He wants you to have something far better than gold, namely, a helpless dependence on Him, that He may have the privilege of supplying your needs day by day out of an unseen treasury.

The Lord may let others be honoured and put forward, and keep you hidden in obscurity, because He wants you to produce some choice, fragrant fruit for His coming glory, which can only be produced in the shade. He may let others be great, but keep you small. He may let others do work for Him and get the credit for it, but He will make you work and toil on without knowing how much you are doing; and then to make your work still more precious, He may let others get the credit for the work which you have done, and thus make your reward ten times greater then Jesus comes.

The Holy Spirit will put a strict watch over you, with a jealous love, and will rebuke you for little words and feelings, or for wasting your time, which other Christians never seem distressed over. So make up your mind that God is an infinite Sovereign, and has a right to do as He pleases with His own. He may not explain to you a thousand things which puzzle your reason in His dealings with you, but if you absolutely sell yourself to be His love slave, He will wrap you up in jealous love, and bestow upon you many blessings which come only to those who are in the inner circle.

Settle it forever, then, that you are to deal directly with the Holy Spirit, and that He is to have the privilege of tying your tongue, or chaining your hand, or closing your eyes, in ways that He does not seem to use with others. Now when you are so possessed with the loving God that you are, in your secret heart, pleased and delighted over this peculiar, personal, private, jealous guardianship and management of the Holy Spirit over your life, you will have found the vestibule of Heaven.

G.D. Watson, in *Living Words*.

From here on, my life continues. I have been blessed to achieve a few good things, but many mistakes I have made. My prayer is that my mistakes be stepping stones, but above all this there is a place I'm setting my eyes on, which is not in this life but the life to follow. I wish that if it were possible I would be able to see all who I have seen in this life. I know not where the Lord will lead me from now on, all I do is follow.

May God be with you as we all journey on ahead.

Acknowledgements

TO THE ONE WHO KNEW ME BEFORE I WAS EVEN IN MY MOTHER'S womb, who in His wisdom created me and continued to perfect me, I am forever humbled by your love and grateful for the gift of life.

Margaret Taibu, my mother, my first love, thank you for all the hard work and sacrifices that you made to keep the family together. Joseph Zuze Taibu, my father and my first life coach, the whippings didn't go in vain. I am what I am today because of your tough love. I hope I continue to make you proud. Mum and Dad, Rest in Peace.

My cricket coaches, because of you, a dream became a reality. My fans, your support and love kept me motivated and gave me the drive to score more, catch more and even bowl.

My friends, the family I had a privilege of choosing for myself, I thank you for being there for me always. You encouraged me to chase my dreams, and for that I remain eternally grateful.

Jack Gordon Brown, you are tall and I am short, you are a bowler and I'm a wicketkeeper, you are white and I am black, so how you managed to articulate this story the way you did is nothing short of inspirational. Thank you for catching all the emotions that were hiding for years.

Tatenda Junior Taibu, thank you for being so cheerful and being a part of making our home so irresistibly happy. Gershom Paul Taibu, thank you for being a happy, witty son who makes parenting such a joy.

Loveness, you have been all that I could ever ask for.

Last but not least, thank you to my good friend Nick Gordon, who helped me find a publisher, and to deCoubertin for allowing me to open my journey to the world.

Tatenda Taibu
March 2019